The Humbled Anthropologist

The Wadsworth Modern Anthropology Library

The Humbled Anthropologist
Tales from the Pacific

Edited by

Philip R. DeVita
State University of New York, Plattsburgh

Wadsworth Publishing Company
Belmont, California
A Division of Wadsworth, Inc.

Anthropology Editor: *Peggy Adams*
Editorial Assistant: *Karen Moore*
Production Editor: *Deborah Cogan*
Managing Designer: *Donna Davis*
Print Buyer: *Barbara Britton*
Copy Editor: *Dave Cole*
Compositor: *Kachina Typesetting, Inc.*
Cover Designer: *Donna Davis*

Printed in the United States of America 49

1 2 3 4 5 6 7 8 9 10—94 93 92 91 90

Library of Congress Cataloging-in-Publication Data

The Humbled anthropologist: tales from the Pacific / [compiled by]
    Philip R. DeVita.
        p.   cm.—(The Wadsworth modern anthropology library)
    Includes bibliographical references.
    ISBN 0-534-12570-0
      1. Ethnology—Oceania—Fieldwork.   2. Oceania—Social life and customs.
    I. DeVita, Philip R., 1932– . II. Series.
    GN662.H85   1990
    306'.09—dc20   89-37243
                                                     CIP

The map of the Pacific Islands (Map 1) as well as maps showing the Solomon Islands and Vanuatu (Map 3) and the Eastern Caroline Islands and Kiribati (Map 4) are based on *The Pacific Islands,* a comprehensive, detailed map published by the Hawai'i Geographic Society in 1987. A 25-inch by 32-inch wall map of *The Pacific Islands* is available from Hawai'i Geographic Society Publications, Post Office Box 1698, Honolulu, Hawaii 96806.

The maps of Papua New Guinea (Map 2), Kiribati, Gilberts Group (Chapter 5), and Vanuatu, including maps of Tanna and Ambrym, Epi, and Efate (Chapters 13, 15, and 19), are based on maps rendered by Sherwood Keyser.

This volume, the first of two begun by us, is dedicated to the memory of Edwin Aubrey Cook (1932–1984), friend and mentor, committed anthropologist, the wearer of so many hats and that rare, occasionally irascible human who most often knew what was best for those for whom he cared, but not necessarily for himself.

> *I see you now*
> *(even in this present sunlight)*
> *Clay feet and all*
> *Whistling and dancing finally*

> EXCERPT FROM A POEM BY
> KEN HOECK, ONE OF ED'S
> STUDENTS AT FLORIDA STATE

 Contents

After 35 years as an anthropologist, Professor Billings argues that anthropology might still be a discipline in search of a methodology. Reflecting upon her own extensive experiences as a student and colleague of a few of the world's most renowned anthropologists, she provides examples from her own fieldwork in Melanesia to show that meaningful discoveries were those for which she was not prepared. How much can we be taught to prepare for the important "unexpected" prior to our ventures into the field?

A young anthropologist is sent to a remote island in Polynesia and, beforehand, establishes a set of rules that he intends to follow to successfully complete his first fieldwork. By total accident, while in transit to the island field site, he meets a maintenance worker at a resort who turns out to be the highest ranking member of the society he intends to study. The pre-established rules go by the wayside and the education of the ethnographer begins.

In his welcome to the field, Mac Marshall encounters two unexpected situations of violence. In the second instance he becomes personally involved in a local dispute that, once reconciled, will lead to important ethnographic studies that become the primary focus of his professional career.

What do we do when we know that someone is taking advantage of us? A more complex question would be, what *can* we do when, as guests conducting fieldwork in a remote Melanesian village, we discover that we are being taken advantage of? Can we be taught to prepare ourselves for such situations or do we have to devise novel and uncertain strategies in the course of conducting our fieldwork?

Fieldwork often has many inconveniences, especially on remote Pacific islands. However, these may be inconveniences only to us and not to the residents. There is much that we take for granted and, even in the most personal of matters, we may have trouble adjusting to the habits of our hosts. Our hosts, however, often find it easier to accomodate the personal necessities of the ethnographer.

The Abelam people of Papua New Guinea teach the young anthropologist much about themselves. But in this case, as with most fieldwork experiences, the Melanesians are really teaching the anthropologist about himself.

What does the anthropologist do when a major earthquake hits a small island in New Guinea? In a letter to friends informing them that she is well, we get a vivid description of fieldwork in time of physical disaster, community sorrow, and personal suffering.

EIGHT
Reflections of a Shy Ethnographer: Foot-in-the-Mouth Is Not Fatal   46
Juliana Flinn

Fieldwork entails personal involvement with the people whom we are trying to understand. What happens when the ethnographer is admittedly shy? This ethnographer finds, by accident, that she has gained acceptance in the Micronesian community she is studying.

NINE
What's So Funny About That? Fieldwork and Laughter in Polynesia   53
Richard Feinberg

Because he is laughed at by the people on a small Polynesian island, the anthropologist attempts to understand what laughter means to *them*. He discovers that laughter means something quite different to the Anutans than it does to us.

TEN
Cultural Baggage   61
Joyce D. Hammond

We owe more than we can ever repay to the people whom we study. In an effort to reciprocate for the kindness and help in her ethnographic work, the ethnographer purchases what she believes to be a most important present for her Polynesian hosts. The present, however, turns out to be both inappropriate and embarrassing.

ELEVEN
Raising a Few Eyebrows in Tonga   69
Elizabeth P. Hahn

As an outsider on a Polynesian island, and as a female in an unfamiliar society, the anthropologist must somehow learn about certain cultural nuances that she hasn't been taught and that, once understood, will make her work easier.

TWELVE
The Projection from Pohnpei   77
Glenn Petersen

Why should the men of a high Micronesian island be interested in the American presidential election? How does their perception of leadership and power compare with that of the Americans? More important, what features of their own cultural values do they use to make sense out of the American political situation?

THIRTEEN
The Politics of Ethnography: Americans on Tanna   84
Lamont Lindstrom

How does an outsider gain entry on a Melanesian island when the neighboring villages are divided into different, and often conflicting, religious and political factions? This is the island of the famous John Frum cargo cult. One must walk a very fine line not to offend anyone. In this case, Monty Lindstrom employs a novel strategy to assert and clarify his own identity.

FOURTEEN
'Pigs of the Forest' and Other Unwritten Papers   93
Terence E. Hays

The anthropologist accidentally discovers something about sorcery and curing in the New Guinea Highlands that has never been documented by an outsider. Furthermore, this discovery, if proven true, has anthropological implications which will certainly shake the academic world. However, upon further investigation, we're made to question the absolute or shared quality of cultural beliefs.

FIFTEEN
To Die on Ambae: On the Possibility of Doing Fieldwork Forever   101
William L. Rodman and Margaret C. Rodman

Most often, the anthropologist is adopted into a society, as was the case with this husband and wife team. One becomes a son, or a daughter and is treated as such by the host parent. What happens when, in a life-threatening situation, the children reject the advice of the father and, in this instance, seek the care and treatment of Western "scientific" medicine instead of trusting local cures and sorcery?

SIXTEEN
A Letter from the Field   121
Marty Zelenietz

This anthropologist went to Melanesia to study sorcery but had little luck and began to suspect that sorcery had either disappeared or that the villagers simply refused to talk about it. But an accusation of sorcery surfaces and not only does the ethnographer learn of sorcery, but a renowned sorcerer from a different village offers to teach him the techniques of sorcery. What does one do, especially when the host villagers don't want one with special powers living among them?

By chance, in meeting a self-professed rainmaking sorcerer, the anthropologist
is taught the procedures and then is given a "magical" rainstone. That night,
during the dry season in Highland New Guinea, there is a lengthy and violent
rainstorm that destroys village gardens. Who created the rain?

In this shrinking world, especially with extensive contact with the Western
world, indigenous peoples everywhere are changing, for better or worse, to
the techno-economic strategies of the more developed nations. In the New
Guinea Highlands, during different periods of fieldwork, the anthropologists
trace the career of one villager who attempts to succeed in new enterprises
and, in each new venture, miserably fails.

How many people know what cultural anthropologists really do? Don't most
people equate anthropology with those things found in museums or on "digs"?
An anthropologist is asked to write a travel article about his years of work in
Vanuatu and, unlike the experiences of some others (especially Ali Pomponio,
Mac Marshall, and the Rodmans), his fieldwork has been essentially a pleasant
interlude in a South Seas paradise.

Ben Finney provides us with an example of anthropological fieldwork of an
important and untraditional type: *active ethnography,* involving the reconstruc-
tion of lost Polynesian art and technological skill that was so important in the
discovery and settlement of the Oceanic islands. Unique and problematic in its
conception, the construction and operation of a traditional Polynesian sailing
vessel has helped to bring a renewed sense of Polynesian pride.

🦋 Foreword to the Series

Modern cultural anthropology encompasses the full diversity of all humankind with a mix of methods, styles, ideas, and approaches. No longer is the subject matter of this field confined to exotic cultures, the "primitive," or small rural folk communities. Today, students are as likely to find an anthropologist at work in an urban school setting or a corporate boardroom as among a band of African hunters and gatherers. To a large degree, the currents in modern anthropology reflect changes in the world over the past century. Today there are no isolated archaic societies available for study. All the world's peoples have become enveloped in widespread regional social, political, and economic systems. The daughters and sons of yesterday's yam gardeners and reindeer hunters are operating computers, organizing marketing cooperatives, serving as delegates to parliaments, and watching television news. The lesson of cultural anthropology, and this series, is that such peoples, when transformed, are no less interesting and no less culturally different because of such dramatic changes.

Cultural anthropology's scope has grown to encompass more than simply the changes in the primitive or peasant world, its original subject matter. The methods and ideas developed for the study of small-scale societies are now creatively applied to the most complex of social and cultural systems, giving us a new and stronger understanding of the full diversity of human living. Increasingly, cultural anthropologists also work toward solving practical problems of the cultures they study, in addition to pursuing more traditional basic research endeavors.

Yet cultural anthropology's enlarged agenda has not meant abandonment of its own heritage. The ethnographic case study remains the bedrock of the cultural anthropologist's methods for gathering knowledge of the peoples of the world, although today's case study may focus on a British urban neighborhood or a new American cult as often as on efforts of a formerly isolated Pacific island people to cope with bureaucracy. Similarly, systematic comparison of the experiences and adaptations of different societies is an old approach that is increasingly applied to new issues.

The books in the Wadsworth Modern Anthropology Library reflect cultural anthropology's greater breadth of interests. They include introductory texts and supporting anthologies of readings, as well as advanced texts dealing with more specialized fields and methods of cultural anthropology.

However, the hub of the series consists of topical studies that concentrate on either a single community or a number of communities. Each of these topical studies is strongly issue-focused. As anthropology has always done, these topical studies raise far-reaching questions about the problems people confront and the variety of human experience. They do so through close face-to-face study of people in many places and settings. In these studies, the core idiom of cultural anthropology lies exposed. Cultural anthropologists still, as always, go forth among the cultures of the world and return to inform. Only where they go and what they report has changed.

James A. Clifton
Series Editor

🎋 Preface

In August 1983, Ed Cook and I sat talking on a porch overlooking Lake Champlain. There I proposed the ideas for this particular volume, which was originally to be edited by both of us. For the remaining three days of his visit we retreated to my farmhouse in the Adirondacks, where we formulated strategies and developed scenarios for the completion of what we believed was to be a unique collection of essays by anthropologists— essays which focused on unexpected encounters in Oceanic fieldwork, written in a style comprehensible to a general audience and, we hoped, of some interest to the specialist.

I had developed the idea for a single Oceanic volume. Ed enthusiastically argued that we develop two volumes, one on the Pacific Islands, a second on similar problems in ethnographic problems throughout the world.

The ideas for the collection germinated over my fourteen years of friendship with Ed Cook. They derived from four essential realizations that had coalesced during that juncture of Ed's pilgrimage to visit old friends— a pilgrimage which Ivan Brady and I suspected was, more honestly, a farewell journey. First, Ed's great success in the classroom, especially at the undergraduate level, was due to his genuine concern for his students as participants in the anthropological experience. As a graduate student, I sat in on many of his undergraduate classes. Whether teaching a course on the Pacific, on kinship, or on language and culture, he had an engaging habit of emphasizing a critical intellectual issue by referring to a particular personal event in which he, a most rigorous and dedicated social scientist, had either misunderstood the situation or had screwed up in his field-work. Unknowingly, I stole this practice from him and soon thereafter employed similar practices in my own teaching. I have found this method of accenting an issue by displaying oneself with egg on one's face to be most successful—not as a strategy for amusement, but as a means of providing a personalized account to complement, and often confound, a particular anthropological point.

Second, from attending national anthropological meetings for the primary purpose of spending time with Ed, I discovered another fact. During our extended social hours many of *his* friends, colleagues, and former students would join us and I listened to humorous tales of how they had also screwed up in their fieldwork. However, as in Ed's classroom stories, these anthropologists were telling more than humorous stories. There were, in most cases, important lessons embedded in the content of their experiences. If one listened closely and paid attention not only to what was said but to what was left unsaid, there were lessons to be learned—lessons about the anthropologist, about the people being studied, and about human experiences in a cross-cultural context. I stole these stories also and, where applicable, used them with success in my lectures.

Third, especially in teaching the introductory course in anthropology, I earlier decided not to make the mistake that I'd found evident during my undergraduate training in engineering, mathematics, and philosophy. Whether valid or not, I remain convinced that the problem most educators have is with their approaches to teaching the particular subjects in their particular discipline. I've publicly argued in past guest lectures, particularly to students and professors of mathematics and computer science, that they might seriously reconsider their pedagogical approaches to the general classroom audience. If they are, as seems to be the case, teaching in order to train students to become mathematicians or computer scientists—in other words, to become like the teachers themselves—they might be missing the boat. A more pragmatic and successful approach might be to show students (who at the undergraduate level is often enrolled in these classes simply to fulfill some college requirement) what mathematics or philosophy can teach them about issues such as human problem solving, decision making, or human social issues, and how the subject matter might further contribute to the excitement of logical thinking and a sensitivity to the human situation.

Whether or not this approach has been as successful as I intend, it continues to be my approach to teaching lower division classes. I do not teach to convert students to the discipline of anthropology. I make every effort to expose the introductory audience to what anthropology can teach us about others and ourselves—to help us better understand the complex nature of the human condition, our own and others', especially in this rapidly shrinking world. In the introductory course, the less traditional, more personal, literate, and humanistic writings of Richard Lee, Laura Bohannan, Colin Turnbull, Napoleon Chagnon, and a few others have measurably tendered more productive seeds to the initiates to this discipline. These writings have been the honey that makes the vinegar more palatable, the humanistic interlude that breathes life into the otherwise sterile theoretical and methodological concepts in anthropology. Where, in anthropology, beyond the classroom, do our students discover social scientists to be the humanists that they are—each a real person, so much more than a reference in a text or an author in a collection of readings?

The fourth idea behind the form and substance of this project has a direct relationship to the enterprise of ethnographic fieldwork. I had spent approximately fifteen years living outside the United States—not as an anthropologist, but in various capacities on sailing and motor vessels. I'd prefer to forget many of the personally embarrassing encounters in foreign places but cannot. Too many times, especially when younger, I found myself screwing up on someone else's turf—doing something that would be proper in my own country but later learning that the behavior was quite inappropriate in the host's arena. As the years passed and as I grew wiser, I developed a strategy to follow whenever finding myself in a new place: Keep my big mouth shut and drink a lot of water!

I had to learn not to impose my behavioral rules and expectations on others. I had to learn *how to learn* about others instead of innocently but inconsiderately operating within a set of preconceptions based on my own Western value orientations. I was, after all, a guest in someone else's home.

Once I began to open my eyes, to develop a sensitivity to the contrasting worlds of my new friends in South American jungles or South Pacific islands, I began to learn another important fact. From all of the traveling, from these wondrous experiences, I was indeed learning about others, but more importantly I was learning about myself, about my own society's values, and about my place in a world of differing realities.

The focus of this volume is not on the significant "others" that are so important in the ethnographic enterprise. The focus is foremost on ourselves as anthropologists and the lessons we've learned in living with and trying to understand others.

The project did not turn out entirely as Ed Cook and I had envisioned. First of all, Ed died five months after we began the project. In working to complete the project as a memorial to a special friend, I discovered that many of his colleagues did not wish to put down in writing those precious stories they had shared in a private forum. Second, in the six years it has taken to complete this editorial project, I've discovered that, unlike Ed in his fieldwork and I in my sailing adventures, most anthropologists haven't really screwed up as much as we thought, or else they have chosen not to write about these experiences. However, as will become evident from the readings in this collection, we found that much of what anthropologists have learned about themselves and others was totally unanticipated. These lessons, for which none of their academic training had prepared them, remain perhaps the most memorable and critical lessons of ethnographic fieldwork. They are lessons about *us,* the Western anthropologists, which we learned from *them.*

There are many people responsible for the completion of this memorial to Edwin Aubrey Cook. The unwavering enthusiasm of Mac Marshall, Jim Watson, and Dorothy and David Counts was especially instrumental at a time when I was ready to scrap the project in favor of a more traditional collection of ethnographic readings. Dorothy was so generous in providing a forum for the contributors to openly share their experiences. Sue Pflanz-Cook, a friend since graduate school, has held my hand through the annual meetings of the Association for Social Anthropology in Oceania, knowing full well, especially without Ed, that I am not at all comfortable at public gatherings. Richard Robbins, friend and colleague, readily found time from his own work to keep me and my word processor fired up. Dean H. Z. Liu and Sue Spissinger have, over these years, displayed unwavering confidence in me and this project by digging for funding to support my attendance at these annual Oceanic meetings. Sherwood Keyser, friend and artist, has generously given his time to rendering the maps so necessary to the volume. Elizabeth Klauber gave of her time to edit and comment and search for errors resulting from too many hours at the screen. And, most important, Jim Clifton's commitment and editorial efforts were the cornerstones upon which all of us were able to build.

Finally, I'd like to thank each of those anthropologists, especially those whose works were not included in this collection, for their willingness to share their personal experiences in ethnographic fieldwork. No one has written for monetary gain, as any and all profits from this gamble will be established in an Edwin A. Cook Trust Fund to support travel for foreign Oceanic scholars to attend annual meetings of ASAO in the United States.

Phil DeVita
Plattsburgh, N.Y.

🌀 The Anthropologist Has No Clothes: Revealing Experiences from Fieldwork

MAC MARSHALL

This is a set of stories about anthropological fieldwork. I use the word "stories" advisedly because the contributors to this book have not written standard academic anthropological pieces in the pages to follow. Instead, they treat us to written accounts from anthropology's oral tradition—the sorts of field stories ethnographers share with one another over a drink but seldom recount for outsiders. Perhaps it signifies the discipline's maturity that anthropologists feel increasingly comfortable in revealing their own "tribal secrets" without finding this threatening—in exposing themselves by showing that sometimes they "have no clothes." Indeed, many ethnographers now count it a strength that they can write openly about the trials, tribulations, triumphs, and humorous episodes of anthropological field research.

Most of the stories that follow are a product of anthropology's recent reflexive turn. They illustrate an inward-looking self-examination in which anthropologists reveal themselves to be active interpretive agents in the fieldwork process—less than omniscient individuals in search of cultural meaning. This way of presenting information contrasts with the dominant mode of ethnographic writing of an earlier era when the anthropologist seldom appeared as an identifiable individual in the text, and where "facts" were presented as "the way things are" rather than as one among several possible readings of a sociocultural system. In such an earlier style of anthropological writing, the ethnographer maintained both distance from and control over the subjects and subject matter being treated and revealed little or nothing of him- or herself.

To employ a phrase recently made popular by John Van Maanan (1988), the stories in this book are mostly "confessional tales." Van Maanan characterizes confessional tales by their highly personalized styles, self-absorbed mandates, and the hope of making fieldwork respectable and convincing the audience of the researcher's human qualities. These tales involve "how the fieldworker's life was lived upriver among the natives.

They are concerned primarily with how the fieldwork odyssey was accomplished by the researcher" (p. 75). The reader of a confessional tale should gain insight into the ethnographer's shifting point of view: "Common features of research confessions are episodes of fieldworker shock and surprise. Subjects include the blunders of fieldworkers, the social gaffes they commit or secrets they unearth in unlikely places and ways" (p. 77). This self-exposure via confessional tales is not without its pitfalls and pratfalls, as we shall see. Such stories are of great human interest, but unlike many anthropological accounts the humans we end up learning most about are the anthropologists themselves and attitudes common to their own societies, rather than the people and societies with whom they work.

Many of the stories in this volume deal openly with the anthropologist's feelings and emotions. In this sense they bear a relationship to what Marcus and Fischer (1986) have called "contemporary experiments in psychodynamic texts"—experimental ethnographies in which the authors try to capture people's "self-reflective commentaries on experience, emotion and self" (p. 54). All of the tales in this book show how anthropologists gain experience and understanding of self and others during fieldwork via a complex process of planned, active encounters and impromptu, unexpected happenstance. And the tales also reveal that the most insightful glimpses of another way of life often come to the researcher "at a gut level" via a highly emotional incident.

Most of what we have here, then, are stories about anthropological mishaps and mess-ups. They are accounts of the researchers' foibles, mistakes, idiosyncrasies, blunders—situations in which the anthropologist was embarrassed, afraid, ashamed, one-upped, perplexed, humbled. In short, these stories reveal anthropologists as adventuresome, vulnerable, teachable, tenacious, sometimes gullible persons willing to struggle and learn from and in a host of awkward or uncomfortable situations.

Perhaps a word of explanation is in order for the volume's regional focus. Several years ago the idea for the book was conceived by two anthropologists with research experience in the Pacific Islands: Ed Cook and Philip DeVita. When Cook died prematurely, DeVita resolved to carry the project forward as a memorial to his teacher and friend. Discussing the idea with other Pacific anthropologists at the annual meetings of the Association for Social Anthropology in Oceania, DeVita convinced many of his colleagues to set down their field stories for a volume dedicated to Ed Cook. The work that follows is the result of this endeavor.

Since the settings for the stories in this book are all located in the Pacific Islands, the work might be subtitled "tales from the South Seas," but for the fact that several of the societies discussed are situated *north* of the equator. Within the Pacific region a good geographical distribution is represented in the volume. Five of the cases are set in Polynesia (Anuta, Hawaii, Rotuma, Rurutu, and Tonga), four in Micronesia (Kiribati, Pohnpei, and Moen, Namoluk, and Pulap in Truk State), and eleven in Melanesia, four of them on the island of New Guinea proper. (All of the culturally Melanesian cases are from the nations of Papua New Guinea and Vanuatu.)

While some might find this regional focus a limitation, I believe a strong argument can be made that the issues addressed by the contributors are not constrained by the fact that they all happen to occur in Oceania. These kinds of episodes are common to fieldwork wherever it occurs, be it in Africa, Asia, Argentina, or Arkansas.

Each story in this book stands by itself—a unique revelation of the personal side of the anthropological calling. But while the stories are distinctive in specific incident and location, there are certain common themes that emerge and certain shared topics addressed that bear comment.

One such theme concerns the preconceived ideas we all have for how we ought to act in given sets of circumstances. Every culture provides rules—codes for conduct—that those who share in it master unconsciously in the process of growing up and learning how to behave. Anthropologists are no exception. Not only do anthropologists carry with them to the field the cultural rules they acquired as children and as adults in their own society, but they also learn a set of rules in their graduate training for how fieldworkers ought to comport themselves.

This last point is important. Many of the incidents related in this book happened to the authors during their first period of fieldwork, often very soon after their arrival (e.g., Flinn, Chapter 8; Hahn, Chapter 11; Hays, Chapter 14; Howard, Chapter 2; Lindstrom, Chapter 13; Marshall, Chapter 3; Zelenietz, Chapter 16). For most of these authors this was their first time abroad, their baptism under fire, their opportunity to prove that they could competently and successfully do fieldwork. Years of study, preparation, and investment of time and money were now on the line. It should come as no surprise that the ethnographer—like most people in such circumstances—felt at times uncertain, insecure, unsure about how to behave properly in a different culture. To this must be added the anthropologist's concern to be accepted by those in the host community. Many of these tales, then, involve an untried researcher grappling with the new experience of living in a foreign society and coping with the strains that inevitably accompany such an adventure. As such, the tales are relevant to the potential experiences of others whose work may thrust them into cross-cultural situations: international businesspeople, diplomats, development workers, Peace Corps volunteers, missionaries, employees of private voluntary organizations, and even tourists who set out on their own for something more than a three-day whirlwind tour of another country.

Most of the selections in the first half of the book play on the ethnographer's recognition that his or her rules for proper behavior not only may be different but they may also be highly inappropriate! When should one laugh and when not (Feinberg, Chapter 9)? How does one contend with an islander who understands Shakespearean verse (Howard, Chapter 2)? Is it a mistake to intervene in a fight (Marshall, Chapter 3)? What should one do when given a gift (Counts, Chapter 4), and how should it be acknowledged (if it should)? Ought it to be repaid? If so, in what manner and with what (Hammond, Chapter 10)? What does one do when he comes face-to-face with his own ethnocentrism (Scaglion, Chapter 6)? How does one contend with people's radically different notions of privacy surrounding basic bodily functions (Goodenough, Chapter 5)? How does a woman (in particular) cope with a situation in which she believes a man in the host society is making a pass at her (Hahn, Chapter 11)? Such questions pose problems which fieldworkers solve in novel and sometimes humorous ways.

A second theme contained in several of the stories involves sorcery—the use or potential use of malevolent magic to do harm to others. How do anthropologists understand sorcery? How do they come to terms with it when they encounter practicing sorcerers? Do they (or should they) learn sorcery themselves? If they do, what are the possible consequences for them and for others in the society? As the reader will discover, these are not idle questions to be passed over lightly (e.g., Watson, Chapter 17; Zelenietz, Chapter 16), and they raise important ethical and practical issues for those of us who come from societies in which sorcery does not form a regular part of our background.

A third theme is the shock of recognition most anthropologists experience when they are forced to reexamine their own cherished beliefs—things they have always taken for granted—as a consequence of experiences with people who view the world through very different lenses. To play on my title for this introduction, this dilemma involves "stripping away" the pretexts of one's own cultural background preparatory to gaining an understanding of why people in the newly encountered place think and act as they do. In Hammond's (Chapter 10) nice word play, this requires divesting oneself of one's own "cultural baggage." What makes people sick and how should they be treated to make them well (Rodman and Rodman, Chapter 15)? What is considered edible (Tonkinson, Chapter 19)? What is the nature of the supernatural? Who is "in charge" (who is "the boss") in the fieldwork encounter (Howard, Chapter 2; Rodman and Rodman, Chapter 15)? How does one explain natural phenomena like gravity (Scaglion, Chapter 6) or natural events like earthquakes (Pomponio, Chapter 7)? How does one know his explanation is any "better" than that given by those operating on different premises for how the world works?

The story writers in this book take up a host of topics, some having to do with anthropological field methods and others having to do with matters of ethnographic description. How can (or should) the novice prepare for fieldwork? Should the scholar have a predetermined research design or not (Billings, Chapter 1)? If so, what if it becomes necessary to modify or even discard it in the face of the reality of the fieldwork situation? What is the role of serendipity in the development of anthropological insights? What happens when one acts on impulse (Marshall, Chapter 3)? What if one is shy (Flinn, Chapter 8)? How do other people see us ("us" being the foreigners among them; Petersen, Chapter 12)? What role does nationality play in their assessment (Lindstrom, Chapter 13)? Ethnicity (Finney, Chapter 20)? Gender? Age? What are the advantages (or disadvantages) of having an opposite-sex partner with one in the field (Rodman and Rodman, Chapter 15; Zelenietz, Chapter 16)? Of having one's children accompany one to the field (Flinn, Chapter 8)?

Many of the ethnographic topics discussed in these stories provide information about subjects that Pacific anthropologists have written about elsewhere at great length. We learn about alcohol use and drunken behavior, kava ceremonies and cargo cults. Some of the stories mention kinship and adoption; others introduce the spirit realm and celestial navigation. Nonverbal communication, quilting and plaiting, World War II, canoes, motorboats and ships, tourism, colonialism, traditional politics, gardening, and fishing—a large amount of ethnographic information is nestled within the story lines so that the reader comes away with a sense of what Pacific societies are like even though that is not the express purpose of the book.

North Americans are accustomed to personal privacy and value it highly. However, such privacy often is unavailable in other societies, and for those—like anthropologists—who take up residence in local communities rather than in "world class" hotels, this lack of privacy can be troubling or sometimes even traumatizing (Feinberg, Chapter 9; Flinn, Chapter 8; Goodenough, Chapter 5).

Citizens of the United States frequently do not realize how informed people elsewhere in the world are about selected aspects of American life. Informed or not, though, all of the world's peoples have a tendency to envisage the structure of *other* societies in terms of their own. This tendency is illustrated by Petersen's (Chapter 12) account of the meaning of Teddy Kennedy to Pohnpeians, and also by the ways America figures in at least two Melanesian cargo cults (Billings, Chapter 1; Lindstrom, Chapter 13).

Like the sailors aboard the Polynesian sailing canoe, *Hókúle'a,* described by Finney (Chapter 20), anthropologists of late have embarked on a voyage of rediscovery. Whereas the crew of the *Hókúle'a* sought to rediscover lost navigational arts and their own cultural roots, anthropologists have been in search of a better understanding of the human factor in field research—of the ways fieldworkers' personal characteristics and reactions influence the kinds and quality of information they acquire. Anthropologists hope that from this search will come new ways of knowing about themselves and others, as well as innovative styles of anthropological writing. The stories in the pages that follow represent one aspect of this anthropological voyage of rediscovery—that having to do with the old dictum: Know thyself. This sampler from anthropology's tribal lore about fieldwork provides you, the reader, with the naked truth that anthropology graduate students all learn in their classes: Sometimes—often—the anthropologist "has no clothes." Knowing this basic truth, let us now go "backstage," in Erving Goffman's terms, to learn what doing anthropological fieldwork is really like.

REFERENCES CITED

MARCUS, GEORGE E., AND MICHAEL M. J. FISHER

1986   Anthropology as Cultural Critique: An Experimental Moment in the Human Sciences. Chicago: University of Chicago Press.

VAN MAANEN, JOHN

1988   Tales of the Field: On Writing Ethnography. Chicago: University of Chicago Press.

Maps

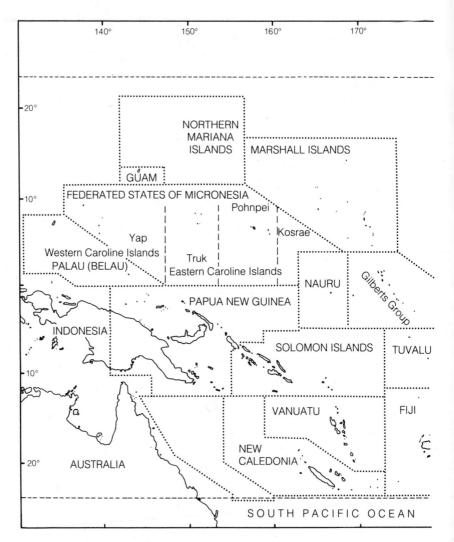

MAP 1 *The Pacific Islands*

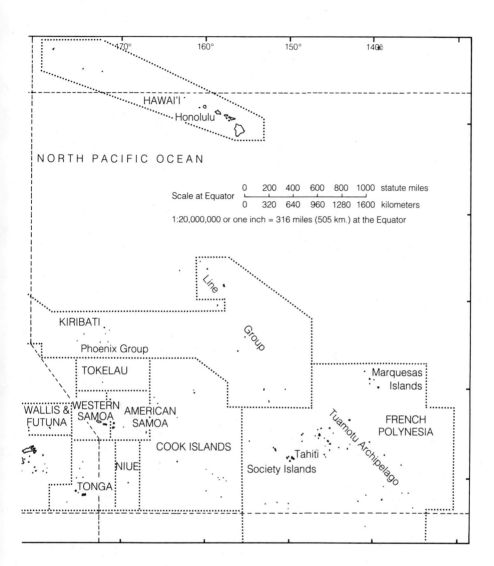

170°   160°   150°   140°

HAWAI'I
Honolulu

NORTH PACIFIC OCEAN

Scale at Equator

| 0 | 200 | 400 | 600 | 800 | 1000 | statute miles |
| 0 | 320 | 640 | 960 | 1280 | 1600 | kilometers |

1:20,000,000 or one inch = 316 miles (505 km.) at the Equator

Line

Group

KIRIBATI

Phoenix Group

TOKELAU

Marquesas
Islands

WALLIS &   WESTERN   AMERICAN
FUTUNA   SAMOA   SAMOA

FRENCH
POLYNESIA

COOK ISLANDS

Tahiti

Tuamotu Archipelago

NIUE

Society Islands

TONGA

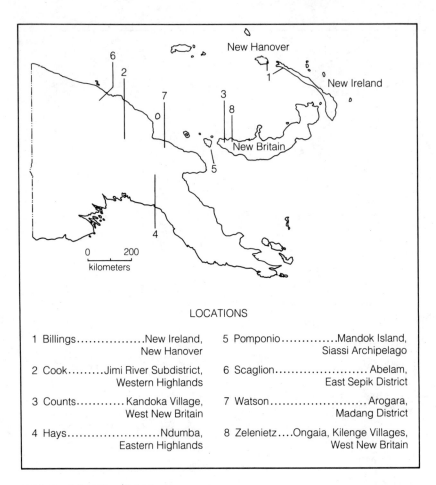

LOCATIONS

1 Billings..................New Ireland, New Hanover

2 Cook.........Jimi River Subdistrict, Western Highlands

3 Counts............Kandoka Village, West New Britain

4 Hays.......................Ndumba, Eastern Highlands

5 Pomponio.............Mandok Island, Siassi Archipelago

6 Scaglion....................... Abelam, East Sepik District

7 Watson........................Arogara, Madang District

8 Zelenietz....Ongaia, Kilenge Villages, West New Britain

MAP 2 *Papua New Guinea*

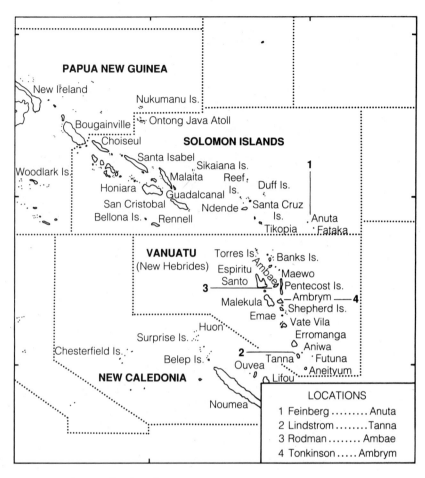

PAPUA NEW GUINEA

New Ireland

Nukumanu Is.

Bougainville :· Ontong Java Atoll

Choiseul

SOLOMON ISLANDS

Santa Isabel

Sikaiana Is.

Woodlark Is.

Malaita   Reef.

Honiara   Is.   Duff Is.

Guadalcanal

San Cristobal   Ndende ᵒ Santa Cruz

Bellona Is. · Rennell   Is.   Anuta

Tikopia   ·Fataka.

1

VANUATU   Torres Is.· ·Banks Is.

(New Hebrides)   Espiritu   Maewo

Santo   Pentecost Is.

3   Malekula   Ambrym   **4**

Emae   Shepherd Is.

Vate Vila

Huon·

Surprise Is. ·   Erromanga

Aniwa

Chesterfield Is. ·   Belep Is. ·   **2**   Futuna

Ouvea Tanna   Aneityum

NEW CALEDONIA ·   Lifou

Noumea

LOCATIONS
1 Feinberg .... Anuta
2 Lindstrom .... Tanna
3 Rodman .... Ambae
4 Tonkinson ..... Ambrym

M A P 3   *Solomon Islands and Vanuatu*

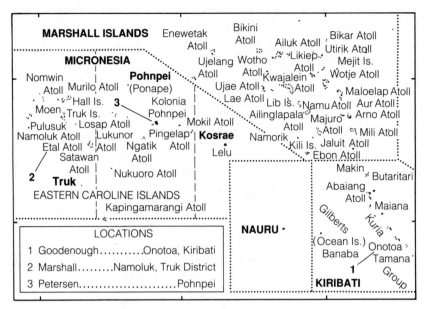

MAP 4 *Eastern Caroline Islands and Kiribati*

ONE

🪷 Is Fieldwork Art or Science?

DOROTHY K. BILLINGS
Wichita State University

Should the anthropologist enter the field with a scientific research design spelled out, with a predeveloped set of procedures and inquiries ready to be operationalized? Or might a research design interfere with creative, receptive responses to actual field situations? Does a research design produce useful data or generate ethnocentric fantasies? What of the unspoiled anthropologist, the one who happens upon, if any longer possible, an unspoiled population? Does he or she achieve rapport without system, resulting in a pristine grasp of a pristine reality? Or, more simply and accurately, is the outcome nothing more than some romantic grasp, a hodgepodge of impressions in some fashion simulating nothing more than the anthropologist's own reality?

Many of us agonized over the generalities and the particulars of these issues during our formal preparation for anthropological fieldwork. Most of our mentors and colleagues offered advice on the basis of their own experiences. Debates persist and I doubt that we're any closer to consensus or resolution on these critical issues. And though I doubt that my own experiences will lead to definitive conclusions, some reflections on this subject from an experiential perspective may provide some clarity, or perhaps compound the existing confusion.

While studying anthropology at Auckland University College in New Zealand in 1955, I had the privilege of participating in a senior seminar which addressed the question, "Is anthropology an art or a science?" Professor Ralph Piddington, who with arresting wit delivered a clear, heavy dose of Bronislaw Malinowski in his lectures, plunked down for science. So too did Jack Golson, who was then beginning his brilliant career in Pacific archaeology. Senior Lecturer Dr. W. R. "Bill" Geddes turned the question over, argued possible positions, played devil's advocate, pondered at length, and said finally, "I think it is . . . an art."

I have never forgotten that particular session. Even the outstanding practitioners of our trade disagreed, respectfully and with extreme concern for the fundamentals of our discipline. I also value the heavy doses of Malinowski. Piddington defending this pedagogical tactic on the grounds that Malinowski gave us a comprehensive research design to clearly accept or clearly reject, a defense I accept. Of course, Malinowski told his students to do precisely what he himself did not do: go into the field with a well-developed research design.

Even if one believes it is essential to have a research design, it is not easy to find one. In the 1950s, I was interested in what Clifford Geertz (1973) had later identified as "What the people are up to," some vague relationship to culture and personality. Casting about for a relevant and systematic research design for which I could hope to receive support for field research, I discovered the work of Florence Kluckhohn and Edward Strodtbeck (1961), *Variations in Value Orientations.* I found minimal support, however, for this approach, or for the study of values, among my academic colleagues or superiors. My interest was greeted with indifference, snarls, ad hominem remarks, and the usual array of verbiage that substitutes for argument and evidence in too many academic settings. At this lowest of points in my journey toward becoming an anthropologist, I was fortunate to have had occasion to meet Ed Cook, just back from his first field trip to Papua New Guinea. It turned out that not only had he been studying values, but he had also used the questionnaire suggested by Kluckhohn and Strodtbeck. I wanted to know what he thought about it: How did he translate, how did he proceed, how did the people feel about it all? In short, did it work? "No," Ed said calmly, "but it had not done any harm." Basically, he confessed that it had worked like any other kind of interview or interactional device. The protocol had elicited responses, from these responses he had learned some things which he might otherwise not have learned.

Many times over the years I have thought of Ed Cook's wise, unpretentious, and forthright gift of honesty. I then—a novice and to Ed a stranger, in spite of our mutual interest in the issues—was left without resolution to the particular problem.

I have learned that those students who proclaim confidence that they have developed an excellent research design still do not seem to know exactly what to *do* in the field. Making maps, collecting genealogies, visiting door to door or hut to hut, conducting systematic interviews, participating in gardening, and attending ceremonies are all things that one can infer anthropologists have done by reading their books, but it is usually not clear how these fundamentals were accomplished. Here we are moving from design and method to what might be called technique and procedure.

Professor Peter Lawrence was extremely conscientious about preparing students for fieldwork experience. Just before my first trip to Papua New Guinea, he sat me down with another novice and poured forth: probable scenarios, potential disasters, ethics, and etiquette. With regard to gathering information about classical anthropological concerns, he said, "Now, don't worry if you cannot find out right away about clans. It's surprisingly difficult sometimes to get to clans, and do not keep questioning them until they lie. That sets up a pattern of lying. Wait awhile, three weeks or so, and then just sit down with your best friend and say, "Now, Charlie, I'd like to know a little bit about how you are related to these other people here."

As it turned out, on our second day in Mangai Village in New Ireland, a man from a neighboring village told Nic Peterson and me, in clear English and without our asking anything, "We have six matrilineal clans here." Peter Lawrence's advice was based on his own fieldwork and was as valuable for being wrong as it would have been had it been right. The experience provided a contrast one does not usually discover in print and alerted us, correctly in this case, to the great importance of matrilineal clans in northern New Ireland.

No one tried harder than Margaret Mead to give her audience and her students a sense of what happens in the field. At Columbia University, she taught a graduate seminar in fieldwork methods, which I attended. Class periods involved, for example, recording observations, by note taking and photography, of a mother and child interacting. We also did outside observations in sandboxes on Riverside Drive. I was genuinely perplexed to find myself in a sandbox with a respected professor of musicology (who was branching out into studying rain dances in Africa), and the Swedish ambassador to the United Nations.

Naturally, I valued all of these encounters. I heard many of Mead's stories and was personally inspired by her interpretations of her films. Many of the details of her own field experiences at one time or another came back to me when I got to the field.

But was I learning *method*? My teacher and colleague, C. W. M. "Steve" Hart, did not believe you could teach other people field methods. He enjoyed telling the story of meeting Margaret Mead at a conference, and of her enthusiastic comment that she was now teaching a course in field methods—a great improvement, she apparently thought he would agree, over the old days when students were just sent off to cope. "But Margaret," Hart said, "what on earth can you actually teach them?" "Oh," she responded, "there are lots of things you can teach them, like, for example, date your notes." Hart then opined to his listeners that any guy who was such a damned fool that he did not know enough to date his notes should not be let loose in the field anyway.

Another point which Mead often emphasized appears to support a position *against* highly developed research designs. She warned against overstructuring questions, which might push people into agreeing with the anthropologist for fear of being embarrassed, accommodating, or for other reasons responding in ways counterproductive to the anthropological task. This advice worked well for me with the Lavongai people of New Hanover. Wanting to attain the material wealth of the Americans, a wealth they had earlier experienced during the war in the Pacific, they held an election and voted for then-President Lyndon B. Johnson to be their leader. Assuming that their duly elected boss would arrive to lead them to Western riches, they were not at all pleased to hear my view that Johnson probably would not come. Their own views poured forth into my tape recorder, while I kept mine to myself. In this case, Dr. Mead's advice seemed to be realistic.

But in New Ireland I found a very polite society of people who did not want to push *their* views on me. They waited politely for me to express my views, and I just as politely waited for them to express theirs. Much time was wasted in polite silence.

New Ireland was my first fieldwork site. I was convinced that I was a hopeless fieldworker. Before I was rescued by the talkative Lavongais, I sustained myself by recalling Mervyn Meggitt's stories about the difference between two groups with whom he had worked. The Walbari of Australia would go on for hours explaining their ceremonies, and when he was exhausted from listening and recording they would say, "Now tell us what you people do." By contrast, the Enga of the Papua New Guinea highlands had few ceremonies, little to say about them, and asked nothing of Meggitt.

Many would support Steve Hart's view that fieldwork methods cannot be taught. We certainly have not come close to the development of a flawless way to teach each other how to "get the hang" of a culture. The key insights on which I have based my interpretations of the two cultures I studied came not from a successful research design but from two field-work accidents. The first accident was my chance meeting with a blind woman in New Hanover. She detained me with cheerful, desperate, and interesting talk, while I tried to break away to find some important bigmen to interview. I was inwardly annoyed that the local women around us did not come to care for the blind woman so that I could get on with my important work. Gradually I gave up my efforts to leave her, and when the boat on which I had hitched a ride was ready to depart, I felt convinced I had wasted my time.

The second accident occurred a month later when I was in a New Ireland village to attend a *malanggan* (funeral) ceremony. I noticed a woman with a little girl, both dressed in new red wraparound skirts and blouses, and each sporting a head of hair dyed red. I thought the woman must be an important person in the ceremony, but I could discover nothing special about her relationship to the dead being memorialized. Finally a man told me, "Her ears are closed and she does not speak." She was deaf and dumb. This New Ireland handicapped woman had clearly been given whatever help she required to bring her fully, even elegantly, into the group. This was such an evident contrast to the unfortunate counterpart in New Hanover, the only person I met on either island whose person and clothes were in need of washing. I had earlier wondered why I had met so many handicapped persons in New Hanover and none in New Ireland. It now seemed apparent that I had indeed met handicapped persons in New Ireland, but because they were not isolated and were cared for, I had not noticed their disabilities.

These purely accidental meetings with two handicapped women brought to focus a whole set of data within which I had not previously been able to observe any pattern. In New Ireland, the weak (children who rarely cried, the old and infirmed, foreigners from elsewhere in Papua New Guinea, the handicapped) were given special assistance while the strong were pressured to serve, and so were encouraged to remain part of an egalitarian group. By contrast, the weak or unable in New Hanover were left to fend for themselves, while the strong appropriated whatever meager spoils there were, in a peck-ordered collection of individuals. While there was nothing in my formal education that suggested we might receive crucial information from the least likely soul, I think I have Margaret Mead to thank for the confidence with which I wrote down everything: She always argued that you never knew when something would become relevant.

One major insight did not work its way into my research reports for fifteen years. It was suggested and supported by comments made by Europeans, amusing comments which I wrote down (which irritated some of them), partly out of habit, partly because I sensed that such sharp wit might carry some truth. The jokes were about the President Johnson cult of the Lavongai, and while some of them served only the interests of the dominant European group, some touched a quality I too had observed. Father Bernard Miller, M.S.C., the American missionary who helped the cultists turn their vote for Johnson into an economic development organization, had said to me in 1967, "You're not going to write this up as a dissertation, are you? You should write this up as a musical comedy!" And Australian medical assistant, Carroll Gannon, who was counted a friend by hundreds of people in New Hanover, teased me about the complexity of the situation with this: "Has it ever occurred to you that they're just acting? They're all Academy Award winners here." Teacher Jim Handcock had said, independently, "They're great actors!" I had noted this quality myself and confirmed the distinction between New Irelanders and New Hanoverians when I saw a high school play: The teacher had unwittingly assigned all the leading roles to children from New Hanover, while children from New Ireland hung back shyly, playing their supporting roles softly and correctly. Trying to save the data from all these experiences, I began to interpret the cult as an improvised drama, in contrast to the traditional drama of *malanggan* ceremony in New Ireland, which was a performance repeated over and over again, cherished for its familiarity, like a medieval morality play.

One further interpretation of the Johnson cult came about as a result of an ethical conflict I felt in telling the story. Whenever I did, people laughed. Worse yet, I laughed. Anthropologists clearly should not laugh at the people they study: It is patronizing. I would have to stop. But I found that I could not tell the story straight-faced, and when I tried to do so, I did not do it justice. I don't know why it took so long for me to see what was so obvious—that is, the cultists, too, thought the cult was funny. They also loved to tell stories about it, and they also laughed when they told them—at themselves, at the election they had mocked, and at the predicament of the government officers they had embarrassed. The Johnson cult, I finally realized, was a satiric drama; and, like all satire, it was humorous as well as serious. It grew from a sense of injustice in social and political realities, but also from a sense of helplessness and of the absurd. The "beliefs," ideologies, and activities of the cult were neither rational nor irrational plans of action of historical perceptions and interpretations; they were dramatic satire, meant to make the colonial Australian administrators squirm.

If there is a message here, it is one of both art and science, and of ethics as well; ethics required me to justify my own laughter, science required me to interpret the data concerning other people's laughter, and art provided the missing explanations. When we interpret the complexities of the human drama with the ponderous solemnity that has characterized a puritanical social science, we very easily and often miss the point. Carroll Gannon offered an analysis of the cult in comparison to a festive party he organized to mark the opening of a hospital in New Hanover. Carroll said, "The party was just like the cult: Those who were in it had a wonderful time, and those who were not always wondered what was happening." What he said may be applied by analogy to some anthropologists. Perhaps we too often go to the party, or the cult, but nonetheless always wonder what was happening.

All fieldwork survivors know how difficult it is to join the "party" in a new culture, and hard work alone cannot guarantee success. I suspect that the people we study could write some interesting books about us that would reveal that they see us more clearly than perhaps we would like. I suspect quite often we are terrible bores to most people, and they probably wish we could fish or make baskets and were less dogged in our pursuit of kinship data. However, we have all made some true friends with those kindred spirits who have found us.

I shall always be particularly grateful to one who found me early in my fieldwork in New Ireland. Eruel was an old man, a bigman, and a carver, who allowed me to watch him for two weeks while he carved a mask. When the time came one morning for the whole village, and the mask, to go to another village for a ceremony, Eruel gave me a long look and said, *"Missus, iu savvy peddlim weely-weely?"* ("Missus, do you know how to pedal a bicycle?") Well, yes, I guessed I did. Eruel then announced to the dozen people standing around that I was too fat for him to pedal me, but I could pedal him (weighing in at about ninety pounds) on the back of the bicycle. So off we went, on a boys' bike, the pedals of which I could not reach while sitting on the seat: seven miles on a coral rubble road, a spectacle noted with whoops of laughter all along the way. Finally Eruel said, "Missus, stop! *As bilong mi pen*" ("My ass pains"). I noted that my ass, too, pained; and from then on, Eruel and I were friends. But it wasn't really because we had shared this humiliating and excrutiating experience together; it was because he could see that I was really interested in his art, interested enough to journey forth with him, by bike, in quest of understanding.

This incident says something about the role played in fieldwork by the genuine qualities of one's person. In the end, one cannot fake it. If Eruel had been a fisherman instead of an artist, we would not have discovered our rapport with each other. Another of Steve Hart's stories speaks to this issue. It seems that a party was in session for Barbara Aitken, who was about to go into the field. W. H. R. Rivers and A. C. Haddon were in attendance. Barbara Aitken, so the story goes, was suddenly seized by apprehension over her imminent departure, and she asked Professor Rivers, "But what will I do when I get to the field?" Rivers is said to have looked puzzled, as though it had never occurred to him to consider this question. He excused himself, went across the room to consult with Haddon, and then returned, smiling. "Don't worry a bit, my dear," he reassured, "Haddon and I agree completely about what you should do. Just be your usual charming self!" All things considered, that's not bad advice, I think. Not bad at all.

But then, of course, being your usual charming self can also get you into a lot of trouble.

REFERENCES

GEERTZ, CLIFFORD
1973   The Interpretation of Culture. New York: Basic Books.

KLUCKHOHN, FLORENCE, AND EDWARD STRODTBECK
1961   Variations in Value Orientations. New York: Harper & Row.

🌺 The First Rotumans

ALAN HOWARD
University of Hawaii

Even after twenty-five years it is not difficult to recreate the mixture of feelings that overcame me when the plane I had taken from Hawaii, itself rather exotic in my eyes, landed at Nandi in Fiji. The Qantas flight arrived at five in the morning, and while we were disembarking the glow of dawn made its appearance. The air was soft and tropical, but still cool, and the Fijian policemen, whose presence (in the theatrical sense) was most impressive, added drama to the scene. A mixture of strange smells, some sweet, others pungent, filled my nostrils. I was overcome with a sense of being in an exotic place and, my anthropological training notwithstanding, was overcome with a mixture of excited anticipation and anxiety. I was twenty-five years old, naive and full of wonder for the mysteries of cultural differences. The airport experience did nothing to dispel the images I had in my mind of the culture I was planning to study, or what "my subjects" would be like. If anything, the island of Rotuma, which was governed from Fiji by the colonial administration, would be more exotic, and more primitive, than Fiji. I had read the meager literature describing Rotuman culture, and something about its history, and it left no doubt that I would find a people steeped in traditions and beliefs I would find initially bizarre and irrational. But I would work hard and eventually unravel their twisted logic so that it would appear sensible. I would be translator for these people, would transform their exotic remoteness to comfortable familiarity. It was a mission of sorts, born of a need to make sense out of a world I was (and still am) struggling to understand. I could not help but run over the rules I had set for myself:

Be observant and careful not to offend.

Do not show disapproval, no matter how strange the behavior or how silly the beliefs (which recalls a dictum I read in an early version of *Notes and Queries in Anthropology,* the fieldwork manual published by the Royal Anthropological Institute of Great Britain and Ireland, that an anthropologist should not show his revulsion, no matter how disgusting the customs of the natives really are).

Concentrate on communicating, by learning the Rotuman language and being careful to talk simply and clearly when using English.

There were other rules—there must have been, for I remember rehearsals as taking quite some time—but I have forgotten what they were. In retrospect it seems they helped me deal with anxiety, but they were soon displaced by the realities of interaction, which made any preconceived code of conduct untenable.

It was in this frame of mind that I met, quite fortuitously, my first Rotuman. I had left Nandi and taken a taxi to Korolevu, a resort on the way to Suva where I would later have to confront colonial officials, for whom I had prepared another set of preconceived behaviors. In Suva I would have to be on my best behavior and would have to recall all the rules of etiquette and table manners my mother tried to teach me as a child. With them I would use the elegant parts of my vocabulary (learned mostly in studying for my entrance exam to Stanford) so as not to sound like a dolt. My advisor had suggested that I buy a tuxedo and dinner jacket, which I couldn't afford, just in case I got invited to formal affairs in Suva. Lacking the right attire, I was even more determined to talk properly. With Rotumans I would talk simply and clearly, with colonial officials I would turn into a pedant.

But before facing these ordeals I would spend a day at Korolevu, which lived up to its advertisements as a resort that captured the full flavor of Fiji. The hotel was located on a splendid beach, with palm trees and all the other romantic symbols of the South Seas. The hotel rooms were *bures* (thatched huts) and the service personnel were frizzy-headed Fijians who by physique and bearing gave new meaning to my visions of "the noble savage." I was enthralled, to say the least. After dinner—itself an exotic experience for me, although the fare was curry rather than dalo and roast pig—I got into a conversation with one of the hotel clerks. He asked what I was doing in Fiji and I when I told him about my plans for doing research on Rotuma he said, "Oh, we have a Rotuman working here as maintenance manager. Would you like to meet him?" My heart skipped a beat. "Sure," I replied, and quickly rehearsed the rules. So I was taken to meet my first Rotuman.

Alex Rae was an impressive-looking man by any cultural standard. He stood about six-feet-four and had a mane of white wavy hair and a beautifully bronzed complexion. Despite his casual European clothes he appeared the epitome of the Polynesian chief. He was in his mid-sixties at the time—a very handsome man indeed. As soon as he spoke I realized my rules were a waste of time, for his speech was as elegant as his appearance. To my untutored ear it sounded like Cambridge or Oxford, but it turned out to be simply good Fijian English. Mr. Rae was a charming and gentle man, who made me feel at ease right away. I guess I learned my initial important lesson from him in the first few minutes of our encounter—that Rotumans were gracious, perceptive hosts, and that any attempt on my part to act the role of anthropologist would be ludicrous.

He held full command of our conversation, asking first one question, then another. He listened patiently to my answers and showed a full appreciation for my purposes. We started out slowly, talking about practical matters related to life on Rotuma, and then he gradually shifted toward more theoretical concerns. I don't remember the specifics, for in retrospect it was his sophistication and style of conversing that sticks in my mind. However, I do remember my first blunder. We were talking about the issue of Polynesian migrations and he mentioned some of Peter Buck's theories. I seized that moment to make one of those Batesonian statements—a statement framed in such a way as to carry an implicit message about our developing relationship—that one is often tempted to make to people one is patronizing. I said, simply and as a matter of fact, that Peter Buck was a Maori, that his true name was Te Rangi Hiroa. What I was trying to do, of course, was to use Peter Buck as a common denominator between us. I am an anthropologist; Peter Buck was an anthropologist; Peter Buck was Te Rangi Hiroa, a Polynesian; you, Alex Rae, are a Polynesian; therefore there is a social equivalence between us. I am not really your social superior by virtue of being white.

Perhaps I am making myself sound more arrogant than I in fact was, for my manner was gentle and appreciative of his obvious intelligence. I was simply trying to consolidate our developing relationship. His response caught me off guard, for he corrected my error. I don't remember his exact words, but the message was that I was not quite right, that Te Rangi Hiroa was only half Polynesian. His mother was a New Zealand Maori but his father was Irish. In truth I did not know this, or if I once did had forgotten it, and felt properly chastised. I don't think Mr. Rae was trying to chastise me or was making a statement about our relationship by correcting my error. I think he was much more at ease and less self-conscious than I was during the entire encounter. But his remark made me aware of how inappropriate my initial framework had been for our interaction. Lesson two: Don't assume I know more than another person, Rotumans included, unless I'm prepared to be embarrassed.

Our conversation extended for hours and I enjoyed it immensely. It was in no sense an anthropological interview. If I had entertained that thought to begin with it soon dissolved in the sheer pleasure of conversing with a delightful and knowledgeable companion. This simply wasn't the context I had associated with anthropological interviewing. I could not see Alex Rae as a "subject," only as a remarkable human being. He did talk about his life, especially about the period in his youth when he became a professional boxer. This led him to discuss various professional boxers, past and present, and to my astonishment he knew the succession of world champions in every major weight division from the beginning of records to the present. Since I took pride in my own knowledge of sports trivia—I could recite the New York Yankees lineups back to the 1920s—Rae's knowledge of boxing was the final persuader. Here was a formidable intellect—a man from whom I could, and did, learn much.

I left Korolevu in a rather different frame of mind from the one I had brought to Fiji. The landscape was still exotic enough, but I was no longer burdened by notions of "primitive" natives. In Suva I met Alex Rae's sister, Faga, her son, Oscar, and her daughter, Liebling. All were sophisticated urbanites who further demolished my preconceptions. Liebling had been the first Miss Hibiscus and had traveled extensively abroad; Oscar was a draftsman for a government agency. Perhaps it was one of the jokes Oscar told me that put the final nail in the coffin of my ill-conceived notions. It went like this:

There were two men who were fond of poetry. One man was an ardent fan of Tennyson, the other was equally committed to the poetry of Shakespeare. They would frequently go on walks together and when they came upon interesting scenes would make up poems in the style of their favorite bards. One day when they were on such an excursion they saw before them a man approaching with a severe hernia. The Shakespearean turned to his companion and asked, "How would Tennyson describe this scene?"

With only a moment's hesitation the second man offered his verse:

"Down yonder hill there comes a wag,
legs spread apart,
balls in a bag."

"Not bad," remarked the first man. His friend then challenged him to compose a poem in the Shakespearean manner, and without hesitation he came forth with his composition:

"Lo! What manner of man is this,
that comes with his balls in parenthesis?"

As it turned out, Alex Rae and his sister, Faga, were by genealogical reckoning among the highest ranking Rotumans alive at the time. They were grandchildren of the great chief Marafu, who was in power when the island was ceded to Great Britain in 1881. It was, I think, fortunate that I met them first, since it might have been easier to maintain my illusions had I gone directly to Rotuma. Not all Rotumans were as sophisticated as Alex or Oscar, but then again, I have met few people since who can match them.

SUGGESTED READINGS

HOWARD, ALAN

1970   Learning to Be Rotuman. New York: Columbia Teachers College Press.

PLANT, CHRIS, ED.

1977   Rotuma: Split Island. Suva, Fiji: Institute of Pacific Studies, University of the South Pacific.

THREE

🌀 Two Tales from the Trukese Taproom

MAC MARSHALL
University of Iowa

It was nearing sundown in Mwáán Village on Moen Island, Truk, as we bounced slowly along in the Datsun pickup. The landscape glowed, and the Pacific island blues and greens heightened in intensity as the shadows lengthened. The village's daily rhythm slowed, and the moist air was heavy with incompatible aromas: acrid smoke from cooking fires, sweet fragrance of plumeria blossoms, foul stench of the mangrove swamp, and the pleasant warm earth smells of a tropical island at dusk. All was peaceful, somnolent, even stuporous. And then the quiet was shattered by an ear-splitting shout out of nowhere: "Waaaaa Ho!" The horrible roar was repeated, and its source—a muscular young man clad only in blue jeans and zoris—materialized directly in the path of our truck, brandishing a two-foot-long machete.

The three of us in the pickup were all new to Truk. Bill, the driver, was an American anthropologist in his sixties traveling with his wife through Micronesia en route home from Asia, and he'd only been in Truk for a couple of days. Leslie and I, the passengers, had been there for approximately a month awaiting a field-trip ship to take us to our outer island research site on Namoluk Atoll. In the interim she and I were staying in a small guest facility on the grounds of a Protestant church–sponsored high school a couple miles from the town center. We had met Bill and his wife by chance the day before at a local restaurant. The four of us had spent this day voyaging by motorboat to another island in Truk Lagoon to explore the ruins of the former Japanese headquarters that had been destroyed in World War II. On our return we agreed to meet for dinner, and Bill had just come for us in his rented truck to drive back to town for supper. None of us had ever before heard the frightening yell, "Waaaaa Ho!" Nor had any of us been confronted by a young Trukese man built like a fullback and waving a machete over his head.

"What in the hell?" Bill asked, but before I could respond we were nearly upon the young man. Fortunately, the bumpiness of the dirt road limited our speed to perhaps five miles per hour, and Bill avoided hitting our challenger by swerving to the left just in time. As he did so, the young man brought the machete down with all the force he could muster on top of the cab, once again announcing his presence with a loud "Waaaaa Ho!" The machete cut into the edge of the cab approximately half an inch deep right where I had been holding on to the door frame a split second before. As steel bit steel, Bill panicked and floored the truck, but our attacker managed to strike another powerful blow with the knife on the edge of the truck bed before we escaped. We jolted along at fifteen miles per hour the rest of the way to town, the maximum we and the pickup could sustain given road conditions. We were completely shaken by what had just befallen us.

"Why in the hell did he do that?" Bill wanted to know. I was new to Truk, there to study and learn about Trukese society and culture. I had no answer to Bill's question. We literally did not know what had hit us, or more accurately, why we had been attacked. Over dinner we speculated on the possibilities. The young man might have been angry with foreigners and decided to take out his bad feelings on us. No, we rejected that hypothesis because it was clear that the young man would not have been able to tell who was in the truck when he burst out of the bushes and lunged at us. It all happened too fast. A second thought we had was that the young man had it in for someone who owned a blue Datsun pickup, saw our truck approaching, and mistook us for someone else. But this hypothesis failed for the same reason: Because of the dwindling light and the thick brush along the roadside it seemed unlikely our attacker could see the color and make of the truck before he leapt into its path. Finally, based on our collective experience as persons reared in American culture, the four of us concluded either that the young man was emotionally distraught over a recent major trauma in his life or that he was mentally ill and a clear danger to the general public.

We were puzzled and truly frightened. What made the incident all the more bizarre was that Leslie and I had been treated with unfailing kindness by all the Trukese we had met from the moment of our arrival. We had walked through Mwáán Village several times daily for four weeks, many times after dark, and always we had been greeted by warm smiles and a cheery *"Ran Annim!"* What could have provoked this attack? Why in the hell *did* he do that? Although I could not know it at the time, this incident presaged much of my later research involvement with the people of Truk and directed my attention to a series of questions and puzzles that I continue to pursue.

I can now, with some degree of confidence, provide an answer to why the young man did what he did: He was drunk. The fearsome yell announced that fact immediately to anyone who knew the code surrounding drunken behavior in Truk, but we were ignorant of this as outsiders and novices in the subtleties of Trukese life. When young Trukese men drink, they are perceived to become dangerous, explosive, unpredictably aggressive. Given the option, the received wisdom is to avoid Trukese drunks if at all possible. We, of course, did not have that option and we became yet one more target of the violence associated with alcohol consumption in contemporary Truk. In fact, we were lucky that no one was hurt. Quite often the aggression of Trukese drinkers results in injuries and occasionally deaths.

How long has alcohol been available in the islands? Why do young men drink in Truk and why do women almost uniformly abstain? Why do drinkers so often become violent after consuming alcohol? What happens to the perpetrators of such violence? Questions such as these surrounding the Trukese encounter with alcoholic beverages are legion, and when pursued they open myriad windows into Trukese personality, culture, history, and social organization. Before I came to understand this, however, I had another traumatic experience involving Trukese and alcohol.

By the time this second incident occurred, Leslie and I had been in Truk for four months. We had left the headquarters island of Moen and sailed 130 miles to the southeast to a tiny and remote coral atoll which was to be the focus of my dissertation research. Namoluk was idyllic, an emerald necklace of land surrounding a turquoise lagoon bounded by the deep sapphire blue of the open ocean. Namoluk was a close-knit kin community of 350 persons where people knew one another in terms of "total biography": All the details of one's life and the lives of one's relatives and ancestors were part of local lore and general public knowledge. Everyone had a particular role to play that in some senses seemed almost predestined from childhood onward. Namoluk was fascinating, an integrated yet intricate community with a long history of its own which had been studied only briefly half a century before by a German scholar. I became totally engrossed in my research and in trying to master the local language.

We had taken up residence in a comfortable new cement house with a corrugated iron roof located more or less in the center of the village area. Our house sat at the intersection of two main paths and in between the locations of two of the island's three licensed bingo games. Since bingo was played daily by a large part of the population, a steady stream of islanders strolled past our front door. The family on whose homestead we lived slept in a wooden house next door, but members of the family were in and out of our house continually.

Soon after our arrival on Namoluk I learned that alcohol use was the subject of considerable controversy. Technically the island was dry by local consensus, but the legality of the local prohibition ordinance was questionable because proper procedures for enacting such a law had not been followed. At the time we came on the scene an intergenerational struggle was under way between men over roughly the age of forty or forty-five and younger men for control of the elective municipal government. Alcohol became a central issue in this struggle, with older men supporting prohibition and younger men enthusiastically drinking booze whenever possible. Even so, drinking was certainly not a regular event on Namoluk and when it did take place it often led to nothing more than boisterous singing and loud laughter late at night in the canoe houses. I began to get the impression that drunkenness on Namoluk was categorically different from what we had experienced on Truk a few months before.

And then it happened. Late on a Sunday afternoon we were lolling about our house, just being lazy and chatting with our landlord, when suddenly a huge commotion arose in the distance. Sounds of anguish, anger, and anxiety swirled toward us and then, out of the milling mob of men, women, and noise, came that unforgettable yell: "Waaaaa Ho!"

I sprang to my feet, jumped into my zoris, and dashed out the door to find a crowd of twenty to thirty agitated people at the intersection of the two paths, yelling, shouting at one another, and keeping two persons separated. As I took in the pattern of what was happening, I realized that a fight was threatening between two men who had been drinking, Each was being upbraided by female relatives to refrain from fighting, while at the same time men were standing by to make sure that their own male kinsman was not injured. Before I could stop to cooly assess the situation and record it objectively in my data notebook I found myself next to the antagonists. The larger man suddenly jumped on his opponent, wrestling him to the ground. Instantly he began pummeling and pounding the smaller man with his fists. I acted almost instinctively. Before I fully realized what I was doing I had a full nelson on the larger man, had pulled him off of his victim, and was trying to convince him to desist from such behavior.

Though strong enough to protect myself from harm, it occurred to me as I stood there that I had made a terrible mistake. All through graduate school my professors had emphasized the importance of not taking sides or getting involved in local political or interpersonal squabbles in the research community, lest one make enemies, close off potential sources of information, or even get thrown out of the research site. All of those warnings flashed through my mind as I pressed the full nelson on the struggling man. I was convinced that I had blown it and that this whole sorry episode would have nothing but negative repercussions for my work—and just at a time when things seemed to be progressing so splendidly and Leslie and I were beginning to feel like we really fit into the community.

But, oh, how wrong I was.

In learning why I was wrong, I also learned an important lesson about masculinity and how masculinity relates to fighting and to alcohol use in Trukese culture. And I had taken a major step toward what has become the central focus of my research over the past fifteen years: the study of alcohol and culture.

Once tempers calmed and it was clear that the fighting was over I released my hold and returned to my house, shaken and chagrined. How could I have been so stupid as to get involved in a silly drunken brawl? As I sat there feeling sorry for myself, a knock on the door roused me from dejection. It was two of the teenagers on the island, boys of about fourteen years of age, who were among our most loyal and patient language teachers. They asked if they could come in and, though I didn't really feel like company, I said, "Sure." The three of us sat on the woven pandanus mat on the floor and one of them immediately commented, "Wow, you were really strong out there a few minutes ago!" I wasn't sure whether I was being flattered or mocked, but before I gave a snide response I glanced at the boys and recognized the earnestness in their faces. I made some uncommittal answer, and they elaborated. My behavior had been thought impressive and salutory by everyone present: They said it demonstrated strength and bravery or fearlessness. If they only knew, I thought, that it actually demonstrated nothing more than the ignorance of an interloper endeavoring to keep the peace according to the inappropriate canons of his own culture!

Later that evening the man I had restrained, who was among the most influential and important of the younger men in the community, and on whose bad side I could ill afford to be, knocked on my door, accompanied by an older male relative. My landlord was with me and, while he knew what was about to take place, I was completely in the dark. The older man spoke long and rapidly in the Namoluk language and I understood only a little of what he said. Then the younger man spoke directly to me in English, asking my forgiveness for any problems he may have caused and noting that he would not have acted the way he had if he hadn't been drinking. "It was the alcohol that made me do it," he said. "We Trukese just don't know how to drink like you Americans. We drink and drink until our supply is gone and then we often get into fights." I was enormously relieved that *he* wasn't angry with *me,* and we begged one another's pardon through a mixture of Trukese apology ritual and American-style making up after an unpleasantness.

What I didn't recognize at the time, and only later came to fully understand, was that this incident that upset me so for fear I had botched my community rapport not only *improved* my rapport (including with the man I had restrained!) but also contributed to the development of my personal reputation on Namoluk. I noted earlier that Namoluk persons know one another in terms of total biography. As a foreigner from outside the system, I was an unknown quantity. Initially, people didn't know whether I was a good or a bad person, whether I would prove disruptive or cooperative, whether I would flaunt local custom or abide by it. Like every Trukese young adult—but especially like young men—I had to prove myself by my actions and deeds. I had to create and sustain an impression, to develop a reputation. At the time I didn't know this. Luckily for me, and purely by accident, my actions that afternoon accorded closely with core Trukese values that contribute to the image of a good person: respectfulness, bravery, and the humble demonstration of nonbullying strength in thought and deed. What I first believed to have been a colossal blunder turned out to be a fortunate coincidence of impulsive action with deepseated cultural beliefs about desirable masculine behavior. Now I, the unknown outsider, had begun to develop a local biography. But this was something I came to understand only after several more years of fieldwork in Trukese society.

SUGGESTED READINGS

MARSHALL, MAC

1975 The Politics of Prohibition on Namoluk Atoll. Journal of Studies on Alcohol 36(5):597–610.

1979 Weekend Warriors: Alcohol in a Micronesian Culture. Palo Alto, CA: Mayfield.

MARSHALL, MAC, AND LESLIE B. MARSHALL

1989 Silent Voices Speak: Women and Prohibition in Truk. Belmont, CA: Wadsworth.

FOUR

Too Many Bananas, Not Enough Pineapples, and No Watermelon at All: Three Object Lessons in Living with Reciprocity

DAVID COUNTS
McMaster University

NO WATERMELON AT ALL

The woman came all the way through the village, walking between the two rows of houses facing each other between the beach and the bush, to the very last house standing on a little spit of land at the mouth of the Kaini River. She was carrying a watermelon on her head, and the house she came to was the government "rest house," maintained by the villagers for the occasional use of visiting officials. Though my wife and I were graduate students, not officials, and had asked for permission to stay in the village for the coming year, we were living in the rest house while the debate went on about where a house would be built for us. When the woman offered to sell us the watermelon for two shillings, we happily agreed, and the kids were delighted at the prospect of watermelon after yet another meal of rice and bully beef. The money changed hands and the seller left to return to her village, a couple of miles along the coast to the east.

It seemed only seconds later that the woman was back, reluctantly accompanying Kolia, the man who had already made it clear to us that he was the leader of the village. Kolia had no English, and at that time, three or four days into our first stay in Kandoka Village on the island of New Britain in Papua New Guinea, we had very little Tok Pisin. Language difficulties notwithstanding, Kolia managed to make his message clear: The woman had been outrageously wrong to sell us the watermelon for two shillings and we were to return it to her and reclaim our money immediately. When we tried to explain that we thought the price to be fair and were happy with the bargain, Kolia explained again and finally made it clear that we had missed the point. The problem wasn't that we had paid too much; it was that we had paid at all. Here he was, a leader, responsible for us while we were living in his village, and we had shamed him. How would it look if he let guests in his village *buy* food? If we wanted watermelons, or bananas, or anything else, all that was necessary was to let him know. He told us that it would be all right for us to give little gifts to people who brought food to us (and they surely would), but *no one* was to sell food to us. If anyone were to try—like this woman from Lauvore— then we should refuse. There would be plenty of watermelons without us buying them.

The woman left with her watermelon, disgruntled, and we were left with our two shillings. But we had learned the first lesson of many about living in Kandoka. We didn't pay money for food again that whole year, and we did get lots of food brought to us . . . but we never got another watermelon. That one was the last of the season.

LESSON 1: *In a society where food is shared or gifted as part of social life, you may not buy it with money.*

TOO MANY BANANAS

In the couple of months that followed the watermelon incident, we managed to become at least marginally competent in Tok Pisin, to negoti- ate the construction of a house on what we hoped was neutral ground, and to settle into the routine of our fieldwork. As our village leader had predicted, plenty of food was brought to us. Indeed, seldom did a day pass without something coming in—some sweet potatoes, a few taro, a papaya, the occasional pineapple, or some bananas—lots of bananas.

We had learned our lesson about the money, though, so we never even offered to buy the things that were brought, but instead made gifts, usually of tobacco to the adults or chewing gum to the children. Nor were we so gauche as to haggle with a giver over how much of a return gift was appropriate, though the two of us sometimes conferred as to whether what had been brought was a "two-stick" or a "three-stick" stalk, bundle, or whatever. A "stick" of tobacco was a single large leaf, soaked in rum and then twisted into a ropelike form. This, wrapped in half a sheet of news- print (torn for use as cigarette paper), sold in the local trade stores for a shilling. Nearly all of the adults in the village smoked a great deal, and they seldom had much cash, so our stocks of twist tobacco and stacks of the Sydney *Morning Herald* (all, unfortunately, the same day's issue) were seen as a real boon to those who preferred "stick" to the locally grown product.

We had established a pattern with respect to the gifts of food. When a donor appeared at our veranda we would offer our thanks and talk with them for a few minutes (usually about our children, who seemed to hold a real fascination for the villagers and for whom most of the gifts were intended) and then we would inquire whether they could use some tobacco. It was almost never refused, though occasionally a small bottle of kerosene, a box of matches, some laundry soap, a cup of rice, or a tin of meat would be requested instead of (or even in addition to) the tobacco. Everyone, even Kolia, seemed to think this arrangement had worked out well.

Now, what must be kept in mind is that while we were following their rules—or seemed to be—we were *really still buying food.* In fact we kept a running account of what came in and what we "paid" for it. Tobacco as currency got a little complicated, but since the exchange rate was one stick to one shilling, it was not too much trouble as long as everyone was happy, and meanwhile we could account for the expenditure of "informant fees" and "household expenses." Another thing to keep in mind is that not only did we continue to think in terms of our buying the food that was brought, we thought of them as *selling it.* While it was true they never quoted us a price, they also never asked us if we needed or wanted whatever they had brought. It seemed clear to us that when an adult needed a stick of tobacco, or a child wanted some chewing gum (we had enormous quantities of small packets of Wrigley's for just such eventualities) they would find something surplus to their own needs and bring it along to our "store" and get what they wanted.

By late November 1966, just before the rainy season set in, the bananas were coming into flush, and whereas earlier we had received banana gifts by the "hand" (six or eight bananas in a cluster cut from the stalk), donors now began to bring bananas, "for the children," by the *stalk!* The Kaliai among whom we were living are not exactly specialists in banana cultivation—they only recognize about thirty varieties, while some of their neighbors have more than twice that many—but the kinds they produce differ considerably from each other in size, shape, and taste, so we were not dismayed when we had more than one stalk hanging on our veranda. The stalks ripen a bit at the time, and having some variety was nice. Still, by the time our accumulation had reached *four* complete stalks, the delights of variety had begun to pale a bit. The fruits were ripening progressively and it was clear that even if we and the kids ate nothing but bananas for the next week, some would still fall from the stalk onto the floor in a state of gross overripeness. This was the situation as, late one afternoon, a woman came bringing yet another stalk of bananas up the steps of the house.

Several factors determined our reaction to her approach: one was that there was literally no way we could possibly use the bananas. We hadn't quite reached the point of being crowded off our veranda by the stalks of fruit, but it was close. Another factor was that we were tired of playing the gift game. We had acquiesced in playing it—no one was permitted to sell us anything, and in turn we only gave things away, refusing under any circumstances to sell tobacco (or anything else) for money. But there had to be a limit. From our perspective what was at issue was that the woman wanted something and she had come to trade for it. Further, what she had brought to trade was something we neither wanted nor could use, and it should have been obvious to her. So we decided to bite the bullet.

The woman, Rogi, climbed the stairs to the veranda, took the stalk from where it was balanced on top of her head, and laid it on the floor with the word, "Here are some bananas for the children." Dorothy and I sat near her on the floor and thanked her for her thought but explained, "You know, we really have too many bananas—we can't use these; maybe you ought to give them to someone else. . . ." The woman looked mystified, then brightened and explained that she didn't want anything for them, she wasn't short of tobacco or anything. They were just a gift for the kids. Then she just sat there, and we sat there, and the bananas sat there, and we tried again. "Look," I said, pointing up to them and counting, "we've got four stalks already hanging here on the veranda—there are too many for us to eat now. Some are rotting already. Even if we eat only bananas, we can't keep up with what's here!"

Rogi's only response was to insist that these were a gift, and that she didn't want anything for them, so we tried yet another tack: "Don't *your* children like bananas?" When she admitted that they did, and that she had none at her house, we suggested that she should take them there. Finally, still puzzled, but convinced we weren't going to keep the bananas, she replaced them on her head, went down the stairs, and made her way back through the village toward her house.

As before, it seemed only moments before Kolia was making his way up the stairs, but this time he hadn't brought the woman in tow. "What was wrong with those bananas? Were they no good?" he demanded. We explained that there was nothing wrong with the bananas at all, but that we simply couldn't use them and it seemed foolish to take them when we had so many and Rogi's own children had none. We obviously didn't make ourselves clear, because Kolia then took up the same refrain that Rogi had—he insisted that we shouldn't be worried about taking the bananas, because they were a gift for the children and Rogi hadn't wanted anything for them. There was no reason, he added, to send her away with them— she would be ashamed. I'm afraid we must have seemed as if we were hard of hearing or thought he was, for our only response was to repeat our reasons. We went through it again—there they hung, one, two, three, *four* stalks of bananas, rapidly ripening and already far beyond our capacity to eat—we just weren't ready to accept any more and let them rot (and, we added to ourselves, pay for them with tobacco, to boot).

Kolia finally realized that we were neither hard of hearing nor intentionally offensive, but merely ignorant. He stared at us for a few minutes, thinking, and then asked: "Don't you frequently have visitors during the day and evening?" We nodded. Then he asked, "Don't you usually offer them cigarettes and coffee or milo?" Again, we nodded. "Did it ever occur to you to suppose," he said, "that your visitors might be hungry?" It was at this point in the conversation, as we recall, that we began to see the depth of the pit we had dug for ourselves. We nodded, hesitantly. His last words to us before he went down the stairs and stalked away were just what we were by that time afraid they might be. "When your guests are hungry, *feed them bananas!*"

LESSON 2: *Never refuse a gift, and never fail to return a gift. If you cannot use it, you can always give it away to someone else—there is no such thing as too much—there are never too many bananas.*

NOT ENOUGH PINEAPPLES

During the fifteen years between that first visit in 1966 and our residence there in 1981 we had returned to live in Kandoka village twice during the 1970s, and though there were a great many changes in the village, and indeed for all of Papua New Guinea during that time, we continued to live according to the lessons of reciprocity learned during those first months in the field. We bought no food for money and refused no gifts, but shared our surplus. As our family grew, we continued to be accompanied by our younger children. Our place in the village came to be something like that of educated Kaliai who worked far away in New Guinea. Our friends expected us to come "home" when we had leave, but knew that our work kept us away for long periods of time. They also credited us with knowing much more about the rules of their way of life than was our due. And we sometimes shared the delusion that we understood life in the village, but even fifteen years was not long enough to relieve the need for lessons in learning to live within the rules of gift exchange.

In the last paragraph I used the word *friends* to describe the villagers intentionally, but of course they were not all our friends. Over the years some really had become friends, others were acquaintances, others remained consultants or informants to whom we turned when we needed information. Still others, unfortunately, we did not like at all. We tried never to make an issue of these distinctions, of course, and to be evenhanded and generous to all, as they were to us. Although we almost never actually refused requests that were made of us, over the long term our reciprocity in the village was balanced. More was given to those who helped us the most, while we gave assistance or donations of small items even to those who were not close or helpful.

One elderly woman in particular was a trial for us. Sara was the eldest of a group of siblings and her younger brother and sister were both generous, informative, and delightful persons. Her younger sister, Makila, was a particularly close friend and consultant, and in deference to that friendship we felt awkward in dealing with the elder sister.

Sara was neither a friend nor an informant, but she had been, since she returned to live in the village at the time of our second trip in 1971, a constant (if minor) drain on our resources. She never asked for much at a time. A bar of soap, a box of matches, a bottle of kerosene, a cup of rice, some onions, a stick or two of tobacco, or some other small item was usually all that was at issue, but whenever she came around it was always to ask for something—or to let us know that when we left, we should give her some of the furnishings from the house. Too, unlike almost everyone else in the village, when she came, she was always empty-handed. We ate no taro from her gardens, and the kids chewed none of her sugarcane. In short, she was, as far as we could tell, a really grasping, selfish old woman—and we were not the only victims of her greed.

Having long before learned the lesson of the bananas, one day we had a stalk that was ripening so fast we couldn't keep up with it, so I pulled a few for our own use (we only had one stalk at the time) and walked down through the village to Ben's house, where his five children were playing. I sat down on his steps to talk, telling him that I intended to give the fruit to his kids. They never got them. Sara saw us from across the open plaza of the village and came rushing over, shouting, "My bananas!" Then she grabbed the stalk and went off gorging herself with them. Ben and I just looked at each other.

Finally it got to the point where it seemed to us that we had to do something. Ten years of being used was long enough. So there came the afternoon when Sara showed up to get some tobacco—again. But this time, when we gave her the two sticks she had demanded, we confronted her.

First, we noted the many times she had come to get things. We didn't mind sharing things, we explained. After all, we had plenty of tobacco and soap and rice and such, and most of it was there so that we could help our friends as they helped us, with folktales, information, or even gifts of food. The problem was that she kept coming to get things, but never came to talk, or to tell stories, or to bring some little something that the kids might like. Sara didn't argue—she agreed. "Look," we suggested, "it doesn't have to be much, and we don't mind giving you things—but you can help us. The kids like pineapples, and we don't have any—the next time you need something, bring something—like maybe a pineapple." Obviously somewhat embarrassed, she took her tobacco and left, saying that she would bring something soon. We were really pleased with ourselves. It had been a very difficult thing to do, but it was done, and we were convinced that either she would start bringing things or not come. It was as if a burden had lifted from our shoulders.

It worked. Only a couple of days passed before Sara was back, bringing her bottle to get it filled with kerosene. But this time, she came carrying the biggest, most beautiful pineapple we had seen the entire time we had been there. We had a friendly talk, filled her kerosene container, and hung the pineapple up on the veranda to ripen just a little further. A few days later we cut and ate it, and whether the satisfaction it gave came from the fruit or from its source would be hard to say, but it was delicious. That, we assumed, was the end of that irritant.

We were wrong, of course. The next afternoon, Mary, one of our best friends for years (and no relation to Sara), dropped by for a visit. As we talked, her eyes scanned the veranda. Finally she asked whether we hadn't had a pineapple there yesterday. We said we had, but that we had already eaten it. She commented that it had been a really nice-looking one, and we told her that it had been the best we had eaten in months. Then, after a pause, she asked, "Who brought it to you?" We smiled as we said, "Sara!" because Mary would appreciate our coup—she had commented many times in the past on the fact that Sara only *got* from us and never gave. She was silent for a moment, and then she said, "Well, I'm glad you enjoyed it—my father was waiting until it was fully ripe to harvest it for you, but when it went missing I thought maybe it was the one you had here. I'm glad to see you got it. I thought maybe a thief had eaten it in the bush."

LESSON 3: *Where reciprocity is the rule and gifts are the idiom, you cannot demand a gift, just as you cannot refuse a request.*

It says a great deal about the kindness and patience of the Kaliai people that they have been willing to be our hosts for all these years despite our blunders and lack of good manners. They have taught us a lot, and these three lessons are certainly not the least important things we learned.

 "Did You?"

WARD H. GOODENOUGH
University of Pennsylvania

When I was on Onotoa in Kiribati in the summer of 1951, I learned that, like most other Pacific Islanders, people there routinely greeted one another with "Where are you going?" or "Where are you coming from?" to which such replies as "North," "South," "Ocean side," or "Lagoon side" were customarily acceptable answers. The questions and answers were routine greeting exchanges among people who had lived their lives in the same community and already knew one another well.

The novice Westerner encountering Pacific ways may at first react to the opening question as an intrusion into his or her privacy, feeling called upon to explain where indeed he or she is actually going. Not so. When asked "How are you?" at home, we are not called upon to explain our actual state of health. "Fine, thanks!" ends the exchange. The same held in Onotoa.

More disconcerting to the Westerner learning to live with Onotoans was the routine exchange that took place when someone in a group rose to go out to relieve himself or herself. As one stood up to go, one heard the usual question, "Where are you going?" In this case the appropriate answer was "To the sea." Someone returning to a group after "going to the sea" was greeted with "Did you?" to which the appropriate reply was "I did."

Urination might take place almost anywhere that was a little out of the way, appropriately with one's back to anyone else nearby. The beach was the place people went to for more serious relief. Hence the expression "To the sea." There was no attempt at privacy. Indeed, a person squatting on the beach might be holding a conversation with someone at a house forty or fifty feet away without regard to gender. When finished, one completed the toileting by wading out into the water for a quick wash. It was all done very matter-of-factly.

Western colonial officials and missionaries had been unwilling to accommodate to this easy approach to defecation. For their convenience, each village had been required to construct an outhouse over the water in front of the village assembly hall. It was customary for visitors to beach their canoes there and to be housed in the "sitting place of strangers" in the assembly hall, a large, sacred public building whose use was hedged by many formalities. Before there were outhouses, those approaching

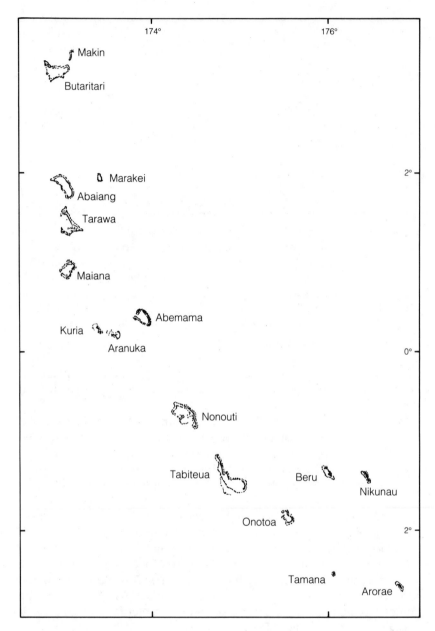

Kiribati (Gilbert Islands)

from all directions had an unimpeded view of this imposing building, which sat just above the beach. Now visitors were greeted by a small hut on piles out over the lagoon's shallows interposed between them and the assembly hall. It did not enhance the majesty of the approach. Even so, when visiting another village with Onotoans, I could sense a contagious, excited tension among my companions as we approached the beach before the assembly hall.

The outhouse itself made few concessions to privacy. Its square frame, resting on the piles, supported two parallel pieces of wood on which to place one's feet. There was a screen of coconut leaf thatch about two feet high, at the most, so that the user's body from midriff down was shielded from outside view in squatting position. About four feet of open space extended above the screen to the roof, providing the user with an excellent view of the beachfront and the various activities taking place along it. It also provided people on the beach with an excellent view of the occupant of the outhouse.

On Onotoa, to reach the outhouse in front of the assembly hall where I was housed, it was necessary to walk out on two long coconut logs, laid end to end. There was no handhold; it was a balancing act all the way. At the beach end of this walkway, the log was about two feet above the sand, requiring the user to clamber up on it, rise to a standing position, and then get into a state of balance before tightroping out the nearly fifty feet to the business end.

Except when the English lands commissioner came to work in the village, I was the only user of this convenience for toilet purposes. I found that, as a Westerner, I was expected to use it. The Onotoans had been required to build it to accommodate the modesty of people like me. My habits in such matters made me happy to use it, in any case.

The structure had other uses, however. It was a place much favored by children for fishing with hook and line when the tide was in. They would stand in the outhouse, hanging over the low thatch wall, or sit on the log walkway just in front of it with their handlines or improvised fishing poles. Their efforts were not signally rewarded, but occasionally they came up with a few small fish. Thus, when I had need to use the outhouse, it often happened that children were out there fishing. I would come to the end of the log, precious roll of paper in hand, and make throat-clearing noises. The young anglers would look up, see me standing there, and quickly scurry in to the beach, clearing my access to the outhouse and giving me such little privacy as it afforded.

Because I had expressed an interest in learning the then-popular form of dancing known as the "Multiplication Tables," which had been imported from Tavalu in postmissionary times, the Onotoans decided that the proper way to keep me entertained and, perhaps, out of possible mischief was to involve me in nightly informal dance sessions in the village assembly hall. Thus, I soon became well schooled in giving the answers "To the sea" and "I did."

There was an occasion when the schooling served me well. One afternoon I was seized with an urgent need to use the outhouse. As I rushed to the beach, clutching the toilet roll, I saw that someone fishing with a pole was sitting on the log about four feet in front of the entrance. It was one of the village's loveliest fifteen-year-old girls. My urgency did not permit the usual throat-clearing routine. I leapt onto the log and proceeded as quickly as possible up to the outhouse. As I approached the girl she reached behind her with one hand to keep from falling off the log while she leaned over to let me step around her. She then serenely resumed her fishing while I entered the outhouse, dropped my pants, and squatted. My performance must have announced itself a good hundred yards in either direction along the beach. The girl remained politely oblivious to it all, seemingly intent on her fishing. At length I finished, pulled up my pants, and emerged to return to the beach. Again, she grasped the log with one hand and leaned over to let me step around her. As I did so, she turned her head, looked up at me, and in a sweet, matter-of-fact voice asked, "Did you?"

Thanks to what I had learned, I managed to keep my balance and replied as offhandedly as I could, "I did."

SUGGESTED READINGS

GRIMBLE, SIR ARTHUR

1957   Return to the Islands. London: John Murray.
1952   We Chose the Islands. New York: Morrow. (English Edition: A Pattern of Islands. London: John Murray, 1952.)

MAUD, H. E.

1963   The Evolution of the Gilbertese Boti: An Ethnohistorical Approach. Memoir No. 35. Aukland, New Zealand: The Polynesian Society.

SIX

🐚 Ethnocentrism and the Abelam

RICHARD SCAGLION
University of Pittsburgh

Ethnocentrism is the belief that one's own culture is superior to all others. Anthropologists have found that virtually all cultures, and indeed nearly all individuals, are ethnocentric to a greater or lesser extent. In its worst forms, of course, ethnocentrism emerges as racism or ethnic prejudice and provides justification for the persecution of others who are "different." In introductory anthropology courses, anthropologists usually introduce the notion of ethnocentrism by explaining that anthropologists try not to be ethnocentric or judgmental in studying, describing, or analyzing other cultures.

Ethnocentrism can take very subtle forms, however, and one cannot easily put aside one's cultural prejudices. In illustrating the concept of ethnocentrism to my introductory anthropology classes, I often tell a story of an argument I once had with one of my friends of the Abelam tribe. The Abelam, a group of horticulturalists living in the foothills of the Prince Alexander Mountains of the East Sepik Province in Papua New Guinea, are the people with whom I have done most of my fieldwork. Abelam men traditionally pierced their nasal septa and wore ornaments in their noses for certain ceremonial occasions. On one such occasion, a friend of mine, dressed for a ceremony, came to see me at my field house. As I was temporarily occupied inside, I shouted out for him to rest on my veranda, and I would be out to see him shortly.

Earlier in the day, I had been reading several months' worth of *Sports Illustrated* magazines, which had been sent to me by sea mail, and which I had left on the veranda. I could hear my friend leafing through the magazines (obviously looking at the pictures, since he couldn't read). Suddenly he burst into uproarious laughter. Remembering the general hilarity that a trick photograph of a two-headed man had once occasioned in the village, I expected something similar. I rushed out to see what was so funny. My friend was laughing so hard that he couldn't speak; he merely pointed down at the page. I didn't get the joke. I saw a very elegantly dressed woman in what I think was a liquor advertisement, looking quite properly attired for the opera. She wore a black strapless evening gown with beautiful diamond jewelry, including a necklace and tiara, and had elaborate diamond pendant earrings. I would have thought he would consider her to be finely decorated. I asked him why he was laughing.

For a while he was still laughing so hard that he couldn't speak, but finally he managed to gasp out, "This white woman has made holes in her ears and stuck things in them." I looked at him, sitting there with an ornament in his nose, and pointed out that he had made a hole in his nose and stuck something in it. "That's different," he said. "That's for beauty, and has ceremonial significance. But I didn't know that white people mutilated themselves!" I pointed out that on the streets of Pittsburgh, where I live, women with pierced ears are fairly common, but that if he walked around with that feather in his nose, people might think it was pretty funny. We argued for a while about where it might be proper to make holes in one's body, and for what purposes, and I finally ended the discussion by dogmatically asserting that I thought it equally odd to have any sorts of holes in one's body other than those present at birth.

This incident illustrates the fact that the Abelam are just as ethnocentric as the members of other healthy cultures. As an anthropologist I was prepared for this, of course. What I was not prepared for was that the Abelam would teach me how really ethnocentric I was myself, and that they would fundamentally change the way I view the world. None of this happened overnight, however. There was no single great revelation, but rather a series of small incidents in which, in the words of Ed Cook, "I made an ass of myself in the field." It has been a humbling experience.

In 1974 all this was yet to come, however, for when I first met the Abelam, I was a smug young anthropologist who "knew it all." I had come to Abelam territory to study the introduction of a court of law, based on a European model, which had been set up by government officials in the preceding year. I was curious to learn how the Abelam were reacting to the Western law which had been introduced to keep peace in the villages. I quickly learned that they were not using the court at all, that they totally rejected this imposition of a foreign government. Having relatively little to do in "town," I decided to move into Neligum Village, in the northernmost part of Abelam territory. My education was about to begin.

It didn't take me long to see why the Abelam weren't using the introduced courts. Very simply, they had their own methods for resolving disputes, which were very effective. Whenever an argument broke out in the village, respected elders were quick to arrive on the scene and cool down the parties involved. The elders immediately mediated in the dispute and were generally successful in reaching a solution that was satisfactory to all. A communal meal usually followed, which further smoothed things over and served to underline the fact that peace had been restored.

The longer I stayed with the Abelam, the more I began to respect their traditional way of life, and the better I came to appreciate why they did the things they did. The Abelam are a horticultural people whose staple foods are yams, bananas, taro, and sago, which they supplement by hunting wild pigs and small game in the forest. They are famous for their artwork and for their majestic, towering men's houses which dominate the village skylines. They have a fairly comfortable life by any standards. Famine was unknown in Neligum Village. Abelam have a rich and fulfilling ceremonial life. Their knowledge of the local ecology is truly remarkable. They have names for all the local plants and animals and know all of their characteristics and uses. Once, early in my fieldwork, I foolishly stumbled into a patch of stinging nettles and my leg immediately reddened with an accompanying sharp pain. My Abelam companion searched for a few moments in the forest, while I sat in severe pain, feeling sorry for myself. In short order he produced an herb, which he applied to my leg, almost magically eliminating the pain. Hmm, I thought, these people know what they're doing.

With my general respect for their way of life firmly established, the Abelam began the next step in my education: giving me a good dose of much-needed humility. The incident that most vividly sticks in my mind occurred the second time I went hunting for wild pigs. The first time out was very interesting and enjoyable for me. I observed the Abelam's hunting techniques and took photographs of what turned out to be a very successful hunt. The Abelam set up nets in a semicircular arrangement wherever there were breaks in the forest undergrowth. Men then hid just beyond the nets, sending women and children out to make lots of noise and drive the game into the nets. When the game became entangled in a net, the men hiding nearby then dashed out and secured or dispatched the animal. As soon as the men dashed out, I dashed out with my camera, and we all had a good time.

About two weeks after my first successful hunt, a group of Abelam men came to my house and asked if I'd like to go out hunting with them again the next day. In my anticipation, I hardly slept that night. Anthropologists are very concerned with rapport, or getting along with people in the study community. They want to be accepted. Here, I thought, is a big breakthrough. This is the first time they have asked me to do something with them. Always before I had intruded myself into their activities, and they had let me go along. Wow! I thought, They *like* me! They *accept* me.

The next day a large party set out, and I helped the men carry the pig nets. After the nets were all set up, I started to take my place with the men behind the nets. "Nah," they said, "we want you to go with the women and children and beat the bush. We've never seen anyone who makes as much noise in the jungle as you!" I was crushed, but had to admit to myself that they were probably right, since, in 1967, a sergeant in the U.S. Army had made essentially the same observation more than once.

For a while, the Abelam continued to have a good laugh at my expense, as I gradually achieved some measure of competence at their tasks and understood their way of life more fully. They smiled when I got lost in the jungle, they laughed at my misuse of their language, and their amusement knew no bounds when I slipped and fell on my rear end in the mud. This last was a fairly common occurrence, and to the credit of the Abelam, they usually held their uproarious laughter until they were sure I was un-injured. Sitting there covered with mud and surrounded by Abelam friends doubled up with glee, it was very hard to maintain an attitude of cultural superiority.

Despite their own ethnocentrism, the Abelam were smart enough to realize that many items of Western technology were useful for them, and they were always willing to try new things. I finally got to the point where I began to think I knew enough to help them. While steel tools (mainly axes and machetes) had been used by the Abelam for many years, I had noticed that they were still using digging sticks for making holes in which to plant their root crops. These instruments were heavy, pointed sticks which were thrust repeatedly into the ground at an angle in the same hole. Once they had penetrated deeply, they were used as a lever. The hard-packed earth exploded out of the ground, leaving a hole suitable for planting. I thought I might introduce a shovel to make their task easier.

A large crowd gathered to watch the crazy anthropologist dig a demon-stration hole with a shovel. After watching me struggle for several minutes trying to sink my shovel into the hard-packed soil, someone handed me a digging stick, asking me to "try this." I was amazed to see how easy it was to use, and how quickly even my own inexperienced hands could dig the hole. Later that day, several people mentioned to me that everyone knew about shovels, and various people in the village owned them, but they were rarely used for garden planting because they didn't work well.

I like to think that at this point certain of my Abelam friends and I were beginning to learn from one another. It had taken me fully six months of living in Neligum Village to learn enough even to talk to people in their own terms. I was now beginning to sense a real change in many people's attitudes. Whereas, to be honest, I was originally seen as a somewhat bizarre and curious oddity, I now felt I was beginning to be taken more seriously and people were more likely to listen to my ideas.

Throughout the period of my "initiation," one of the individuals most understanding of my ignorance was an elder named Moll Apulala, who subsequently adopted me as his son. He never faulted me for not knowing or understanding something in the first place, but was completely in-tolerant when I misunderstood or misapplied something he himself had taught me. Illiterate himself, he believed (and probably still believes) that reading and writing have turned my own brain to mush and totally ruined any ability for memorization and analytical thinking that I may once have had. Of course, his own powers of memory are uncanny.

After I became his son, my education became more intense, and I began to rethink certain ideas. For example, Pacific scholars believe that dogs have been present in New Guinea for a very long time, probably arriving with early Melanesian migrants, whereas cats are a more recent European introduction. I expressed this idea, which was immediately contradicted by my Abelam father, who asserted that both had been present in Abelam territory since "the time of the ancestors." I thought I could offer him some linguistic evidence to convince him he was wrong. "What is the Abelam word for *dog?*" I asked him in Tok Pisin, the lingua franca of the area. "*Waasa,* as you know perfectly well," he replied. "Okay," I said, "and what is the Tok Pisin word?" "*Dok,*" he replied. I pointed out that "now we have a pattern. The English word for dog is *dog.* So you can see what happened. When Europeans arrived, you had dogs and had your own word for dogs, so you didn't need to borrow the pidgin English term for them. But what is the Abelam word for *cat?*" I asked. "*Pusi,*" he replied. "Well, there you have it," I said. "As you know, the Tok Pisin word for cat is also *pusi,* and in English we often call cats *pussies.* So what has happened is obvious. Unlike the case with dogs, where you had your own word, since you didn't have cats before we brought them to you, you had to borrow our word for them."

"There's where your logic is faulty," he countered. "Clearly, it was you who borrowed the word from us!"

I never did believe him, nor did he believe me, but I confess that this discussion made me think much more clearly about what I think I know, and what evidence I have or should accept about certain "facts." But as yet I had not begun my fundamental rethinking of the natural world. It all started innocently enough. I had been asking the usual questions about Abelam conceptions of natural phenomena, such as the moon, sun, rain, night, and day. Being generally courteous people, my Abelam friends asked about Americans' beliefs in these areas. Having been well trained in science and technology, I felt on safe ground here. I gave them the usual lecture that all of us have had in the second or third grade. I picked up a coconut and explained that the earth wasn't really flat, as it appeared, but was actually a large sphere. I showed them where we were in New Guinea, and where the United States, Australia, Japan, and other places were. I could sense that they were willing to accept this idea, since they live in a mountainous region that doesn't apear very flat anyway. I then waxed eloquent, picking up a flashlight (the sun) and a citrus fruit (the moon), and demonstrating how the earth moves around the sun, and the moon around the earth, creating the phases of the moon and such. My friends listened politely, and I thought everything was fine. Everything *was* fine until the next week, when I overheard some elders discussing how it was that the Americans all walked upside down!

I of course tried to disabuse them of this notion. I picked up another coconut and showed them how New Guinea could be on top and the United States on the bottom, as I had originally portrayed them, but if the earth rotated (here I inverted the coconut), the United States would be upright and they themselves would be upside down. They argued that this couldn't be correct. They were here now, and they could see that they were standing straight up. Furthermore, they were old men who had lived for many years, and they had *never* been upside down. Now they had me, although I didn't know it yet. I thought about this problem (in English, of course). I had taken several physics courses in college, and a statement of Newton's law of universal gravitation came to mind: "Every body in the universe attracts every other body with a force that is directly proportional to their masses and inversely proportional to the square of the distance between their centers." Unfortunately, I couldn't rely on this English jargon. I had to explain "grabity" (as my friends pronounced *gravity*) in real, concrete terms in either the Abelam language or in Tok Pisin. I quickly became so confused, speaking in these other languages, that I began to realize that I didn't understand "grabity" either. It was just something that I had accepted since the third grade. Why *don't* those people on the other side of the earth walk around upside down? I still don't *really* understand.

I think I now believe that "grabity" is merely a model of the natural world, and is not necessarily "real." It is just a heuristic device, something that is useful for organizing and predicting natural phenomena. I also think that certain beliefs held by the Abelam—things regarding ancestral ghosts or water spirits, for example—may not be any more real than "grabity," in that none of these things can be tangibly verified. But they are no less accurate predictors and organizers of the observable world, and as such are just as valid. In short, I don't know what I believe anymore, but I do know that Western culture doesn't have a lock on knowledge.

I stayed with the Abelam for a little more than a year on that first field trip. Since that time, I've revisited them often. As I write this paper, I'm preparing to visit them yet again, for the first time in several years. I first lived with them as a young man; now I'm firmly established in middle age. What will they think of me? I remember once, after an absence of three years, I arrived in the village to be greeted with the observation that "Oh, you're bald now!" (Actually a bit of an exaggeration, in my opinion.) The humbling of the anthropologist will be ongoing, no doubt, and I'm sure my education will continue. I still have a lot to learn from them. I can only hope that, in some small way, they are also learning something from me. But if nothing else, at least I know I am contributing to the village by being an almost endless source of amusement.

SEVEN

What Did the Earthquake Mean?

ALICE POMPONIO
St. Lawrence University

On February 9, 1987, the Vitiaz Strait off the northeast coast of New Guinea was rocked out of its predawn somnolence by an earthquake that measured 7.4 on the Richter scale. The epicenter was eventually determined to lie under the sea off the west coast of Umboi, the volcanic island which is the focal geographical feature of the Siassi Archipelago. Tiny Mandok, a ten-acre coral islet off the southern tip of Umboi, was not spared.

The earthquake struck at a time when the villagers of Mandok and I were already physically and spiritually depleted by a series of sorrowful and confusing events. Then without respite we were shocked by the terrible earthquake. Each tremor compounded our confusion. Fear of a possible tidal wave added terror to our sorrow. I was scared. It is most difficult to maintain scientific perspective and objectivity when one's own tiny speck of the cosmos seems about to be obliterated.

The people of Mandok kept asking me, "Ali, what did the earthquake mean? Why did it come? Was it sent to punish us?" Each question was followed by an interpretation reflecting their shared concerns regarding this new catastrophe. I was reminded of E. E. Evans-Pritchard's classic account of Azande witchcraft. In it, the major factor requiring explanation was not why a dilapidated silo fell, but why it did so at the exact moment in which a man happened to be sitting under it. We all needed reassurance badly. Many Mandok expected me to supply some. I couldn't, really, but felt obligated by the bonds of friendship and loyalty to people who had taken me into their confidence and trust to at least try.

This was my second trip to Mandok, in the Siassi Archipelago. On my first, six years before, I was adopted into the family of a village bigman, and thence into the village. This permitted me to live with the people on Mandok, learn their language, and participate in their daily life to the extent to which I was able. I lived on Mandok for some fifteen months and, using Mutu, the local vernacular, did an extensive study of the impact of Western education on this rural island community. My family and my village relationships were real and most rewarding. We got along fine, for the most part. I asked, they answered. They asked, I answered. They were very patient with me in my struggles for clarity in their language and my awkwardness as an outsider trying to live among them. When I returned to Mandok in October 1986, I was treated to a real homecoming and seemed to pick up more or less where I had left off before. My Mutu was rusty, but my linguistic recovery was swift.

When the earthquake struck, however, I was humbled to learn that in times of severe duress, the usual gaps in the multidimensional process of cross-cultural communication can become almost unbridgeable chasms. Explanations of any sort suddenly become most difficult to convey.

What did the earthquake mean to me, coming when it did? As I mentioned, just prior to the earthquake we of Mandok suffered a most disheartening series of personal and village disasters. During the entire time I was suffering from a back injury I sustained in the process of getting to Mandok. This caused me constant pain. Just as I was again becoming mobile after three months of virtual immobility, there was a sudden and unexplained death in my village family that threw the whole village into sorrowful turmoil. The attendant frustrations of the death, the funeral, and the general malaise of the whole village had me depressed. Then came the *coupe de grace,* the last straw—a 7.4 earthquake, unheralded, full-blown, and terrifying. I didn't need it at all—really I didn't.

I was beginning to feel that perhaps some local spirits were angry with me. Maintain objectivity, indeed! What about sanity? What about life? I really was down in the depths of a blue funk.

And yet a little voice inside me, outside myself yet from somewhere inside, kept insisting that I had to record these events, and the Mandok's reactions to them. After all, how often has an anthropologist been so fortuitously positioned to record this kind of a disaster as it happened? (And lived to tell about it? asks a cynical voice from another side.) There was just one problem: I could not hold a pen steadily enough even to start writing. In time I decided to write a letter. But to whom? Not my family, for sure, because I hoped they never even heard about the earthquake. (They had, as it turned out.) I had friends in Lae who I knew would know about the earthquake and be worried about me, so I decided to write to them. I thought that if I could focus my attention on informing them of the state of Siassi as I knew it, I could unwind enough to do the necessary. The decision itself lifted my spirits and calmed me down.

I present the letter here in edited form, expanding it to include subsequent events.

Thursday, 12 Feb.
Mandok

Dear Rae and John,

The sky is cloudy, the air leaden. The sea is in a flat, dead calm. There is only the barest occasional breeze to ease the smoke from a smouldering fire past my nose. On Monday night this village was a real ghost town of only fourteen die-hards, too stubborn (or stupid) to leave. Today, Thursday, the village is still virtually deserted—we now number about forty-odd. An occasional staccato whirring announces the arrival of yet another helicopter or plane. Short of another *guria* (Tok Pisin for "tremor, earthquake"), these are the only events that cause anyone to move from the apathetic stupor that grips us all. The sagging, deserted houses hang indifferently, their sad slump the constant reminders that jolt one's senses from an otherwise almost euphoric calm. The proverbial lull-before-the-storm effect is all-enveloping.

If I were a superstitious type (famous last words!), I would by now be resigned to the fear that the gods were not entirely well disposed toward my research. My back injury causes me constant, unrelieved pain, despite the medication I am taking. Doing fieldwork upside down is *not* fun. Thanks again for the sun lounger, it helps immensely. At least now I have some mobility to move around in the village and take my "therapeutic bed" with me. (Aren't euphemisms wonderful?) The teens are very good about carrying it and setting it up for me. Just as I was beginning to believe I was coping with all of this, we were struck with an unmitigated sequence of events, disastrous to all concerned.

My village brother, son of a bigman and a bigman in his own right both on Mandok and in town, died suddenly. Incredible—there was no apparent cause or reason to expect it. He had finished off his feasting cycle for the masked figures on Mandok just two days before. All of us were whisked to Finschhafen (the seat of his authority) in a state of frenzied disbelief and shock. It was true, despite our secret hopes to the contrary. Pandemonium erupted. I am getting ahead of myself. Let me backtrack a bit and explain. Bear with me.

On Saturday, January 24, a speedboat came racing into Mandok, just ahead of the *M. V. Salamander* (the boat that services Siassi between Finschhafen and Lae). The messengers delivered a letter to our compound which was marked URGENT in red ink. This was the incredible report of my brother's death, which I had the dubious honor of reading aloud to my village father and family. We all packed small bags hastily and boarded the *Salamander* for Finschhafen.

Once there, and at the family's request, I called the attending doctor for the cause of death. His diagnosis: "asymptomatic natural death" (isn't that an oxymoron?) that was either a heart attack or an embolism. The family rejected the diagnosis as inadequate to explain the death of a seemingly robust forty-one-year-old man who they had seen just days earlier. They requested an autopsy. Since there is no embalming in PNG and the body had been frozen, there had to be a thirty-six-hour delay for the body to thaw. The order was given on Monday for the autopsy to be performed on Wednesday. Meanwhile, my brother's second-in-command (and very close friend) and I cleaned out his desk. He had been executive officer of the local development authority.

Siassi mourning custom forbids a bereaved family to speak out in public. In any case, they were much too grief-stricken to do so, hence they asked me to represent them in the funeral arrangements. This honor was fraught with emotional trauma on many levels. As a result, I was afforded an inside look at Melanesian reasoning. It was not always very logical or reassuring to my Western culture–oriented thinking.

There was much debate over the burial site. Because my brother and his family were very important Siassi, the family won this one: Their son would be buried on Mandok. A second debate ensued which almost nullified the first. My brother must be honored in a Finschhafen funeral service before the body was shipped back to Mandok. The Finschhafen bigmen set Friday as the date for their service. There was only one thing wrong with this plan: The family was leaving on the prior Wednesday night's boat! That tug-of-war was squared away in time, but not without a lot of talking and much aggravation. It was just one of *many* examples of the week's frustrations. There is much to tell that really isn't renderable in writing, without sounding picayune, paranoid, or ethnocentric. Suffice it to say the entire affair was an emotionally grueling week of shock, horror, frustration, and confusion.

The autopsy, which was inconclusive, added to the malaise. The surgeon who performed it was a nice man, well known and liked by the Mandok. His surgical skills were obvious, but his communicative skills left something to be desired. He did not speak Tok Pisin well, and this fact added much confusion to his report for the Mandok. The autopsy revealed that, for a bigman, my brother had extraordinarily small blood vessels. Other than that, nothing pertinent to the cause of death was found. My brother's wife had explicitly requested that his head remain untouched. However, when examination of the torso revealed nothing conclusive, she was prevailed upon to sign a release permitting examination of the brain. It was done, but to no avail. Nothing definitive indicating possible cause of death was revealed. The doctor concluded that some sort of (bodily?) electrical disturbance interrupted the rhythm of his heartbeat and caused his heart to stop. It just *stopped.* Lights out. The blood samples have been sent to Port Moresby for analysis. We await the final report.

The Mandok, however, have a different explanation for the death. Also present at the autopsy was a policeman friend of the deceased. Sometime near the end of the autopsy he asked the doctor if *poison* could have been the cause of death. As you probably know, *poison* here, is a polysemous term which also means "sorcery." The doctor apparently did not know this. He answered that it could be poison, it could still be a heart attack, or something in the brain—it could be anything. We simply do not know yet. To a Westerner, this kind of an explanation seems fair enough, cautious, and reasonable in light of the available evidence (or lack thereof, in this case). In PNG, however, translated through vernacular categories and local worldview, this response engendered an entirely different conclusion. Utilizing their own concepts of what *poison* means to them, the Mandok who were present at the autopsy (in PNG, family members have the right to view it—in fact, so does virtually anyone else who happens to stroll by the room at the appropriate time, but I am getting ahead of myself again) jumped instantly to the conclusion that the cause of my brother's death was sorcery.

It was a simple bridge that the doctor unwittingly provided. It all stems from this incident. Some months ago (May 1986), my brother was involved in a tragic accident at sea. It started out to be a happy family outing of related men and their sons. A "brother" from Aronaimutu, wearing his work overalls and boots, was one of them. They had all been drinking heavily. As they were coming into the harbor, not far from one of its encircling islets, suddenly the boat flipped over and went down. My brother and all of the Mandok on board somehow managed to swim safely to shore. The Aronaimutu man did not. He was never seen again.

One day, this man's brother was in Finschhafen. With my brother present, he publicly declared that my brother would pay for his brother's death and follow his brother to the grave. In Melanesia this constitutes a direct sorcery threat. To the Mandok, it was now a threat fulfilled. This Aronaimutu man cemented that notion in the Mandok's minds by his subsequent, very strange behavior. He was here on Mandok when the messengers came in by speedboat (or he came with them, I'm not sure now which). As soon as he read the letter he let out a cry and gave it to me to read aloud. He then took off. At the time, I thought he ran to the men's area or some other private place to grieve. I learned later that instead he ran for the speedboat and fled to Aronaimutu. Upon arrival at Aronaimutu, without mentioning the Mandok death to a soul, he went to sleep. Odd. To the Mandok, this behavior provided conclusive proof of his guilt. The reason he did not speak, according to my Mandok relatives, is that his great guilt silenced him. If he admitted to the "murder," then he would know that his own death would soon follow.

As far as the Mandok are concerned, the case is closed. The death is viewed as a sorcery payback. Some people have attributed the earthquake to my brother's spirit. They are convinced he is angry and lashing out at the world at large to destroy all of his personal worldly works, etc. Since this last interpretation was offered for the first time just one hour ago, I can't say yet how seriously it will be taken.

Papa hasn't mentioned anything of the sort. Two priests who were visiting the Mandok mission came by to view the damage and to console the few people left. One asked Papa why he hadn't gone to Umboi with the others. He looked at them, shifting his direct gaze from one to the other, and said; "If a man tries to shoot us, or throw a bomb at us, all right, we must run away and hide. But this is an act of God. How can you hide? Where can you run? No way. No. There is no running or hiding from the hand of God."

I can still hear the ever-so-faint smugness in Papa's voice as he delivered these lines—I guess it isn't often that an old Papua New Guinean man gets to lecture a pair of white priests on theology.

As for me, I feel generally numb inside. This death bore many similarities to the death of my own brother less than two years ago. That death also was sudden, shocking, and remains unexplicable to this day. (Since I started to write this letter, aftershock number two just trembled—we get a lurch about every hour or so.) The faces kept changing in my mind, back and forth, back and forth. Don't ask me how or why, I had *no* intention of being there, but events occurred in such a way that before I realized it I was standing behind his head, watching the autopsy. Actually, it was quite interesting, when I could (force myself to) "forget" who it was on the table being dissected. It wasn't as much of an ordeal as I had anticipated. In case you were wondering, that is how I know so much about what happened and what was said. I was there.

After the family members left the room I did point out the doctor's error (regarding "poison") to him. He did what he could to amend it in his later more formal and public statement, but it was too late.

So at the moment I guess I have some problems, eh? We still don't know (1) if this is a simple earthquake or volcanic activity, (2) if it is over, (3) if it is just cranking up for a biggy (8.0 is classified on the Richter scale as "major"—7.4 is "major" enough for me), or (4) how or why my brother died. Back to square one and no moves visible. I have this uncanny feeling that at any moment Rod Serling is going to peer out from under one of the sagging houses and welcome me to the *Twilight Zone.* Someday I should write a movie script entitled, "The Day the Earth *Wouldn't* Stand Still." Oh, to have Michael Rennie's pal Gor, the gigantic robot, and say to him, "*Gor, klatu barata nikto!*" (which in loose translation means "Get me the hell out of here!"). The air does have that quality to it that suggests that I am in the middle of a movie. The only problem is, none of us has a script! Eeesh. However, the plot continues, even though many of us would have walked out on this film days ago.

One week after the burial, just as the folks were settling into quiet, subdued mourning, the earthquake ripped us all out of our sorrow and dumped us into terror. As it is, I am starting to think, just because I'm getting paranoid doesn't mean they are not out to get me. This will certainly be a research period that will live long and vivid in my memory, provided of course I do live to tell the stories over again!

Well, on to the earthquake. Saturday night I was not feeling too well. Something got my gut in Finschhafen and had not yet let go. I fell asleep in the now-open half of the big house. It is the same house in which I lived on my first field trip. It was "open" because they tore down the walls to make a large clear space for the funerary vigil. It must have been about ten P.M. I was awakened from my "nap" by a low rumbling noise. The house trembled, then began to shake violently. Mama, who was sleeping beside me, started screaming, over and over. We were stunned, too stunned to move. But it was soon over, ending just as suddenly as it had begun. We all sprang from a deep, tired sleep and ended up rattled and wide awake. After talking about it a bit and calming each other down, we all went to bed. I had to get up several times that night, due to my own gastrointestinal gurias, so I didn't get much sleep. I did sleep Sunday afternoon a bit during siesta time. There were several aftershocks, but nothing serious. By Sunday afternoon, we were all inured to them. This was a big mistake.

Sunday night. I went to bed ready and virtually desperate for a good night's sleep. I had not yet recovered from the grueling ordeal of the *week*-long funeral. I needed a good, long, full night's sleep. I didn't get it. Once again I was awakened from a dead sleep by the shaking and rumbling. But this time, unlike the night before, it did not stop in an instant. It kept on getting more and more violent. I sat straight up in bed—a feat in itself when the whole house is shaking against one's own bodily movements. I swung my legs to the floor and groped in the almost total darkness for my flashlight with one hand, my netbag with the other. I found neither. During that time the hurricane lamp on the veranda was swinging insanely. It either fell or was taken by my "brother-in-law" as he fled from the house. Now it was pitch dark. In the blackness I sensed more than saw one of my bookshelves topple over. Things from the other bookshelf on the opposite wall went flying. The tremors ran in a north-south direction, so everything fell straight out from the walls, which ran east-west. Things fell all around me and blocked my way. I ripped the chair out from under the table (adjacent to the bed) and tried to dive under it. No dice. Fallen objects wedged the chair, so I could only fit my head and shoulders under it. (This was a real scene from the Three Stooges—too ridiculous to be plausible.) Brief moment—no rumble, no rock—I decided to escape from the house rather than hide under the table.

I scraped, crawled, and clawed my way out of the house. The distance is only two or three meters but it seemed endless at the time, what with the rocking, rolling, and dodging of catapulted books and things. (It was almost like the film sequences in horror movies in which, at the climactic moment, the action is viewed in slow motion. I was moving as quickly as I could with my stiff back, but however quickly I moved, it wasn't quite fast enough to avoid "the monster.") I got to the top of the ladder, and things calmed as suddenly as they started. I got an adrenaline afterrush and felt my head lighten and legs weaken. I was shaking, so I sat down. My butt did not hit the step before the rumbling and shaking started again. Without even thinking about it, I bounced off the ladder and flew down the stairs. Fear, the motivator par excellence, evaporated all weakness *wan-tu* (Tok Pisin for "one-two," "in an instant").

Free of the house, I called to my "brother-in-law." No response. My father appeared about three meters away, so I called him. He came and grabbed my hand and pulled me out of our yard. I resisted and tried to insist that *under* the house was the best place to be. He yelled at me, in loose translation, "Are you mad? Don't you see that the houses are all falling down around us? You come!" He then yanked my arm and led me to the clearing next to the church. Here, Mama took me in tow. She led me by the hand to the *maran,* the ceremonial clear space in the center of the village. Well, I was certainly not the paradigm of the objective scientist at this undignified moment, but frankly I didn't much care. Besides, I had plenty of company. The whole village emptied into this center. All were as shaken as I, but no one was really hurt.

Whoever gave the advice that during an earthquake you should stay inside and duck under a table or bed did not live in a bush hut on stilts, I can tell you that! Nor did this person store Siassi bowls on elevated shelves. These houses rock at the slightest bodily movement, let along a full-blown earth tremor. And kwila is a very heavy wood. Carved into the oblong shape of a ceremonial bowl (over a meter in length), it can be deadly if it falls on you. Thank goodness no one got seriously injured. Some people did get crowned with clay pots and flying Siassi bowls (the big ones), but no serious injuries were sustained.

We retreated back to the church clearing which sits on the edge of our compound. Some teenage boys were sent to watch the sea for signs of a tidal wave. None, thank goodness, but they still feared one. (What anyone would or could do if they saw one coming, I don't know. Disappear in a swoosh, I guess. The thought was too horrible to contemplate at that moment.) We all just sat glued to our places and waited for the sun to rise. It eventually did as, of course, it always does. I don't think a sunrise ever looked so beautiful to me, though, I can tell you that.

When word came that Aromot Island was cracked and many houses were down, most Mandok cleared out and went to the Muru garden area on Umboi. Here on Mandok our count was four houses demolished or fallen, and about eleven more tilted because of stilts that were knocked out from underneath. I have already taken some pictures—I'll take more and get double prints made.

Malai Island is supposed to have several houses down and a large crack that admits the sea, or water up from the lens. FKC sent a scouting team out yesterday. Lablab has some bush huts down, and a demolished wharf. The Kovai side (northwest) of Umboi seems to have borne the worst. The government station at Semo is *flattened.* All of its toilets and water tanks are demolished. Some people saw smoke coming from the mountain (Tarave) and we can see reddish brown landslide scars from Mandok. Our wharf, too, is down. A couple of teachers' houses on Por are tilting or destroyed.

I thought of calling you on Monday but Father Ansgaar told me it took two hours to get through to Lae on the radio, so I didn't. I sent chloroquine to the Muru refugees to be taken as a prophylactic, because by next week they will all be down with malaria. We have had rain and thunderstorms for the three nights they have been there, and most have only worn tarpaulins for protection. Every news bulletin we have managed to receive on our radios is dominated by news of cyclone Uma in Vanuatu. So a lot of people are really scared by the rain. The Siassi earthquake gets only the briefest mention, one to two lines at best. The first report, on Monday morning, put the epicenter on West New Britain. A number of people conflated the two events into one traveling maelstrom: They feared that whatever the "cyclone" was that hit Vanuatu was moving quickly toward us. I tried to explain the difference in the reports as best I could, but have to admit I was stuck on one very perceptive question. Can an earthquake cause that kind of a disruption in weather patterns? This seemed a logical question to some of the more educated younger people. If an earthquake can cause a tidal wave, why not a cyclone? The moon causes higher tides when it is full, and also, according to the Mandok, calms the seas. Knowing all of this, and given my own terror and lack of sleep, it sounded good at the time.

We have aftershocks *still*—day and night. But people are slowing dribbling back to Mandok. The Pindiu Road is down, Lablab and Mandok wharves are down, and the Semo/Gomlonggon Road is also buried under a landslide. Some people are saying that my brother's spirit is lashing out, since these were all "his" projects through the development authority. Is it true? At this point, even I am willing to say, "*Husat save?*" (Tok Pisin for "Who knows?").

Once the mundane details of finding and cooking food were taken care of, once some people started trickling back into the village, all were consumed with the question of what the earthquake meant. What exactly was it, and what did it mean? they asked me. I tried to explain plate tectonics by using a punctured soccer ball and enamel-coated tin plates.

Picture the following scene. We are sitting around a hip-high veranda. There is a fire. I am on the veranda because I still can't sit for very long or be up at all for more than forty minutes maximum. But there I am, like a gawky stork, balancing this deflated soccer ball and three enamel plates of different sizes, in between my two hands and my raised knee (ugh!). "You see," I say, "the earth is round like this soccer ball—when it is filled with air, that is. We see land, mountains, and sea (pointing with my chin), but we don't see that there is land underneath the sea, with mountains and valleys just like on the surface."

A hiss of wide-eyed amazement ripples around the fire, all eyes glued to the soccer ball and my clumsy hands and knees straining to keep the plates on it and my lap-lap discretely tucked.

"The problem is," I continue, "that the formations of land cover the earth's surface sort of like these plates are covering this ball. As you can see, they do not fit too well." I break out into a sweat, trying doggedly to reclaim the knowledge of introductory geology that was once mine. I grimace at the thought of my brother Al's reaction to my rendition of his chosen field. But the trouper in me says, "The show must go on, the mail must get through." The stress of knowing that my adoptive family and friends are depending on me to say something plausible (and understandable to them) translates into, "Just *do it*." With my back now screaming for relief, I continue.

"Now, these plates don't fit, you see? And underneath them the earth is very hot, like a *mumu* (Tok Pison for "stone oven") that is so hot it melts the stones and starts boiling."

"Ah," someone says, "underneath the ground the earth is hot—so hot it melts the stones in a mumu? *Xoraa!*" (Mutu for "Wow!")

"Ye-es," I say tentatively, "and sometimes it breaks through the surface, sort of like when a boil breaks—like a volcano."

Eager noises of assent—I think they've got it now!

"But sometimes the stuff doesn't come out of a volcano. Sometimes it just sort of ripples these plates a bit, like a wave moves a floating canoe"—maybe a maritime metaphor will cinch it—"and they bump together," I say, shifting two plates together until they clang to illustrate the point. On cue, Mother Earth, as if to nod assent, shakes a little in silent aftershock. A few bottles rattle, house posts creak. We all stiffen and hold our breaths.

My father, who has been silent until now, wags his head from side to side, emitting a low, noiseless whistle, and concludes, "God surely does work in strange ways."

So much for science. Setting down my show-and-tell props, I accede to the querulous demands of my aching back and stretch it flat on the veranda. The lively chatter that ensues is encouraging. I think I gave them something to chew on, at least.

Well, that's it from here. You asked for a long letter, and you got it. Take care, *write soon*—with some good news, please, if there is any.

Cheers from the rock
and roll capital of PNG

Ali

So there I was, stuck in a dilapidated and deserted village, with no place to go and no way to get there, anyway. After the earthquake I got Papa to tell me the story of the Great Gitua Shipwreck, another in which *he* was involved, and of course past tidal waves, earthquakes, and other cataclysms in Mandok history. I also got two-thirds the way through *Grant's Guide to Fishes* with him. Showing him the pictures, he recited the Mutu terms for each, the conditions of fishing, etc., that I would eventually use to create a taxonomy of fish and other sea creatures. I also finished my lexis, *finally,* the day before the earthquake. Funny, it seems every time I did a full day of linguistics a disaster struck. Were these omens?

We all have our ways of dealing with trauma, however it comes packaged at any particular moment. My own behavioral response, to the extent to which my aching back allowed, was to record the Mandok's feelings, reactions, and above all their explanations for the series of cataclysms that hit them, their village, and the entire area. I was already behind in recording their reactions to the tragic death and funeral. Part of this was due to the fact that for so long I was genuinely in mourning with the family in Finschhafen. I felt it was appropriate to allow an intervening period to diminish the emotional charge pervading the entire village. Before any of us could recover from that trauma, however, the earthquake gave us all something new to worry about.

My emotional response was to try, as much as my shattered nerves allowed, to keep calm. My attempts to explain my brother's death and the earthquake as best I could were genuine. The people's responses to my explanations, and to the events surrounding them, were equally genuine. Each of us tried our best to communicate—really we did. But, as the old adage goes, some things get lost in the translation. In this case, much got lost, but other things got added. I did have the sense that I was in a movie. There was something surrealistic about the entire sequence of events and relentless trauma that encouraged that sense. The alternative sense was to insist to myself that just because I was getting paranoid did not mean they (whoever "they" are) were not out to get me.

Now, after the fact, it almost seems as if it was only a movie. But it wasn't. Oh no, not quite. That much I do know. I *lived* through this one.

EIGHT

🐚 Reflections of a Shy Ethnographer: Foot-in-the-Mouth Is Not Fatal

JULIANA FLINN
University of Arkansas, Little Rock

I am shy. This proclamation is nothing more than a simple indicative fact that under ordinary circumstances would mean little. However, preliminary to ethnographic fieldwork, the issue presented problems of an extraordinary nature. Before I went to the field in Micronesia, I fretted over my shyness—worried that it would severely interfere with my research. Completely convinced I would make a fool of myself, I nonetheless dug deeply in the commitment to play the role of the child in remote surroundings and to learn, explore, and mostly, test myself. By accident, through an incident with a Micronesian informant and friend, I grew. Surviving chastisement, I learned something of both shyness and friendship, and more importantly I was compelled to face my own ethnocentricity.

Preparing to leave for the field, I discovered a reference to an article titled "Memoirs of a Shy Ethnographer." I eagerly sought a reprint, anxious for any tips dealing with shyness in the field. Simply knowing that others had contended with this personal problem would itself be comforting. Anthropologists had, in print, discussed culture shock, adjustment problems, even anxiety, but nowhere had I uncovered a discussion of shyness in the ethnographic enterprise. After all, cultural anthropologists are by the nature of their profession nosy: They have to enter a society, build rapport, gain some appreciable degree of acceptance, observe, participate, and ask people questions. I was moderately confident that I could do all that, but I dreaded the trauma that was likely to result. I wanted some hints. I needed some hints. And I needed the comfort of knowing I was not alone in worrying about shyness in the field.

My shyness essentially manifested itself as a fear of making mistakes and appearing blatantly foolish in public. I was apprehensive—worried at not presenting myself as perfect, the results of which would find me neither acceptable nor likable. I probably also had a touch of what is today being called the "Imposter Syndrome," the conviction that I only appeared to be a good graduate student and professional candidate. I suspect that women may be more prone than men to this particular problem. I recall echoing the feelings of a colleague who described her reaction at passing her doctoral examinations: "I can't believe it! I fooled them again, and they passed me. They still haven't found out that I don't know anything!"

Shyness, especially in dealing with graduate faculty, had disturbed me. Suspicious that shyness was preventing me from learning the social and political skills necessary for survival in a university, I often considered quitting, once especially after an awkward meeting with an advisor who seemed to have no idea why I consulted him. Perhaps because of a stubborn streak that counters my shyness, I persisted. I had more or less quietly pursued my own course in school without actively seeking advice and I decided to continue my unobtrusive ways. In fact, I put them to the test. If I failed in graduate school as a result of my own personal attitudes and approaches, I would then receive some confirmation that I was unsuited for the academic life.

I was not at all certain, however, that I would continue to remain successful quietly pursuing my work in the field. Perhaps I could manage graduate school without lengthy and frequent consultations with faculty, but I could not keep to myself in the field forever. Even though I had already been in Micronesia for two years as a Peace Corps volunteer, I prepared for fieldwork with a lingering sense of dread. I worried about approaching and talking to people—strangers, many of whom would probably have minimal or misconceived ideas of why I was there.

I looked back nostalgically on those Peace Corps years. They seemed so easy and free of stress compared to what was now facing me. In the Peace Corps I had a specific job to do, a clear role to play with structure and expectations that at least provided some degree of comfort. In fieldwork I would have to build my own structure, my own relationships, my own role—all of which seemed daunting.

I devoured articles about field experiences, especially about gaining entry into the field, building rapport, and interviewing. None of these dealt with shyness. Trusting that I was not unique, I wanted to know how other people had dealt with the problem. So I eagerly searched the library for the "shy ethnographer" article.

I was disappointed. The article had absolutely nothing to do with shyness. In fact, I never did figure out exactly what the title had to do with the article. I was on my own. To this day I remember the sick feeling in my stomach as I stepped into the jetway in San Francisco. How had the adventurous and persistent half of me forced the terrified half of me into this situation? What in the world was I doing?

Even more vivid is the memory of a sea of eyes swooping down the beach when my boat came ashore at the atoll. A wave of curious children descended to see a white woman carrying a blond toddler. But it was that same blond toddler who helped me contend with my shyness. He made my fieldwork easier. In fact, while I was in the field, I vowed that one day I would write my own article and finally thoroughly address the issue of shyness in ethnography—"Memoirs of a Shy Ethnographer, II." I soon discovered I was managing to deal with my shyness and even felt I had a few tips to pass along. I also decided that my first recommendation would be to beg, borrow, or steal a two-year-old child, preferably a gregarious and outgoing one like mine, though how I ended up with such a self-possessed and friendly child is still a mystery.

I had deliberately selected a remote field site on a coral atoll in Micronesia, more remote even than my earlier Peace Corps assignment. Yet this remoteness had positive effects which somewhat alleviated the problem of shyness. For example, the islanders held different notions of privacy than Americans, so I could easily watch and participate in many daily activities. I could easily wander by a homesite without feeling as though I was intruding into someone's privacy. This was, for me, thankfully a more comfortable environment.

Furthermore, I already knew several of the residents. Many had been my students several years earlier. The island residents knew who I was, since students had returned from school with tales of their American teachers. Some were initially confused about why I had come to their island, assuming I was returning as a Peace Corps volunteer, but I explained as best I could about my new role. Most saw me as a woman interested in learning about their customs. More important than my reasons for coming to their island seemed to be the fact that I was returning to Micronesia and had chosen to live with them instead of on the neighboring atoll where I had been assigned by the Peace Corps. I felt as though I was being treated as a long-lost friend, and they were convinced I genuinely liked them because I had chosen their island for my return.

Even more convincing to them, however, was the fact that I had brought my son, who was then about nineteen months old. The islanders were familiar enough with Americans willing to live with them because of years of Peace Corps service, but the majority of volunteers had been single and male. For a woman to come—and to bring her child—was a new experience which they interpreted to mean that I not only liked them, but I trusted them and their way of life to be good and healthy for my son,

Having a child with me in the field offered other benefits. I was much more real a person and woman in the eyes of my hosts. At my age and married—but deliberately childless—while in the Peace Corps, I presented an enigma. Although I now discovered the island women were curious about why I had only one child in the field, it was easier for them to now understand and relate to me and my situation. They might have to struggle with the notion of "anthropologist" but they had little trouble with "mother." And with a small child, I also found it much easier to be casual with people; my son often accompanied me and eased awkward moments when I felt compelled to talk about something. Even without a particular research purpose in mind, I could wander the island with him and simply stop and visit when he seemed so inclined. And several issues came to light because people would tell me of dangers to him. I was warned, for example, about walking with him on the beach in the evening for fear of malevolent ghosts.

Yet I was, in effect, myself a child in the field—a foolish and unknowing child. Intent on learning but still fearful of mistakes, it was important to me that the islanders learn to develop a concerned willingness to correct my blunders and misunderstandings. Much of my learning and questioning had to be public. I well remember exploring the island feeling like the pied piper because of the trail of children I attracted. I had forgotten what it was like to be noticed all the time, no longer anonymous.

Nonetheless, I contended as best I could with my shyness as I began learning their way of life. For example, I had ambivalent feelings about a young girl in the family with whom I lived—a girl who was a bit more outspoken than most. She was personally valuable precisely because of her lack of tact. Old enough to notice and explain my mistakes, she was at the same time either not mature enough or not inclined to politely ignore them. Most of her remarks centered on my speech. I arrived speaking a different Micronesian dialect, that of another island. Whenever I slipped into a word form or expression from the other island, she was the first to publicly correct me. Perhaps this young girl understood earlier than others. She chided me when I used a word from my Peace Corps experiences, especially when the local word forms were quite different. With bluntness she told me to learn to use the language of her people. Adults, on the other hand, tended to switch to the dialect from the district center—another dialect in which I was not well versed—when I had difficulty understanding. It took time for me to convince people that I could understand better if they just tried again in their own language.

These were valuable lessons. Considering that I wanted to explore attitudes toward people from other islands and that my hosts disliked the people from my Peace Corps site, I realized I could easily be given misleading answers if I sounded like one of those other islanders. Nonetheless, I was not accustomed to being scolded by a twelve-year-old girl. I swallowed my pride, reminding myself how useful she was.

Another outspoken woman was Camilla, a friend and participant in one of my greatest blunders. She had been a student of mine when I taught as a Peace Corps volunteer. Since then she had finished high school, returned home, married, and become pregnant with her first child. I cultivated a relationship with her for a variety of reasons. First, she was typical of the sort of persons I had come to study, a woman who had gone away to school, graduated, formed ties with other islanders while away, and returned to her home island. She was articulate, witty, patient, and seemingly comfortable with me. She was also a bit more outspoken than most. Since she knew I wanted to learn the ways of her people, she graciously volunteered information and provided instructions about how I should behave in local events and ceremonies.

One of the other reasons I liked Camilla was that she felt free to ask me questions. I discovered that I was much more comfortable answering questions than asking them; perhaps she should have been conducting the ethnographic research. But I learned much from the questions people asked me, perhaps as much as I learned from the questions I asked. For example, one woman, convinced that one of us misunderstood the other, pumped me for information about adoption in the United States. She very carefully set up her case: "Come on now, Julie. If you had ten children, and your sister didn't have any at all, wouldn't you share at least some of them with her?" Americans were immensely selfish creatures in her eyes.

When I asked about clans, people sometimes seemed surprised. "Why? Don't you have clans?" I had to answer no. "Well, then how do you know who your relatives are?" I enjoyed their candor and gained insights into how they viewed kinship.

One day I had gone to see Camilla and we had finished discussing the particular subjects of interest. I stayed, as was my habit, to talk as friends. Since she was pregnant with her first child, we began sharing stories about our experiences. In the back of my mind, I realized we were having this discussion in part because I had a child of my own—again an example of the advantages of conducting fieldwork as a mother.

Curious about local beliefs, I asked if she had any sense of whether she was carrying a boy or a girl and if she had any preference for one or the other. She said, "Some women say they know if it's a boy or a girl, and maybe before, in older times, there were people who could tell." Like the American I was, I also asked about names, wondering which ones she was considering and what meaning the choices had. She couldn't understand my curiosity. "We pick names after a child is born. How can you know what name to give before that?"

We had also been talking about the possibility of my returning sometime to her island and whether or not I would have any more children. She, like others, couldn't understand why I had only one child—especially at my age. Here I thought, compared to my experiences in the Peace Corps, arriving with a child would make such a difference. It did, but people also wanted to know why I had only one. In fact, they felt sorry for my mother. Many women lamented her fate: "The poor woman, she had only five children."

Thinking of how often people asked if my son and I would come back and how often they said they would like to see him when he was older, I said, "Well, maybe you'll have a girl, and maybe my son will come back when he's twenty or so, fall in love with your daughter, and get married." Camilla was appalled at what I considered an innocent remark. In fact, I meant the remark as an indicator of my close feelings. She glared at me, taken aback. I began to get the sense that I had said something I shouldn't have.

"Julie, you shouldn't say things like that. What an awful idea!" It was small comfort right then that I valued Camilla for her slightly atypical bluntness.

Now I had done it! I blushed, inwardly cringed, convinced that I had indeed made a fool of myself and that she'd never again take me seriously but would continue to treat me like some silly child. I had obviously said something I shouldn't have. How stupid had I revealed myself to be?

"Our children could never marry. You shouldn't say such a thing."

There it was again. Why couldn't she just drop it? But on the other hand, I figured I should pursue the issue; after all, I didn't want to repeat my mistake.

"I didn't mean to insult you. What's wrong with what I said? I want to know, so I won't do it again."

"It would be incest," she said, with a tone I interpreted as disbelief that I was so dense and slow to understand.

"Incest?" I thought I knew about that.

"Yes. Incest. Our children can't marry each other—we're sisters!" she responded.

"Sisters!" I liked the sound of that. I knew that the islanders created sibling ties for relationships we label friendships. Here I had been so overwhelmingly concerned about having made a foolish mistake, the result of which was this discovery of how fond Camilla was of me.

"Since we're sisters, our children are brothers and sisters and shouldn't get married."

I understood her point, and I relaxed, no longer concerned about a mistake. But over time I have seen many other implications of what she said.

This is the single strongest memory of my fieldwork, a turning point in so many important ways. First, I was able to take a very close look at the sort of role I wanted to play while living on the island. In this regard, I was made aware of how much my own values affected my behavior. Second, the abstract ideas I had read concerning kinship and Micronesian culture, instead of being an intellectual exercise, became very real and personal. As a result, I gained explicit insights into their meanings of kinship. Finally, perhaps because this was a cross-cultural friendship, the incident with Camilla was the beginning of personal growth for me which led to the realization that I could do or say foolish things and still be valued and liked.

I considered making explicit the created sibling relationship, partly to show I had a certain understanding of the relationship (and to recover some wounded pride!), partly because I was so pleased. But then I found my own personal values coming into play. I immediately realized that by making the relationship explicit—even more explicit than she had—I would have to treat her brothers as she did, including showing all the customary patterns of respect. I was comfortable with general patterns of courtesy and respect, but I disliked the thought of crawling in the presence of all her brothers. I also considered the dangers of inadvertently alienating others. Where would I stop? Who might be insulted or hurt because I had not befriended them?

Another practical concern was relationships with men. I wanted to remain marginal enough to be free to talk easily with men, including Camilla's brothers. There were distinct advantages to my being an American woman. For personal and professional reasons, I recognized the limits of how comfortably "native" I might go.

In one other way I discovered how very American—and ethnocentric— I had been by commenting on our children being potential mates. All the theoretical alliance material I had studied became real: I was trying to validate our relationship, marking it by hinting at an alliance through marriage—a Western pattern. Yet adoption, common in the Pacific, may serve similar functions when marriage ties are not strong. Adoption validates and strengthens ties since the natal and adoptive parents are siblings and share a child. It would have been much more culturally appropriate for me to have suggested that I adopt her child in order to mark our closeness.

This incident made very real for me the islanders' views of kinship as sharing—as behavior, not just biology. Camilla was genuinely appalled at my suggestion, despite the absence of any blood ties.

Perhaps most valuable was the sense of friendship that allows mistakes. I'm not sure why this particular incident was so crucial in this regard. It may have been precisely because I was so consciously concerned with being accepted and not seeming foolish.

I have continued to learn from my experience—and to think seriously about quiet, shy, and unassuming behavior as a possible asset in the field. In later conversations with other anthropologists, especially women, I have found I was not the only one to enter the field thinking I should be actively doing something all the time, seeking people out, asking questions, interviewing, and asserting myself. One woman, for example, talked of initially feeling uncomfortable about just "hanging around." Another woman commented that informants eventually revealed that they came to trust her because instead of beginning with questions, she quietly joined them in activities. Less modest behavior, in this instance, would have resulted in alienation.

My own shyness in the field may have been painful, but it fit local expectations of how a women should behave and may, all things considered, have inadvertently been a productive and useful ethnographic tool. What I value most from the incident with Camilla, however, is what I learned of meaningful friendship.

NINE

What's So Funny About That? Fieldwork and Laughter in Polynesia

RICHARD FEINBERG
Kent State University

On the evening of my third night on Anuta, with darkness approaching and my hut crowded with inquisitive villagers, I tried several times—unsuccessfully—to light my pressure lantern. This Western Pacific kerosene counterpart to the familiar Coleman lantern was somewhat difficult and tricky to operate. A cloth mantle had to be heated with denatured methyl alcohol for several minutes prior to opening the main kerosene valve. At each failure, the assembly broke into hysterical laughter and I, in annoyance and frustration, fought to maintain my composure. Finally, the critical temperature was reached and I ignited the lamp. Then, in the light, in an effort to save irreplaceable alcohol, I removed the wick used to prime the lamp. When I attempted to blow out the flame, however, some of the burning spirits dripped onto my bare leg. As I struggled to extinguish the flames, the gathering, instead of coming to my aid, laughed still more uproariously.

This was my first period of overseas anthropological field research. In 1970 I had been searching for a relatively untouched Polynesian community to serve as a field site for my doctoral research. Raymond Firth was visiting professor at the University of Chicago. Since 1928 he had been involved in an intensive study of Tikopia, a remote Polynesian outlier in the Solomon Islands. When I asked him for advice, he suggested Tikopia's nearest neighbor—still smaller, more remote, and not yet seriously studied. If I really wanted a traditional community, he noted, "Anuta is about as isolated as you can get."

A year and a half later, I was on Anuta to embark upon a year-long study of kinship and social structure. Knowing that Anuta's language would resemble Tikopia's, Professor Firth had graciously taken time to teach me basic Tikopian grammar and vocabulary. From conversations with Firth and examining the few literary references, I had developed a general idea of what I was to find. I would be living on an island just a half mile in diameter with a population of about 150 people. The community would be stratified, led by hereditary chiefs, and divided into a number of ranked clans, which would be among the most important units of social activity. Decades earlier, the people had been converted to the Angelican church; otherwise, Anutans would be but minimally affected by European civilization. I knew that they would be living in leaf houses with no electricity or plumbing. They would produce virtually all of their own food, grow vegetables in local gardens, and catch fish from wooden outrigger canoes. And they would cook their food in earth ovens or over open fires.

For the novice that I was, I felt fairly well prepared for my adventure. Still, there were doubts. Would I be accepted on the island? Would I be able to learn the language? Would I collect sufficient data for a dissertation?

My confidence was bolstered somewhat by events preceding my arrival on Anuta. While awaiting the interisland ship in Honiara, the Solomon Islands' capital, I met a few bilingual Tikopians. In addition, several educated Tikopians traveled with me on the three-day voyage by government ship from the administrative station in the Santa Cruz Islands to Anuta. My companions added to the rudimentary linguistic knowledge I had gained from Firth, so that by the time I reached Anuta I was ready to begin learning the language in earnest. This positive beginning, combined with the urgency of finding myself among a group of Polynesians, almost none of whom spoke English, enabled me learn the language more quickly than I had imagined. Within a month I was conducting census interviews in Anutan. A few months later I was dreaming in Anutan.

But I am getting ahead of myself. Having read Firth's introduction to his anthropological classic, *We, The Tikopia,* my arrival on the island left me with a sense of déjà vu. In those first hectic moments, as I tried to keep track of my gear—already doused from shooting through the surf in the ship's launch—and to protect it from the rain while greeting the island's two chiefs, I failed to notice that the ship had disappeared. Only later did it strike me that I now was completely out of touch with my own culture, family, and friends . . . in new and strange surroundings, until the ship's next visit, perhaps three months hence.

Prepared as I was, from reading and from practice in the language, I was still not prepared for the constant attention, the almost total lack of privacy, the daily bombardment by what struck me as infernally stupid questions, and the incessant laughter at events I viewed as anything but funny— especially laughter at my own expense.

The attention should have come as no surprise. Fieldworkers in non-Western societies—particularly those working in small, confined, face-to-face communities—typically discover that they lack the privacy most Americans have learned to take for granted. We should not be surprised to find our hosts as curious about us as we are about them. Furthermore, in a community where entire families live in one-room houses and people spend little time alone, one should expect to be placed under constant scrutiny, whether writing field notes, reading, eating, or dressing a wound.

On these issues, Napoleon Chagnon pointedly described his personal experience among the Yanomamo Indians of South America:

> The thing that bothered me most was the incessant, passioned, and aggressive demands the Indians made. It would become so unbearable that I would have to lock myself in my mud hut every once in a while just to escape from it: Privacy is one of Western culture's greatest achievements.
>
> But I did not want privacy for its own sake; rather, I simply had to get away from the begging. Day and night for the entire time I lived with the Yanomamo I was plagued by such demands as: "Give me a knife, I am poor!"; "If you don't take me with you on your next trip to Widokaiya-teri I'll chop a hole in your canoe!"; "Don't point your camera at me or I'll hit you!"; "Share your food with me!"; "Take me across the river in your canoe and be quick about it!"; "Give me a cooking pot!"; "Loan me your flashlight so I can go hunting tonight!"; "Give me medicine . . . I itch all over!"; "Take us on a week-long hunting trip with your shotgun!"; and "Give me an axe or I'll break into your hut when you are away visiting and steal one!" And so I was bombarded by such demands day after day, months on end, until I could not bear to see an Indian (Chagnon 1968:8).

Still, in one way or another, most anthropologists do manage to adjust to the lack of privacy.

Thankfully, my hosts were much more pleasant and far less demanding of me than Chagnon's Yanomamo were of him. Nonetheless, Anutans' interest in my comings and goings often took a form to which I found difficult to reconcile myself. In particular, it was hard to suppress irritation at what seemed to me stupid questions. The most ubiquitous of these was the perpetual "Where are you going?" I could be walking from my house to the beach—a distance of perhaps a hundred yards—meet a dozen people along the way, and every one would ask, "Where are you going?" "What are you going in order to do?" And "When are you coming back?"

I could be walking to the beach, hook and line in hand, as a canoe was being prepared for a day's fishing expedition, meet the same dozen people, and each would ask in turn, "Are you going to the ocean?" I could be walking to that section of the beach used as the men's lavatory, carrying a roll of toilet paper, and everyone I met would ask me with a laugh, "What are you going in order to do?" If I were sitting with a group of Anutans and got up to stretch my legs, I would immediately be asked, "Where are you going?" Or if I should join an extant group, I would be asked, "You come?"

This last I found particularly irksome, as I sensed my hosts were being more than just a bit facetious. It seemed to me that even my most minor movements were being magnified beyond all semblance of reason or good taste. Of course, this characterization is quite unfair. Stereotyped questions of such cultural significance are often independent of their denotative content. These types of query are commonplace in many communities (see, especially, Goodenough in this volume) and an Anutan's greeting of "Where are you going?" is no more a request for specific information than our "How are you?"

But how to explain the events of that third night and my disastrous attempt to light my lantern? I could not help suspecting that as a strange new arrival I had been singled out for ridicule. Perhaps fortunately, I did not yet speak enough Anutan to express my feelings.

As time went on, however, I became increasingly aware that what I had experienced was common practice on the island. Anutans typically respond to other people's minor traumas—tripping over roots, stubbing toes, hitting heads on rafters or low-hanging branches, being dashed into the reef by heavy surf, or even mispronouncing words and otherwise displaying ignorance—with full-blown laughter.

The urge to laugh at other people's mishaps is, of course, quite comprehensible in terms of Western culture. Indeed, much of our comedy plays on this urge. However, it is possible to laugh at the Three Stooges with their faces full of pie, or Zonker Harris's traumatic realization that his college days are numbered, precisely because these people are *not* real. When someone we know is faced with an insoluble dilemma or when a neighbor stubs his toe, Americans may feel an urge to laugh; but normally that urge is suppressed. Were one to laugh at someone falling from a tree or slipping on a sheet of ice, the victim would add anger and embarrassment to physical discomfort while the viewer is condemned for lack of judgment and compassion. Anutans, by contrast, seem to feel no such constraints, and laughter at one another's misfortunes is a constant fact of life.

Anthropologically, these observations raise some important questions. Why do Anutans laugh so freely? What message is communicated by laughter at a victim of misfortune? How do victims feel when they discover that they are the target of another person's laughter?

Sometimes an ethnographer is fortunate enough to have informants come forward with a ready explanation that is convincing and consistent with the observed facts. Thus, when Richard Lee was made the butt of an elaborate hoax by his !Kung bushmen friends, informants readily explained the incident as their customary antidote to a successful hunter's would-be arrogance (Lee 1969). But the Anutan case seems more complex.

At first I thought Anutan laughter might serve to promote care and competence in physical activities among a people for whom such routine activities as climbing coconut trees and interisland sailing leave little room for error. Anutans, given this theory, would learn early that the slightest faux pas would result in ridicule and shame; and they would soon become extremely careful to avoid situations which might result in embarrassment and censure. This explanation loses force, however, when one weighs potential costs in terms of social tension against the potential benefits. Moreover, it seems just as likely that the threat of ridicule might make people self-conscious and more, rather than less, prone to errors. And, as I was soon to learn, this explanation suffers from the flaw of making false assumptions about laughter's meaning in the Anutan scheme of things.

Upon further queries, my informants told me that when others laugh at them, they suffer neither shame nor anger; rather, they feel happiness and laugh themselves. The rationale I heard for this response is that when one is hurt, he is unhappy. Happiness is a dominant value in Anutan culture, and laughter is identified with happiness. Moreover, laughter is regarded as contagious. Therefore, if someone suffers a minor injury or misfortune, observers are supposed to laugh. Hearing this, the victim is unable to suppress his own laughter, and his sorrow is converted into pleasure. In contrast with minor mishaps, when someone suffers serious injury involving broken bones or spilled blood, others on the scene should *cry* as they would for a deceased kinsman.

This altruistic explanation is internally consistent and plausible in terms of Anuta's cultural values and dominant symbols. Still we must be wary of accepting it uncritically.

On occasion, Anutans will admit irritation. For example, an informant told me he particularly resented laughter at verbal mistakes in front of a large group. By contrast, if only a few people were present, he felt that laughter was appropriate and served to relieve embarrassment.

Since the Anutan explanation did not always fit with the behavior I observed, I decided to examine the work of Western social scientists for insight. In the process, I discovered suggestions of several psychological and social functions served by laughter. A few even seemed as if they might shed light on the Anutan situation.

Freud (1960) wrote that laughter served to release tension by rendering a potentially threatening situation less so. But in Anuta many of the events which evoke laughter do not appear to be particularly threatening, and it would seem that the most threatening aspect of many of these situations is the prospect of ridicule itself.

Nachman (1982:124–128), in discussing laughter among Melanesians in Papua New Guinea, notes that laughter creates a sense of community among the participants at the expense of the recipient. He argues that laughter is a "potent weapon of social criticism."

In Anuta laughter may be directed at the situation rather than the person, thereby rendering potentially disruptive events harmless and forging a sense of solidarity. While the suggestion may make abstract sense, however, I received no confirmation from Anutans that it accurately describes their situation.

Melford Spiro (1952) suggests that people anywhere, under some circumstances, will develop conflicts and hostilities. Conflicts are repressed in normal social intercourse, and a nondisruptive release mechanism, like laughter, is sought. The Micronesian atoll community of Ifaluk has developed one workable solution: Conflict is attributed to evil spirits which may be destroyed or driven off through collective ritual. The parallel argument for Anuta would offer collective laughter as a cultural alternative to overt expressions of hostility or anger.

There would appear to be less need for such an outlet on Anuta then among the Ifaluk, but Anutans have a variety of release mechanisms available. They do at times get into arguments and accuse each other of misdeeds. One primary function of the chiefs (see Feinberg 1978, 1981), in fact, is to resolve disputes. As on Ifaluk, Anutan hostilities may be openly directed against evil spirits. And hostilities may be acted out through competitive sport, particularly *tika* dart matches resembling our javelin events (see Firth 1930, 1936, for detailed descriptions of this sport on Tikopia).

In former times, Anutans sometimes killed each other—or so it has been related—and presently, aggression against non-Anutans is at times acceptable behavior. But Anutans claim that laughter is not meant to be aggressive; rather, its intent is quite the opposite.

This last protest could well be interpreted as a rationalization rather than a statement of fact. The question, then, is why would Anutans have bothered to construct such an elaborate rationalization, particularly when it might better serve as a release mechanism if it were explicitly acknowledged as such? I felt the answer might lie, in large part, in the cultural prohibitions on expression of aggression toward kin. And this must, in turn, be understood in terms of the place of laughter in Anutan culture.

To smile and *to laugh* are denoted in Anuta by a single word: *kata*. There is a strong positive value associated with such behavior. In fact, one cannot be a "good person" *(tangata rerei)* unless one laughs and smiles a lot. *To laugh* or *to smile* is strongly associated with the prime Anutan value of *vakivaki* (happiness). This is in direct contrast to anger *(konokono)* and sorrow as expressed through crying *(tangi)*.

Anutans are preoccupied with happiness and constantly explain their actions in terms of making us happy. If one asks the meaning of a song, dance, feast, or other act, the answer is most frequently that it is (1) the ancient custom of this island, (2) a demonstration of our *aropa* (love), or (3) to make us happy. While happiness is an important value, however, Anutans are concerned with overt expressions rather than subjective states.

It is for this reason that *aropa* (see Feinberg 1981:67–72 and passim) is only recognized as giving and sharing of material goods or labor. Should one wish to send his "love" to someone overseas, it is in the form of a material gift, and "love" is expressed most potently by sharing membership in one domestic unit, which holds all property in common.

Anutans learn dramatic modes of expression early in their lives. This is seen in their demonstrative wailing at the death of a kinsman or at the destruction of a canoe. It is evident in constant appeals to come and eat, as expressions of goodwill, regardless of the would-be host's true feelings about the invited guest. And it is further apparent in Anutans' readiness to laugh and smile.

The "love ethic" enjoins smooth relations among kin, which in this case includes everyone on the island. Hence, we find a deeply held ethic of nonaggression. Yet conflicts do occur and laughter remains a sanctioned outlet for aggressive feelings. This can only be compatible with *aropa* if the aggressive intent of the laughter is denied—and denied convincingly.

My final clue to understanding the patterns and significance of laughter on Anuta came from an account of a different Polynesian people: the Samoans. In a recent book, Derek Freeman (1983) offers a description of Samoa designed to contrast in important ways with Margaret Mead's depiction in *Coming of Age in Samoa.* Freeman emphasizes rivalry, aggressiveness, and a propensity to flashes of extreme violence as important features of Samoan personality. This, however, is combined with a veneer of grace, respect, and smooth, harmonious relations under most circumstances. Freeman describes meetings in which sensitive issues are thrashed out between rival factions. As the level of tension rises, so does the level of respect, politeness, self-effacement, and formality of discourse.

Indeed, Anutans take pains not to confront each other directly with personal criticism. I have heard people make the most scathing comments about others behind their backs, only to transform themselves into consummate diplomats when dealing with their verbal targets in face-to-face encounters. In 1980, when the Anutan community was being torn apart by rampant factionalism, the adversaries finally resolved the problem, not by openly addressing the points of conflict, but by studiously avoiding mention of the contentious subject.

In this light, Anutan laughter may be seen as a mechanism for releasing hostilities that should not be openly expressed. This conclusion also makes it possible to understand some of the behavioral inconsistencies associated with Anutan laughter. Since behavior on Anuta is so carefully controlled, one cannot assume a cause-and-effect relationship between what people feel and what they do. People wail at funerals because it is the proper way to act, whether they feel grieved at the deceased's demise or not; and consequently, the most pathetic wailing may be interspersed with idle conversation, pipe-smoking, and even jokes. Children's cries of anguish are turned on and off as if on cue. And in like manner, laughter at a victim of misfortune often evokes laughter rather than a grimace.

Perhaps the most important lesson of Anutan laughter lies in the ambivalence of its message. I, like most anthropologists, was hoping to decipher a single unequivocal meaning in the phenomena that I had chosen to investigate. Reality, however, need not be bound by our analytic categories. Symbols, in Victor Turner's words (1967), are often "multivocal," bearing different meanings in different contexts, and sometimes conveying several differnt messages simultaneously. Thus, the same event may be susceptible to multiple interpretations and thereby elicit differing emotions, even in one individual.

For the anthropologist in quest of underlying meanings and definitive analyses, this state of affairs can be most disconcerting. For Anutans, who take the position that internal states are necessarily unknowable by an outside observer and that therefore people can be judged only by their overt actions, it is a nonproblem.

REFERENCES

CHAGNON, NAPOLEON

1968   Yanomamo: The Fierce People. New York: Holt, Rinehart and Winston.

FEINBERG, RICHARD

1978   Rank and Authority on Anuta Island. In Adaptation and Symbolism: Essays on Social Organization. Karen Ann-Watson-Gegeo and S. Lee Seaton, eds. Honolulu: The University Press of Hawaii.

1981   Anuta: Social Structure of a Polynesian Island. Laie and Copenhagen: Institute for Polynesian Studies in cooperation with the National Museum of Denmark.

1986   The 'Anuta Problem': Local Sovereignty and National Integration in the Solomon Islands. Man (N.S.) 21:438–452.

FIRTH, RAYMOND

1930   A Dart Match in Tikopia. Oceania 1:64–96.

1936   We, the Tikopia. London: George Allen and Unwin.

FREEMAN, DEREK

1983   Margaret Mead and Samoa: The Making and Unmaking of an Anthropological Myth. Cambridge, MA: Harvard University Press.

FREUD, SIGMUND

1960   Jokes and Their Relation to the Unconscious. New York: Norton.

LEE, RICHARD B.

1969   Eating Christmas in the Kalahari. Smithsonian Magazine: December, 1969.

MEAD, MARGARET

1970   (Original: 1928) Coming of Age in Samoa: A Psychological Study of Primitive Youth for Western Civilization. New York: Dell.

NACHMAN, STEVEN

1982   Anti-humor: Why the Grand Sorcerer Wags His Penis. Ethos 10:117–135.

SPIRO, MELFORD

1952   Ghosts, Ifaluk, and Teleological Functionalism. American Anthropologist 54:497–503.

TURNER, VICTOR

1967   The Forest of Symbols. Ithaca: Cornell University Press.

 Cultural Baggage

JOYCE D. HAMMOND
Western Washington University

Just before I left for the islands of French Polynesia, I bought a beautiful piecework quilt with a grandmother's flower garden design. The owner of the Quilt Parlor gave me directions to the quilter's house. I knocked on her door, introduced myself, and told her how much I liked it: "When I saw your quilt, I knew it was just what I wanted! I'm leaving soon for Tahiti and the other islands of French Polynesia to learn about Polynesian quilts and the women who make them. Their quilt tradition was partly inspired by American missionary quilts. I decided it would be nice to take a quilt made by a fellow Hoosier to share as an example of what quilts are like here in Indiana. I think that the women in the islands will enjoy seeing the quilt you made."

As I packed the beautiful, multicolored quilt in its own suitcase, I smiled and thought, this is cultural baggage of a different sort! When anthropologists use the phrase *cultural baggage,* they usually mean the attitudes and ideas that they, as members of their own culture, inadvertently take with them wherever they go. Cultural baggage is something many anthropologists would just as soon leave at home, since it is generally felt that one's own cultural biases can distort perceptions of the way in which other people think and feel.

As a graduate student, I thought I knew all about cultural baggage—mine in particular. I had learned that anthropologists were supposed to be objective in describing the life-styles of other people. Aware of my cultural background, I would not let my white American middle-class attitudes and ideas interfere with my perceptions, or so I thought. How surprised I was to learn later that along with my quilt, typewriter, clothes, and other supplies, there was some cultural baggage for which I had not accounted. Yet the hidden stowaway, in the end, turned out to be helpful. I came to realize that cultural baggage, heavy and inevitable as it may be, can be instrumental in the learning process. It is impossible for anyone to be an objective observer of one's own culture or that of others. Participating in the experience of living precludes empirical objectivity. Yet, far from being an encumbrance, my reactions and emotions to various situations I experienced in the islands helped me not only to understand my hosts better, but also to appreciate the impact that I had on my own study.

I arrived in Tahiti, laden with my baggage of one sort and another, eager to begin my research. I engaged a tutor and began practicing my conversational skills in Tahitian. Soon, I felt ready to depart for some of the more remote islands of French Polynesia to live among families and learn about quilts, how they were used, and who made them. It was not long before I heard that the women of Rurutu in the Austral Islands, south of Tahiti, were renowned throughout French Polynesia for their piecework quilts, which they called *iripiti*.[1] I made connections with the daughter of the chief of the iripiti makers. She wrote to her mother about my study, and I received an invitation from Mahana Vahine[2] to stay in her home in Rurutu.

Rurutu was not a tourist island. Although it boasted a new airport in addition to its two harbors, most of the travelers to and from Rurutu were locals or French officials visiting the island on official business. Despite the few foreigners on Rurutu, the influence of Western culture was readily apparent. Among the fifteen hundred or so inhabitants, most of the people were Protestants. The largest buildings in the three small towns on the island were churches. All subjects in the towns' schools were taught in the official language of the territory—French. There was a French doctor and a French policeman on the island. Islanders could buy canned beef and butter imported from New Zealand in the small neighborhood general stores.

Life in Rurutu reflected the accommodation of outside influences on island traditions that stretched back before European contact. This was apparent not only in the *iripiti,* which evolved from the combined influences of indigenous bark cloth and introduced Western quilts, but also in the women's work patterns and plans for the *iripiti* and their other handwork.

I spent many hours with one particular group of women who worked together to sew *iripiti* and hand-weave fine pandanus mats, purses, and hats. The women worked daily, except on Sundays, holidays, and special occasions. They shared their labor with one another on a cooperative, round-robin basis. Each woman, on the day for which she was to be in charge, designated to each of the other women the tasks she wished to accomplish that day. The group created the opportunity for each woman to acquire valued goods in return for her skills and labor. Women might choose to sell their pandanus products to a buyer who shipped them to the Tahiti tourist market. They might also keep some hats, mats, and purses to give as valued gifts to relatives and friends at birthdays, weddings, and farewells. However, the women did not sell the brilliantly colored *iripiti.* Created from Western fabric and hours of painstaking hand sewing, they were much too valuable to sell. Women decorated their homes with them during special holidays and saved them as wedding presents for their children.

The dozen or so members of the women's group convened in one of the Protestant church's neighborhood meeting houses early every morning. At noon, the member whose turn it was to provide the largest meal of the day, as her day's contribution of labor, arrived with the hot food. Children and husbands were sometimes enlisted to help deliver it. Often, it arrived in a wheelbarrow. The fare usually consisted of fish or canned beef in noodles, breadfruit, and taro. A coconut sauce, in which all other foods were dipped by hand, and heavily sugared coffee completed the meal. The cook set the long table and called the other group members to eat. It was also her duty to clean the dining area, the dishes, and the silverware when everyone finished and resumed work for the afternoon.

Day after day I sat among the women for hours, watching them work and listening to their conversations. Sometimes I tried my hand at weaving a pandanus mat or sewing the tiny postage stamp–sized pieces of fabric in an iripiti together by hand, but I was under no illuisions that I could reciprocate with labor or services in a way that made me an equal in the group's functioning. I was very grateful for the women's easy acceptance of me in their midst and their approval of my interest in their work.

After I had been in Rurutu for a time, I decided to travel to Rarotonga in the Cook Islands in order to do some comparative research there. Although I made it clear that I would return to Rurutu, the women's group hosted a farewell party for me. In addition to the abundance of food at the party, which was itself a sign of honor, the women gave me many gifts they had made themselves. Gathered around the feast table, they presented me with three bottles of *mono'i,* a scented coconut oil used by men and women alike to make their skin glisten and their bodies fragrant. They gave me a number of pandanus hats in a variety of styles and several beautiful round pandanus mats. They also gave me quantities of shell necklaces with shells in every imaginable shape and color strung in a multitide of styles. Knowing how much I admired their handwork, the women had given me presents they knew I would treasure. I was over-whelmed by their generosity and thoughtfulness. I openly admired each gift and thanked them profusely and repeatedly. They beamed at me and were clearly pleased at my pleasure.

After the party, Mahana Vahine arranged all the gifts on my bed. She stood over them and said, "These are a sign of the contentment of the people for you. You must never sell them. They are yours to take back to the United States. Show others in your country what the women of Rurutu make." I listened carefully and indicated I was in total agreement. It would never have occurred to me to sell such wonderful tokens of affection and esteem which communicated the women's pride in their own work. I was surprised that Mahana Vahine thought it necessary to tell me what I already knew and felt. After all, I understood gift giving.

After Mahana Vahine finished speaking, she took a piece of paper and wrote down the names of all the women and their presents. I thought she was making a list to help me remember each woman's name and her gift, just as people often do at baby and bridal showers in the United States. At home, it was good etiquette to send thank-you notes to each individual, making specific reference to the particular gift. Was this the custom in Rurutu as well? As I was speculating on the prospects of making thank-you cards in Tahitian, she folded the paper up, placed it in my dress pocket, and asked me, "Do you think about those women?" I guessed at her meaning. "Oh yes! I wish that I could do something for them in return for their kindness to me and the gifts they have given me this evening." I had not thought it necessary before (in fact, it seemed quite inappropriate to me) to tell her that I had already been thinking of presents I could bring back from the Cook Islands to surprise her and the others. Now I assured her that I intended to bring back some gifts for the women. Contrary to my expectations, she proceeded to tell me exactly what I should bring.

"In Rarotonga there are stores with nice fabric. Buy a bolt of *pāreu* fabric. Then each woman can have a *pāreu*." Throughout many of the islands of Polynesia, women, and sometimes men, use brightly colored cotton fabric as an informal garment. In French Polynesia, it is called a *pāreu*. The *pāreu* is one of the most versatile items of clothing imaginable. It is a simple strip of fabric about one yard wide and two yards long. It can be wrapped around a woman's body from chest to mid-thigh to make a cool and attractive dress for casual wear. It can also be wrapped around the waist to make a long skirt or, when the fabric is old and faded, a work apron.

I was not surprised by Mahana Vahine's suggestion of a gift of cloth. It only served to reconfirm the value islanders place on Western fabric, whether for clothing or for an *iripiti*. What did surprise me (aside from the fact that she made the choice of the gift for me) was that I should bring back a whole bolt of the *same* fabric. In American society, women who associate with one another are often embarrassed to wear clothing that is just like that of someone else. In our society, we emphasize the ideal of "one of a kind" in emulation of the designer's original creation. Our emphasis on the individual as distinct from others relegates conformity in dress to the uniform. Well, I thought, if Mahana Vahine thinks it is appropriate to buy the same fabric for everyone, it must be. I went away with the assurance that I would be buying a gift that would be well liked. Carrying a bolt of cloth back to Rurutu might seem odd to me, but it had the advantage of fitting more compactly into my luggage.

Avarua, the capital of the Cook Islands, was a bustling, cosmopolitan city compared to the little village where I had been staying in Rurutu. I found a store that sold nothing but fabric. Row upon row of cloth crowded the aisles. There were cottons, rayons, silks, velvets, and chiffons. There were solids, prints, and plaids. In short, there was variety! Compared with the little shopfronts of Rurutu with their one or two bolts of high-priced, low-quality cottons, the fabric store in Avarua seemed like a seamstress's fantasy come true!

There were plenty of bolts of the inexpensive cottons from which a *pāreu* could be made, but my eyes wandered to bolts of more expensive and better quality fabrics. The cotton blends seemed far superior. The colors were more vivid and saturated; the designs seemed more artistic and graceful; and the cloth itself was a superior quality that could retain its beauty much longer. I did some quick financial figuring and decided that I could and would afford the more expensive fabric. I wanted to thank my Rurutu friends with the kind of fabric that would accurately mirror my feelings. They had spent hours making the gifts thay gave me. I wanted my presents to convey my deep appreciation for them. I picked out the brightest, prettiest cotton blend in the store. How pleased they'll be with my choice, I thought.

I returned to Rurutu with my bolt of fine fabric and handed it to Mahana Vahine proudly. Her expression turned from surprise to disappointment. "This is not what I told you to bring! This is dress fabric! It's of the quality women use to make dresses! I don't know if there will be enough fabric for each woman!"

I had created a dilemma. The fabric I had selected for the women to be fashioned into what I thought would be an especially fine *pāreu* belonged to another cultural category in Rurutu thought. It seemed I had mis-calculated in a manner compared to adding salt when the recipe called for sugar. For, although I had purchased superior quality fabric, I had bought only enough to make *pāreus,* not dresses.

Rurutu dresses are often ankle length and they have sleeves. I had already learned about sleeves. The first Sunday I was to go to church with Mahana Vahine, she had asked me why I wasn't wearing my white dress. I told her I didn't have one. She looked at me in disbelief and generously gave me a white shawl to cover the light yellow dress I was wearing. The next day, I wrote to my mother and asked her to send me a white dress as soon as possible. As it was winter in Indiana and the stores weren't selling white summer dresses, she made me a dress. When it arrived and I modeled it for approval, Mahana Vahine said it was fine—except for the sleeves. They were cap sleeves, not full-fledged, respectable sleeves that completely covered my shoulders and upper arms. Again, I wore the white shawl.

So Mahana Vahine was correct in saying there probably was not enough fabric on the bolt from Rarotonga. She took the fabric from me with a worried look. I hung back, feeling ashamed and embarrassed that I had created such a problem for her. As my host, she had taken pride in my small accomplishments, such as reciting a Bible verse in Tahitian in church. Now she felt responsible for rectifying my mistake. I watched as she unwrapped the long length of cloth, mumbling calculations to herself. She referred to the sheet of paper with the names of the women and their gifts. She worked and worried over the material a long time into the evening. Finally she cut the fabric and wrote the names of each woman on the back side of her allotted piece. I was relieved when she finished, but she offered me no explanation of how she had remedied my mistake. I was too humiliated to ask.

Even if I had erred in my judgment on the type of fabric I had selected, I thought I could express my gratitude to the women when I presented them with my gifts. After all, I reasoned to myself, it's the thought that counts. I envisioned myself calling upon each woman in turn, thanking her once again for her contribution to my work and her presents to me. Instead my plan, based on American ideas of how to give presents, was dashed when Mahana Vahine gave the fabric to her eleven-year-old son to deliver to everyone.

I was greatly disappointed. One of the joys of gift giving I had learned in the United States was to witness the delight (real or feigned) of the recipient. I wanted the satisfaction of having my gratitude, symbolized by the gift fabric, acknowledged. I doubted that Mahana Vahine's shy son would even think to say the fabric was from me.

At least, I consoled myself, I'll hear something from the women after they receive the fabric. I didn't. For several days I searched their faces for a sign that the imagined acknowledgment was forthcoming. As more time passed, I thought I might see one of them appear in something made from the brightly colored cloth. I never did.

The lingering shame that I had made a serious error in judgment in my selection of fabric, combined with a well-ingrained sense of impropriety in asking about my gifts, prevented me from asking anyone, "Did you like the fabric I brought back from Rarotonga?" Maybe the women were so embarrassed for me that they weren't going to say anything. Maybe they didn't like my choice of fabric after all.

It was only later, after several other incidents of gift giving which produced similar results, that I began to think my choice of fabric had nothing to do with the way my gifts were received. I came to the conclusion that the Polynesians and I were operating under different tacit rules. They did not like to draw attention to the gift giver or the gift. To do so, I believe, would underline the unequal relationship established in gift giving in which the recipient "owes" something to the gift giver. A close Tahitian friend later told me it is rare for someone to use the words *māuruuru 'oe* (thank you). The words *thank you,* tossed about so carelessly and often insincerely in American society, are reserved by islanders in French Polynesia, he explained, for rare and special occasions to express a great emotional debt to another.

I had read Richard Lee's account of !Kung San gift giving in his classic story, "Eating Christmas in the Kalahari." He described an experience with gift giving similiar to my own. Yet the story and its parallel were lost on me for a long time because I confused two cultural standards with one another. The Polynesians among whom I lived belong to a society which has interacted with Westerners for over a hundred years. I believe they have come to expect Western reactions in receiving gifts, but they continue to exercise their own norms when they themselves are the recipients. In their acculturated society, which accommodates two sets of cultural rules at the same time, it took several repetitions of gift exchanges before I began to appreciate what I consider to be the adaptability of my Polynesian friends in giving and receiving gifts from Westerners. They would expect me, as the Westerner I was, to demonstrate verbally my appreciation of their gifts, but they would avoid references to mine, although they appreciated the gifts as much as I. Their ideas of how to be recipients of my gifts worked at odds with my American notions of how recipients should act. I was dedicated to the idea of making an individual selection of a gift, of introducing an element of surprise, of presenting the gift in an open, ritual manner, and then of receiving a final verbal acknowledgment in return for my efforts. They, on the other hand, openly expressed their specific preferences for gifts and received the presents in the least conspicuous manner possible.

It has been several years since my stay on Rurutu. Sometimes when I give a present to someone in the United States who unwraps it and makes the appropriate "oohs" and "aahs," I think of the women of Rurutu. I think of the conventions of gift giving in our society that we take for granted and think of as natural. I think of the Polynesians' way of giving and receiving presents. But most of all, I think of the lessons I learned from carrying my cultural baggage with me. My understanding, at times so awkwardly acquired, was in its own way a special and valuable gift.

NOTES

1. *Iripiti* is the Rurutuan name for piecework quilt-like textiles. In the Society Islands, applique and piecework textiles are called *tīfaifai.* In the Cook Islands, they are *tīvaevae.* In the Hawaiian Islands true quilts (with a middle batting layer) are called *kapa,* or simply Hawaiian quilts.

2. Conventionally, anthropologists give people pseudonyms to protect their identity. In some cases, this practice is clearly necessary, as for example in reporting on people who might be in danger from their government or others if their identities were revealed. In other cases, peoples' authentic names might be used in order to credit them for their creations or thoughts. I have used a fictitious name in this account, Mahana Vahine, because my understanding of events is my own interpretation and not necessarily the interpretation of people I mention in my discussion. I have created a name which is plausible as a woman's name in Rurutu. The term *vahine* which follows the marriage name (a marriage name is bestowed on both a man and a woman) is equivalent to *Mrs.,* as in Mrs. Mahana.

SUGGESTED READINGS

HAMMOND, JOYCE D.
1986 Tifaifai and Quilts of Polynesia. Honolulu: University of Hawaii Press.

HANSON, F. ALLAN
1970   Rapan Lifeways: Society and History on a Polynesian Island. Boston: Little, Brown.

LEVY, ROBERT I.
1973   Tahitians: Mind and Experience in the Society Islands. Chicago: University of Chicago Press.

OLIVER, DOUGLAS
1974   Ancient Tahitian Society, Volumes 1–3. Honolulu: The University Press of Hawaii.

ELEVEN

🌀 Raising a Few Eyebrows in Tonga

ELIZABETH P. HAHN
University of North Carolina, Chapel Hill

I had yet to spot land in the ocean that stretched endlessly below but I knew the plane must be getting close to the island of Tongatapu. The Tongan businessman seated across the aisle began searching through his carry-on bag and eventually produced a small mat and length of cord. Other Tongans began preparations for their arrival; a few neckties disappeared, children were summoned and groomed, and several more mats were pulled out. I adjusted my seat belt for the landing. The plane descended toward a sea of coconut palms. At the last minute, a ribbon of runway appeared and we landed at the Tongatapu International Airport. When a few people began to stand up to secure the mats around their waists, the stewardess implored, "Please remain seated until the plane comes to a complete stop."

From my window seat I noticed a throng of people pressing up against the chain-link fence that separated them from the tarmac. They were waving and shouting. Many of the older women were wearing black mourning clothes and almost everyone was girded by a pandanus mat. Witnessing all that energy from the porthole of my plane window was like watching a silent home movie—I couldn't hear a sound above the din of the jet's engines. The warmth of the scene was almost enough to dispel my uneasiness at arriving for the first time, alone, in a foreign country. No one was expecting me, for no one in Tonga knew me. In my more confident moments I had told myself that it was going to be an adventure, but now with the adventure staring me in the face, my confidence was shaky. My mind raced with doubts and fears—what if . . . and what if . . . —but turning to the window once again, I cajoled myself by thinking, look at all those smiling faces anxiously awaiting the passengers! Climbing down the stairs, I was surprised to see no one other than fellow weary travelers—we had taxied to the customs and immigration section of the building, out of sight from the crowd.

After standing in line and obediently answering questions from a formidable immigrations official, my passport was stamped and tagged. Finally I was allowed to enter Tonga. I stepped into the adjoining room. People were running in all directions. The luggage was coming! A huge cart was pulled into the center of the room and as the long handle dropped to the ground, the crowd descended upon it—yanking suitcases several bags deep out of the stacked pile while others caught theirs as they came toppling from above. I stood clear of the melee and in short order I was looking at my two lone suitcases—upended, but safe and sound. I carried them to the rear of the customs line. By the time I stepped into the blinding sunshine, the crowds were gone. The feeling came over me that I, too, had been upended and orphaned. . . .

I checked into a local guest house that was home to expatriates working in Tonga—a pilot, an engineer, a mechanic, an educational administrator, along with the occasional tourist. It was predominantly a household of Tongan women taking care of *palangi* (European) men. I had intended to become part of both households but I didn't seem to fit into either one. To the single working men, I was a woman with an invisible job and no place to report to work. To the Tongan women at the guest house, I was one of the *palangi*. As soon as the male boarders had gone for the day, the women would gather in the kitchen to visit. A few times I appeared at the doorway to say hello, but a casual greeting, much less a conversation, was impossible. A *palangi* entering the kitchen was an interruption. "What is it that she wants?" they would ask themselves. A *palangi* didn't just pop in to visit. I soon found out that a *palangi* wasn't supposed to do a lot of things.

But first things first—I had arrived, had secured a place to stay, and I was in the stage of checking things out. I was learning my way around town as well as what was in town, identifying my possibilities, meeting people, and learning Tongan words as fast as I possibly could. I wanted to be incorporated into the everyday life of a Tongan family. I was disappointed that the guest house had little to offer as an entrance into a Tongan household. The setting was artificial and most of the Tongans who worked there did not live in the compound. Still, it was a foothold.

I was somewhat bewildered as I sat down alone on the veranda each morning planning my day. No one here expected anything of me. I was creating my own reality, my own work schedule, my own set of tasks, many of which would only take form as I learned more about Tongan culture. I couldn't even develop a detailed work schedule of the weeks to come. This lack of structure insulated me from those around me. I was a foreigner on an ill-defined journey. At least Captain Cook's orders constituted a clear, self-contained agenda—find the Northwest Passage and chart, claim, and explore any new lands along the way. But as an anthropologist, I could not describe and catalogue cultural patterns as if they were lifeless features of the landscape. To be sure, I had a clear sense of my own project. But where it would lead me and whether or not the project would be successful depended largely on the locals incorporating me somehow in their life. Meeting people was the first step; ultimately I had to engage them. I had to break out of my isolation and self-absorption. If I was to arrive at an understanding of the ongoing cultural processes, I had to establish a role in the community.

I knew all these things intellectually. As part of my training, I had read everything I could find on fieldwork methods. My advisor had briefed me on ethics, how to behave professionally, the importance of confidentiality. My university had required a "human subjects" review of my project before granting research clearance. None of this, however, prepared me for the reality of being one among thousands. Such preparations, however important for other reasons, tended to inflate the importance of my project and gave a misleading impression of the impact I would have on the people I was studying. My human subjects report, detailing my sensibilities toward the local population and measures proposed to minimize disruptions in people's lives, now seemed bizarre. *I* was the vulnerable party, an impoverished outsider looking on and wanting to be a part of a community of people who shared infinite ties with each other.

I had rehearsed my introductory speech to all of the expatriates and tourists in response to, "An anthropologist, what do you do?" and I was trying to meet those people for whom it was more than an idle curiosity. I began to dread going into town to make my rounds. In these early days, a venture into town consisted of courteous, vacuous interactions. Some people were indifferent. A few were rude. Since I was an unchaperoned young female, teenage boys would often stare and call out to me on the street. But such confrontational encounters were the exception to the rule—most people simply did not care. How could they when they didn't know me?

I had a basic game plan and I knew what little things needed to be done in preparation for the "real" fieldwork. I knew how important it was professionally to build a rapport with the local people. After all, they were my informants. What I didn't anticipate was the extent to which it became important to me personally and emotionally that the Tongans understand and offer some kind of validation of what I was doing.

As a balm to my loneliness and my anxiety over my project's progress, I turned my attention to mastering little tasks and errands—the organizational details of establishing myself in a foreign country. I wanted to master some small piece of interaction. Unfortunately, there were more than a few false starts on the road to competency.

I spent one morning in town doing errands only to find out later that I would spend the afternoon undoing what I had thought I'd accomplished that morning. I had asked, "Where do I buy stamps?" and I was directed to the treasury building across the street, where I bought stamps in the shape of birds and shells. I went into the fabric shop, bought material, and for an additional ten dollars put in an order for a shift to be made to wear to and from the bathhouse. I was uneasy that the Tongan lady had not understood my request and wondered if it would indeed be ready next week. I kept asking her if she understood and she was very quick to assure me with a nod, a smile, and a stream of *"io, io, sai pe"* ("Yes, yes, all right"). I repeated myself to the point of feeling foolish. It was always the same response, regardless of the question—the more I asked, the more *io*'s I got. I decided to take her word for it.

Over lunch at the guest house, I commented that it was surprising that Tongan stamps were only available in such large denominations. Wasn't a dollar a bit much to pay to mail a letter across town? My lunch companions set me straight—my beautiful stamps weren't meant to be mailed. I had bought collectors' stamps instead of postage stamps. Stamp issues generated significant income for the government and were sold in a building separate from the post office.

Luckily, a woman I had met a few days earlier stopped by to see how I was getting along. She was an Australian who was married to a Tongan and she spoke the native language fluently. With her help, I undid all of my errands. She took me back to the treasury building to return the stamps, to the post office to buy stamps, and to the fabric shop, where she found out that there was some confusion as to whether a dress had even been ordered. With a few sharp sentences in Tongan she cut the price in half, demanded a refund for the difference, and made sure my dress would be ready the next day. It was humiliating. What had happened? I was outside the shopkeeper's social universe and odds were that as a *palangi* I would be gone in few days, never to return again.

This was the low point of my early fieldwork. I was tempted to succumb to my cultural isolation and accept it, instead of continuing to try to transcend the cultural barrier. I became discouraged as the difficulties of setting up residence unfolded and the intricacy of Tongan culture grew with closer scrutiny. In short, the complexities were multiplying daily; discernible patterns were not. Rather than growing closer, my research goals seemed to be growing more distant. I kept seeing myself as those two suitcases—apparently in the middle of things but in the end unclaimed. Had I become a Walter Mitty zombie?

At this point, it became painfully clear to me that a large part of self-affirmation comes from others. I needed to tell people about my project and I needed them to understand in some sense what it was I was doing. I was beginning to wonder who *I* was, never mind who the Tongans were.

With more desperation than courage, I tried a different tack. I again approached the Tongan women working at the guest house. These women saw me every day and couldn't ignore me. This time I had something to show them instead of hanging around asking them what they were doing. I waited until the women had gathered around the wash table for midmorning tea and gossip. I reached into my bag for my family pictures and laid them out on the piles of folded laundry. "This is my father, this is my mother, my brother, grandmother . . ." I intoned over their giggles and comments. The photographs were a big success and ever after they greeted me whenever they entered or left the house, where before there had been silence. Finally the *palangi* stereotype had been superseded by friendship.

Heartened by success on the home front, I went in to see a government official in a building on the edge of town. (I was proud of just being able to locate the office.) I did not expect anything from him; I was making the rounds and trying to master a small piece of Nuku'alofa, find various offices, and learn the basics of the Tongan bureaucracy. He was in his office (first surprise) and moreover, he agreed to see me (second surprise).

He greeted me in standard office dress—a white long-sleeved shirt and necktie, a dark brown *tupenu* (a Tongan skirt), and a *ta'ovala* (a Tongan mat) secured around his waist by a braided cord of coconut fiber. The walls of his office were lined from floor to ceiling with the papers and reports of the Central Planning Department. I wondered how to make my vague and observation-oriented project seem like something worthwhile. Here were Tongans themselves engaged in the process of writing about and planning change in their culture and I, a foreigner, was going to have something interesting to say about their social processes, someone who half the time couldn't seem to find her way around the tiny capital of Nuku'alofa? But he was very cordial and soon put me at ease. He seemed to be willing to talk to me for longer than the polite five-minute chat. Here at last was someone to whom I could explain what I was trying to accomplish in Tonga. Indeed, he listened and he asked thoughtful questions. I fought the urge to lean over and hug him. I was having my first "anthropological" discussion—one professional to another. And then it happened—in the middle of one of my explanations, he started raising and wiggling his eyebrows at me. I was taken completely off guard and stammered to a stop. He stopped. No sooner had I resumed talking than he started giving me the eye again. We started and stopped several times. I began to get very angry. There he was, looking so innocent with a quizzical expression on his face, as if *I* were the one doing something odd. How dare he come on to me? How dare he feign interest in my project just so he could flirt with me? I decided to ignore him, but I also made a mental check of other people in the building who might be within earshot of the open office door. I did not want to be alone with him. He acted as if everthing was just fine and made no reference to his pass at me. Both of us ignored the glitch even though we undoubtedly thought the other was a bit strange. As our conversation ended, I thanked him for his time, shook his hand, and departed with my head spinning.

I shelved the incident and continued to meet more people and gather information. One day I was talking to a Tongan woman alongside the road to town. There was a gentle ocean breeze and it was a fine day to be outside. We were in the middle of an animated conversation when she began to wiggle her eyebrows up and down. This time I was more intrigued than confused, for the shock value wasn't there the second time. I began to search for clues in situation. It certainly had nothing to do with sexual innuendo. Had I been wrong about the Tongan bureaucrat? The gesture was in some way a part of the conversation rather than a violation of the conversation's content or context. Unlike a wink that negates or mocks what is being said and suggests questionable intent, this gesture seemed to be congruous with the conversation. It certainly carried a different meaning from its American counterpart.

Was she making a joke or some sort of nonverbal comment? Was she teasing me? Her laughing eyes seemed to draw me in. Had a joke been made that I was too naive to catch? I acted as though I understood, smiled, and after a few minutes, in mindless imitation, I moved my eyebrows up and down as smoothly as possible. It worked well and we had this very lively and civil conversation. I wondered how she could keep it up for so long—it felt sort of like wiggling your ears. Back in my room, I repeated the gesture in the mirror—yep, that's it all right. I felt silly. I felt like an impostor. I was certainly becoming entangled but I had no idea what I was doing. But it was also exhilarating—like flying blindly through the clouds and emerging unscathed.

As I gained more contextual information through subsequent encounters, I became less and less convinced that the gesture involved some sort of hidden joke. That interpretation still harbored an ethnocentric orientation. After all, a joke is a kind of metacomment, akin to a wink, rolling eyes, or crossed fingers. I had not been radical enough in my thinking. What could eyebrow wiggling possibly mean?

One day I was chatting with a woman over tea and as I talked and watched her eyebrows dance in response, I realized that I had missed the point in my elaborate attempts to discern its meaning. It was a simple, elegant expression of affirmation—a gesture that draws the participants to each other's eyes, giving an intensity and intimacy to a friendly exchange. The meaning now seemed so clear.

The scientist in me, however, was not totally impressed with the cry of eureka and withheld judgment until I had falsified the alternate hypothesis. As it turned out, the door of a taxi was my entrance to the perfect experimental situation.

I was riding along, listening to an attractive young driver boast of his exploits in his stay abroad in New Zealand. He was clearly flirting with me and, as many taxi drivers are prone to do with a lone female *palangi* as a passenger, he had propositioned me twice before arriving at our destination. This routine had long since ceased to be flattering, and I had become adept at diffusing the situation by being a good sport. However, this time my heart was pounding with my sudden decision to put myself in mild jeopardy to prove an ethnographic point. It would either be a triumph or, if I were proven wrong, one messy misunderstanding that I would be in no mood to explain.

Somehow the driver managed to keep up a steady stream of banter and dodge pedestrians at the same time. As we bounced over the potholes I waited for my chance. When he reached a particularly amusing part of his tale and turned to me, I looked him square in the eye and wiggled my eyebrows. He continued his story, delighted to have such rapt attention from a young lady. At the end of the ride, I had no problem making him understand that I was not interested in meeting him later. He cheerfully waved good-bye as he roared out the driveway, scattering hens and biddies in his wake.

I was thrilled that my experiment had worked. The final check was to ask a Tongan directly what it was all about. So as not to use up my precious quota of point-blank "stupid" questions, the matter had been delayed for a few days by more pressing stupid questions. You know, the kind of questions that a three-year-old asks, such as why the sky is blue. Such vexing questions are even more tiresome in a (supposed) adult. In my case, I always attempted to couch my "what does it mean" questions in a discussion of a particular concrete incident. Nonetheless, if I did not wish to be considered a complete moron, a couple of such questions a day was the limit.

I found Mele at the beach, squatting at the water's edge, shucking clams for tomorrow's Sunday dinner. She shouted to me to come and join her. I walked over and sat down on a rock next to her, grateful for the opportunity to have a leisurely semiprivate talk while she worked. I told her that I had been talking to a man in town and that he had wiggled his eyebrows at me. I asked her if I was right in understanding an eyebrow wag as simply a gesture of attentiveness. She answered me without words, a habit she was fond of that assured my complete attention. Prying open another clam, she smiled, pleased at the progress I was making in understanding the Tongan way.

I began to think back on all that I had experienced these last several weeks. It seemed to have taken a herculean effort just to get to this point. Then I realized that I had actually asked very few of the questions that had occurred to me and had received direct answers to even fewer. Yet I knew an astonishingly large amount about the minutiae of everyday Tongan life and interaction, the background context upon which the more dramatic events are remembered and written about. The real fieldwork had begun long ago. Here I was, talking with a Tongan woman who had taken on the role of a parent, and in listening to her ramblings about Tongan etiquette that had been sparked by my comments I found myself wiggling my eyebrows in assent. The orphan had been claimed.

SUGGESTED READINGS

AOYAGI, MACHIKO

1966   Kinship Organization and Behavior in a Contemporary Tongan Village. Journal of the Polynesian Society 75:141–176.

GERSTLE, DONNA, AND HELEN PRATT

1974   Tonga Pictorial: A Tapestry of Pride. Photographs by C. A. Gist. San Diego, CA: Tofua Press.

MARTIN, JOHN, AND WILLIAM MARINER

1981   An Account of the Natives of the Tongan Islands, compiled and arranged from the extensive communications of Mr. William Mariner, several years resident in those islands. 4th ed., Volumes 1 and 2 (first edition 1817). Neiafu, Tonga: Vava'u Press.

RUTHERFORD, NOEL, ED.

1977   The Friendly Islands: A History of Tonga. New York: Oxford University Press.

TWELVE

🌿 The Projection from Pohnpei

GLENN PETERSEN
City University of New York

I clambered down from the Air Micronesia plane into the equatorial sunshine and set off to see my friend Anas. It was early June 1979, and I had not been back to the Pacific island of Pohnpei in four years. Anas is *Soulik,* or chief, of Awak, the richly productive part of the island where I do most of my research, and he is more than just a friend. His is an ancient and august title and he is a well-regarded man on Pohnpei. I had learned a lot from him.

At four we left the Land Office, where he works as a cartographer, and started out on the six miles of potholes that lead to Awak. Talk was of our families, our work, our friendship. We had not gone far, though—only to the handsome new bridge spanning the Dau Sokele, an estuary named for Pohnpei's little people, their leprechauns—when Anas turned to me, through with chat, and asked seriously, "So, who's the strongest, President Carter or Teddy Kennedy?"

In good Pohnpei fashion, I first asserted my ignorance, then replied with a question of my own. "I don't know. Who do you think?"

"Teddy Kennedy, he's the strongest. If he'll run. Will he?"

I smiled. Like a crocodile.

I had been thinking about Senator Kennedy, of course. The news had been full of him in the late spring of 1979. And since I first began working on Pohnpei I had been unable to think of him without thinking of the Pohnpei. I had guessed that the topic would again be raised, but I never imagined that it would come up so quickly. Reflecting on it later, I realized that I should not have been so surprised.

In late 1975, as I was finishing up nearly two years of research on Pohnpei (my first fieldwork there), the news from America had been full of speculation about the coming year's presidential primaries. My Pohnpei friends asked me about Senator Kennedy's candidacy with a frequency second only to their inquiries about my family. In the summer of 1979 we were again looking ahead to the primaries, and Teddy Kennedy was still on their minds.

Old Leonardo—who is one of my favorite rascals, and best known in the community for the love potions he brews at the request of young men— was off visiting in another part of the island when I arrived back on

Pohnpei. A week later he turned up at a "forty-day feast" for his brother-in-law, a ritual held two-score days after a death to honor the departing spirit. "Where have you come from?" I asked in greeting.

"Oh, I've been off on a trip to Washington, D.C."

I responded with the customary, *"Ko paid?"* ("You and who else?")

"It was Edward Kennedy and I," he said with a chortle and a slap of his thigh.

Why are the Pohnpei, archetypal South Seas islanders, so interested in Senator Kennedy? And who are they? Pohnpei is one of the Eastern Caroline Islands, in that part of the Western Pacific known as Micronesia. It lies along the equator, twenty-five hundred miles west of Honolulu, twenty-five hundred miles east of Manila. Since World War II, when the United States wrested them from the Japanese (who had in turn followed the Germans and the Spanish), these specks of volcanic rock and coral have been part of the U.S. Trust Territory of the Pacific Islands.

Recent years have seen the growth of a new political consciousness as Pohnpei joined with Yap, Truk, and Kosrae (other islands in the Trust Territory) to form the Federated States of Micronesia. Forty years of trusteeship and more than a decade of political negotiations have provided the Pohnpei with a surprisingly thorough knowledge of the United States. Each year scores of young people go off to colleges in the States. A few weekly newsmagazines and Guam newspapers are passed from hand to hand or read in the library of the island's two-year teacher-training college. The twenty-five thousand or so Pohnpei have during this same period become quite dependent upon the millions of dollars supplied by the United States each year to run the Micronesian government. Participation in this government has acquainted them with elective politics and sharpened their interest in the American political scene.

Yet outside Kolonia, the island's only town, it is still the chiefs who govern Pohnpei. Mountainous and densely planted, with only a single ragged road edging along the shoreline, the island's majestic face is not friendly to large-scale politics. High chiefs head five independent chiefdoms and oversee the work of numerous local chiefs, men like my friend Anas. It is to the reign of the chiefs, not the elected politicians, that we must look if we are to understand the Pohnpei's consuming interest in Edward Kennedy.

A man like Anas lives comfortably in two worlds. Two decades ago he spent a year studying surveying in Hawaii and gaining experience in America. When I first got to know him, he had just succeeded to the chieftainship and was striving to adjust himself to the demands of his new role. In time, though he was a very young chief by Pohnpei standards, he grew comfortable with the authority and responsibility charged to him. He is an acutely political man, a skillful leader, and a thoughtful informant. I turned to him for an explanation of the Pohnpei's fascination with Senator Kennedy.

Asking Pohnpei about their motivations, I must caution, is not a simple thing to do. As sophisticated as they are, they continue to live in their homogeneous communities and have yet to develop the intense self-consciousness of urban civilization. These small clusters of no more than a few hundred people are tightly integrated. People spend so much of their lives together, and know each other so intimately, that they have little reason to inquire into motivation. But some Pohnpei are more insightful than others, and some have accustomed themselves to my peculiar questions. There are those of whom I can ask "Why?"

One night at kava—a mild, tranquilizing beverage that most Pohnpei prepare and drink daily—I sat as Anas's attendant, inside the feast house with twenty or so other members of his chiefdom. Five or six of us were talking together about the recent campaign for the Pohnpei governorship (won, incidentally, by Anas's cousin), and the conversation eventually drifted to America's coming presidential campaign. Anas laughed about an editorial cartoon that had just appeared in the Guam paper: Kennedy riding a donkey and saying, "You're going to whip my *what?*"

I smiled and asked, "Why *is* it that you Pohnpei are so interested in Teddy Kennedy? What is the importance he holds for you?"

Anas considered my question and then answered slowly, obviously thinking the matter through as he spoke.

"It is because of his brothers," he began. "They were very smart men, his brothers, and very brave. John, especially. He was the greatest modern president, we think. Johnson was a warrior, which we admire. Nixon was a very clever man, and this we respect. But in the end both of these men failed.

"John Kennedy challenged the Russians—who were your enemies at the time—during the Cuban Missile Crisis, and he made them back down. He defeated the Russians, a powerful people, and that makes him a strong man, a great man.

"And it was John Kennedy who began providing real funding for Micronesia. Before that we were ignored, forgotten.

"So, you see, it is because of Teddy Kennedy's brothers, because of his family, because of his name. Perhaps we are wrong, but we Pohnpei think these important and that is why we are so concerned with this man."

And then, as he usually does, he probed back. "For whom are you going to vote?" he asked.

"I don't know," I said. "Whom would you vote for, if you could?"

He accepted a coconut shell full of kava, drank deeply, and spit the bitter residue onto the dirt floor. He lit a cigarette, paused, and then asked, "Which of them is smarter, Carter or Kennedy?" He paused again. "Carter is smart, and he is strong right now, because of Camp David and Salt II. Of course, Kennedy is smart too. But he can't run. He'll be killed if he does.

He is the man for the job, but he cannot run: He'll be killed." This he said with conviction. Then he probed again, trying to learn something more, hoping that as an American I would have an understanding that he did not.

It occurs to me, however, that it is just the contrary: The Pohnpei have an understanding of Kennedy's dilemma that Americans do not, and by probing them *we* might learn something. Anas's answer contains the clues, but they are hidden within the unfamiliar shape of Pohnpei culture. Let me be briefly the pedagogue.

Pohnpei is by its traditions a matrilineal society. That is, membership in a clan, access to land, and chances of obtaining a chief's title have depended on one's mother's lineage. Each and every Pohnpei is born into his or her mother's clan and remains a part of that group for life. In the course of many years of missionization and colonial administration, the Pohnpei have come to pass land and last names on through the male line, and they currently ignore a few of the old clan customs, such as blood vengence. But the clans survive, and along with them the chieftainships, all held by men, which remain matrilineal and hereditary.

Chiefly lineages have some freedom to choose their leaders from among contending brothers and cousins, and there are parents who push their sons ahead, eager to see them rise within the hierarchy of titles. Young Pohnpei of ruling lineages are raised to be chiefs. By early manhood they have learned the attitudes and begun acquiring the skills necessary to a Pohnpei leader. They know that they are *soupeidi* (those who look down)—the people who occupy the highest seats in the feast house and gaze down upon the rest of the people working below.

Modern Pohnpei chiefs continue to symbolize their clan's ancestral spirits, and this symbolism guarantees the political system's continued survival. But hereditary rule carries with it inherent flaws: how to be rid of an unsatisfactory chief who rules for life, and how to accommodate competent or popular usurpers. A pragmatic people, the Pohnpei long ago accepted political assassination as a viable element of statecraft. Local legends and oral histories abound with tales of slain chiefs.

Soulik Anas is chief because he is head of the local branch of the Great Eel Clan. One of his ancestors first seized control of Awak for the Great Eel Clan by killing off the chief of a rival clan, and established himself and his clan as the new ruling line. Though the police power of the twentieth-century colonial administrations has moderated this violent streak in Pohnpei politics, people recall the high chief who was shot and killed less than two generations ago, and a fear of assassination remains with them.

When Kava is prepared, for example, the first draught should go to the chief. But many, like Soulik Anas, give the first cup to someone else. This simultaneously confers honor on a guest, friend, or loyal retainer, and makes poisoning attempts pointless.

In addition to hereditary rule, the Pohnpei share another trait common to matrilineal societies. Because the male line is deemphasized, there is no distinct, clear term for the man Americans would call father. Children call their mother's husband and his brothers all by a single term. Thus men we would call uncles are known in Pohnpei by the same term as those we would call father. Or, if you will, a child calls both his father and his paternal uncles "father." And when a man dies, one of his brothers literally becomes the father of his children, charged fully with responsibility for their well-being.

On Pohnpei today, then, some men are born and raised to rule; a Pohnpei man becomes the father of his brother's children should his brother die; and political assassination has traditionally been a practical way of removing a chief.

Though some of their customs may strike us as archaic, the Pohnpei, as I have emphasized, are *not* untouched "primitives," hidden away in an island paradise. It was the grandparents of the oldest people living today who foresook the Stone Age when European traders first appeared on their shores. But the Coca-Cola, Toyota trucks, and Chinese-made cooking utensils that one sees today on the island do not mean that these people are no longer distinctively Pohnpei. It is an island world; what the island-ers know of peoples and places beyond is always framed within the contexts of their island lives.

Edward Kennedy's dilemma, however *he* may experience it, is not perceived by the Pohnpei as being merely a personal or family issue. Nor do they recognize it as some sort of racial scourge haunting American character and society. The questions put to me again and again, "Is Teddy Kennedy stronger than Carter?" (or Nixon or Ford or Reagan) and "Is Kennedy going to run?" are not so much about the U.S. presidency or the American political scene as they are about the contradictions of power itself.

Kennedy, as the Pohnpei perceive him, is a legendary hero in our own time. Born and raised to be chief, he is foreordained to succeed his brother. This is what he knows, what he is. It is his fate. He is the father of not one, but three sets of children, and there is no one to replace him. He will lose his life if he runs; this too is predestined. He must seek the presidency because it is the dynasty's fate, and yet he must avoid this fate because only he is left to truly care for this ill-starred family. Surely the Greeks confronted their heroes with few harsher challenges.

The day before leaving Pohnpei that year, I participated in a ritual feast that confirmed a young man's new title. His white-haired father, a man I knew only vaguely, approached me. He asked what I was doing on Pohnpei. I explained the purpose of my research. He asked with typical Pohnpei modesty if I liked the island: "Pohnpei is a terrible place, isn't it?" And then he asked about Kennedy. "Teddy Kennedy, what about him? Is he still strong? Will he run? He will run, won't he? But then again, maybe he won't." He was speaking to himself as he finished, not to me.

Our conversation echoed many I have had on Pohnpei. People want to know why I am there, and if I like their island—or find it primitive and repelling. And they ask about Kennedy. They are curious about him, they hope I can tell them things they do not know. But I have come to think they are talking to themselves, and to each other, more than they are querying me.

It is with his strength that they are concerned. "Is he the strongest?" they ask. They wonder if he will be strong enough to overcome his fate. In their terms, the strongest chief is the one who not only rules effectively, but has the spiritual power (the technical term is *mana,* the Pohnpei call it *manaman*) to overcome any threats, physical or magical, that might be made against him.

On Pohnpei, the Kennedy saga is much more than an American political drama. The story, for Americans, is history, along with the Teapot Dome Scandal and the *Mayaquez* Incident—significant, but rarely inspiring. But for the Pohnpei it is a moral fable for our time, and a tale for all times, much larger than the lives of the actors who have created the parts.

Though Kennedy's presidential ambitions appear to have waned, the Pohnpei still watch him from afar. I do not know if his is a legend that will in time be added to the rich Pohnpei mythology. Nor do I know what the Pohnpei really think about Edward Kennedy; no anthropologist ever knows what is truly on the minds of the people with whom he works. But it is clear that the Pohnpei's fascination with Edward Kennedy springs from the ways in which his dilemma dramatizes conflicts inherent in their own society. They engage in a most human occupation: projection. They see the contradictions of Pohnpei social life in the lives of those who people the world around them.

Some might want to restrict the term *projection* to the technical realm of psychology, where it refers to a process of unconsciously attributing one's own feelings or attitudes to others. I use it here in a less inhibited and formal sense, but my meaning differs very little. The Pohnpei assume that the slings and arrows of Pohnpei fortune afflict human life everywhere, and they interpret other people's actions in this same light.

Europeans and Americans, among others, engage in projection when envisioning an island paradise or a noble savage. We are given to imaging simple islanders, happy in the sun, and hope that they will not be sullied by the taint of modern life. We long for an innocence that we think once was ours, and as a consequence project it onto the lives of others.

Anthropologists are by and large taught to refrain from projection. Much of the graduate school training we undergo is meant to harden and to sharpen—to forge an unsentimental scholar free of any romantic thoughts about the people he or she goes off to study.

But I have learned from the Pohnpei just how useful this ability to project can be. The Pohnpei are, after all, a colonized people, and they seek to find ways of preserving the autonomy of their own political traditions. Strong chiefs help them to do this—to overcome outrageous fortune, as it were.

Their fascination with the Kennedy saga hinges on questions of fate and fortune, of the will to challenge it, and especially of the strength to overcome it. "Is he the strongest?" they ask me. People on Pohnpei understand the social forces shaping the circumstances of a person's life. But they also believe that the strong chief can prevail. In Kennedy's case they see fate's challenge: the vexed intersection of ambition and responsibility, and the problem of whether he is strong enough to become president and thus challenge the history that threatens him.

The Pohnpei view their own recent history in much the same light. Their grandparents and great-grandparents refused to acknowledge the right of foreigners to rule Pohnpei. The received wisdom of modern politics and economics, the considered opinions of the experts, all argue that Pohnpei and the other Micronesian islands are too small to be truly independent; they are told they must rely on American financial subsidies and "security pacts" for their survival. But the Pohnpei have opted to challenge that fate. They seek autonomy in the strictest sense of the term.

While the Pohnpei no longer wage war in their attempts to achieve autonomy, as they did against the Spanish and the Germans, they still struggle, hoping someday to end foreign rule in Micronesia. They will not agree to a treaty giving the United States perpetual military control over their island; they have negotiated steadfastly and argued articulately against American attempts to coerce them. They have not been entirely successful, but their capacity for projection helps them study the American political scene and enables them to defy forbidding odds against the continued survival of Pohnpei culture.

The projection from Pohnpei is multifaceted and has been remarkably useful, both for them and for me. There is in their vision a quality of force, of grandeur, of intensity, that gives it a fabulous tone. For us, Edward Kennedy has simply had a difficult choice to make; for them the Senator's story not only embodies the specific dilemmas of Pohnpei chieftainship, but also the ancient theme of human challenges to that which fate ordains.

The Pohnpei go on demanding the right to govern themselves, and I have learned to appreciate not only their good sense, but some of the uses of projection.

THIRTEEN

🐚 The Politics of Ethnography: Americans on Tanna

LAMONT LINDSTROM
University of Tulsa

The process of beginning fieldwork is a rite de passage in a double sense. On one hand, it marks the transition from student to working anthropologist. The whole period of field research is definitely a liminal state. On the other hand, the researcher undergoes a transition from being a nominally capable actor in his own society to being an ignoramous in another. This story is a personal description of how my wife and I entered into fieldwork on the island of Tanna in southern Vanuatu.[1]

I came to Tanna to compare the economic activities of people professing different ideologies. This island is a mosaic of competing religious and political factions. These include various Christian sects (of which the Presbyterians are the most important historically), a large community of neopagans, and the now-infamous John Frum cargo cultists. What I needed for a research site was a place where villagers with different ideologies might be found in close proximity.

I was informed of such a site by a friend of a friend. An advisor had met a missionary, currently resident on Tanna, at a conference of Pacific development. This man kindly suggested an area in southeast Tanna that met my requirements; he also asked the people there if they would welcome an anthropologist. Of course, he asked this of Christians. After three weeks of preliminary investigation on Tanna, I took his advice and moved into a Presbyterian village on the flanks of the southern mountains.

I did not expect to have too much difficulty explaining myself to my new neighbors and friends. I am the ninth anthropologist to have spent some amount of time on Tanna, and I expected people to be conversant with the usual anthropological routine.[2] Futhermore, upward of a hundred tourists a month fly to Tanna for a quick afternoon climb of the active volcano, Iasur. Nevertheless, I carefully prepared a small speech in Bislama (Vanuatu pidgin English) explaining what anthropology is, why my wife and I wanted to live in the village, what we wanted to do, what help

From *Canberra Anthropology* 2(2): 36–45, 1979. Used with permission of the journal and the author.

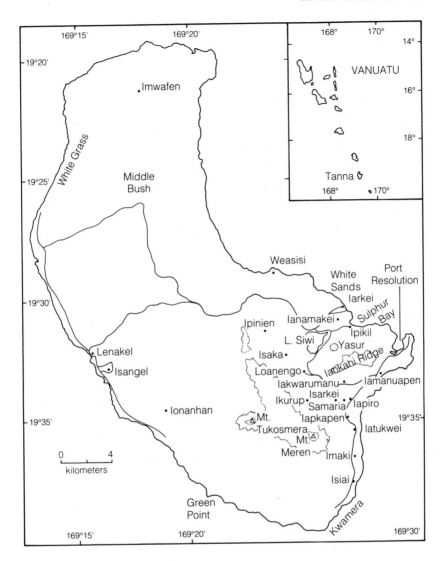

Tanna

we would need, what help we could give, the possible benefits of the study, and the future distribution of its results. I could have thrown this away. No questions or challenges met my arrival.

This does not mean that people understand why I had come to live in their village. On the contrary, in following months I explained again and again the work of an anthropologist. The immediate and unconditional acceptance of me was a political act, consistent with the Tannese pattern of monolithic village ideology and opinion. Once a village bigman agrees, all residents follow his lead. The bigman in our village, an elder in the

Presbyterian church, considered that I had come along "roads" controlled by the Christians (via the local missionary), and this was enough to legitimize me as a village resident.

Comfortable though it was, this immediate adoption by one ideological side did not bode well for the prospects of a comparative study, especially given an aspect of my identity that arouses curiosity and is capable of stoking the political fires on Tanna. I am an American.

Since the 1940s, John Frum cultists have been "singing out" for Americans to come to Tanna to deliver them from whatever their troubles may be. John Frum, a spiritual middleman between America and Tanna, is thought to live in America. He returns to cult headquarters, the village of Sulphur Bay, in times of need. The bigmen of Sulphur Bay control, or at least have influence over, people living in a score of other villages who adhere to their particular version of the John Frum cult.

This cult is the most successful local political organization on Tanna. John Frum believers, however, are not alone in their appreciation of America. Most older Tannese men, now in their sixties, worked for the Americans during World War II at gigantic military supply bases on the islands of Efate and Santo. The trucks, airplanes, ships, and crates of cargo destined for the soldiers and marines fighting in the Solomon Islands to the north made a significant and lasting impression on all islanders.

The current thinking at Sulphur Bay is that Americans must come to help people with business. And Americans must come via Sulphur Bay. In island society, all important economic exchanges proceed along a system of roads. A road *(suatuk)* is an exchange relationship between men, the physical manifestation of which is a path through the bush. Along these roads pass women, pigs, turtles, and (historically) bodies destined for anthrophagy. Each section of road is controlled by a different local big-man. When two men exchange women, for example, intermediate men along the road between the two must pass these women on to their final destinations. In doing so, they gain rights to part of the marital exchange goods that accompnay the women, especially pigs and kava. Where there are no roads, no exchange is possible.

Given the importance of road control, it is not surprising that John Frum leaders do not want America to come to Tanna in any sort of general way. Rather, they want America to come directly to Sulphur Bay, and in doing so to open a new road—a new exchange relationship—that they alone might control. To ensure this, the leading men at Sulphur Bay fly American flags in the center of their village. They raise a U.S. flag every Friday morning at eight A.M. and lower this at four-thirty P.M. Cultists first ran up the Stars and Stripes on February 15, 1978. This flag-raising corresponded to a minor peak in cult activity; Americans were expected at any time.

That February I happened to be in Port Vila waiting for official permission to come to Tanna. The flag incident delayed me. The colonial administration was worried about its consequences. Although the district officer remained unsettled, I eventually made my way to Tanna in April. Instead of immediately proceeding in triumph to Sulphur Bay, I went, in my ignorance, to the Presbyterian mission, where I stayed for three weeks. Worse was to come when I moved into a Christian village. I had obviously come as a result of the raising of the flag at Sulphur Bay, but clearly had been abducted by the conniving Presbyterians. Sulphur Bay sent word that they would club my local bigman the next time they saw him.

Though at the time I was not much interested in Sulphur Bay, which is in a different language area, I immediately sent a message north that I wanted to talk with cult leaders. A reply came back that I was forbidden to come. (Since then, Sulphur Bay bigmen had denied that they ever said this. They accuse the perfidious Christians of presenting me with this lie instead of the friendly welcome they actually sent.)

Sulphur Bay also retaliated by spreading the story that I was not a true "Man America" but some worthless Australian or New Zealander. This interpretation followed directly from the logic of cult ideology, which predicts that John Frum will bring Americans to Sulphur Bay. In that I, a rogue American, came to Tanna without reporting to Sulphur Bay, I threatened prophecy and cultist ideology in general. Instead of altering ideology, it was easier for the cultists to de-Americanize me, which they did.

After several months of ambiguous nationality, I had had enough of John Frum games and decided to play one of my own. The U.S. flag at Sulphur Bay is a powerful cult symbol. Flags are deemed to have the power to pull Americans to Tanna. Popular rumors set forth supernatural origins for the flags. The most common declares that these were gifts from John Frum. But what is exclusive on Tanna is mass-produced in America. I wrote my mother in California. She sent me four examples of the national colors by return mail. I stuck the largest into my thatched roof for an afternoon; the others I displayed casually at my *nakamal,* the local dance ground where both cultists and Christians gather each evening to drink kava.

This symbolic affirmation reinstated me as an American. Only John Frum and I have access to the Stars and Stripes. My flag waving, as it turned out, also improved the chances of making a comparative economic survey.

My original proposal was to situate myself in an area where all three competing ideologies could be readily observed and compared. As I fast discovered, however, island religious sentiments are in reality extremely political. My plans to circulate casually between three villages ran counter to the Tannese notion of *side*—group solidarity that people also call *team, company,* or metaphorically, *canoe.* Furthermore, there is an unpleasant traditional status, that of *kout kasua.* This is a person who betrays his side by opening the gates to enemy attack. A *kout kasua* provides enemies with his village mates' personal refuse for nefarious sorcery, or spoils the war plans of his own side by sneaking off to warn the prospective victims. Recently, several villages near White Sands planned an ambush to rough

up some people of Sulphur Bay. These plans failed because, it was widely believed, a *kout kasua* managed to send word to Sulphur Bay in
time.

I did not want to be perceived as a *kout kasua.* I was rather at a loss
what to do until I discovered the possibility of utilizing a social grouping
that crosscuts ideological differentation. These groupings are named *ter-
ritorial divisions* (which Guiart [1956:25] refers to as *tribes*). In the
Kwamera language they are called "places" or "houses"; the members of
each place form one company in opposition to people of surrounding
places.

To escape my association with one ideological side, I declared that I had
come to study the entire place (as defined by tradition and custom), and
not to study one side (as defined by religious ideology). My place, Imwai
Nasipmene, includes both Christian and John Frum hamlets and thus I
have been able to transcend a complete identification with the Christian
side. The Tannese, too, must sink their ideological differences and hostilities to act together as one place during various socially important neighborhood events, including curing rituals, funeral ceremonies, the pig-
killing *nakwiari* ceremony, and so forth. I have attempted to add anthropology to this list of events.

At this writing, I have begun my economic survey. Periodically, I am
called down from the mountain to Sulphur Bay so that cult leaders there
can assure themselves that I am not distributing too many resources that
evade their control. As I am working with John Frum villagers partially
under the influence of these bigmen, and as I have raised my status by
raising the flag, they are inclined to be friendly. This may or may not last.
Tannese society is a segmentary one and it is easy to fall into the chasms
between the segments. There exist, however, traditional crosscutting ties
that span these divisions. Careful and considerate crossing of these bridges
makes interaction with all sides possible. My status as an outsider, to which
I can retire at any moment when it does not pay to be too much of an
insider, elevates me above some of the fray. This is, however, high-wire
anthropology without a net.

What is the meaning of America on Tanna? I think I might feel more
comfortable in an atmosphere of "Yankee Go Home" and all the usual
sobriquets we have come to expect. The Tannese idealization of America is
sometimes much harder to take. All ideological factions on Tanna adore
America, although the cultists get a little peeved at others squatting on
what they consider to be their ideological turf.

The origins of Americophilia are easy to trace. The four-year presence
of the American military in Vanuatu has become, in the retelling, an almost
mythological golden age of excitement, liberal access to material goods,
and an improved status vis-à-vis Europeans. Only the return of the Americans can restore all this to the people. Those five years sparked the

imaginations of the Tannese and, for four decades now, their illusions have become the building blocks of a number of John Frum organizations and enthusiasms.

This still leaves unanswered the question of why "sing out" to anyone? Why do these people place themselves in a supplicant's position to a fantasized America? An understanding of this begins with knowledge of certain patterns in traditional island society. Two of the most important of these are a kind of patron/client relationship—an important element of bigman political systems—and Tannese notions of the supernatural and of power in general.

Although there are certain inherited titles on the island, everyday power rests in the hands of bigmen. These men achieve their positions through a reputation for knowledge and, to a lesser degree, through material largesse. People support a bigman in order to gain access to the knowledge he controls. Valuable knowledge comprises various magical and medical techniques, the details of historical events, information regarding past exchanges of women, debts, proper custom, land boundaries, and also knowledge of Western society and culture.

During the war, people encountered Americans who manifestly controlled powerful knowledge as well as immense material resources. Americans, moreover, occasionally distributed their goods in a fashion approaching maniacal largesse. As important as its cargo, America also proved itself to possess effective knowledge to produce goods, the ability to restore health to the sick, and a technology of trucks, ships, and planes. America is a perfect bigman, and the Tannese continue to seek roads to America in order to gain access to the goods and knowledge it controls. America, however, has so far proved elusive, failing to assume the proffered mantle of authority. The Tannese remain a group of clients in search of a patron.

The mythic role of America on Tanna parallels that of island supernatural forces. These include various local spirits of place and ancestors. Collectively, people believe these beings to police important areas of human life. Though powerful, the ancestors are manageable, at least to a degree. Men know rituals by which ancestral power might be controlled constructively (as in garden magic) or destructively (as in sorcery).

America, like island spirits and ancestors, is a power that has proved its ability to affect people's lives. If access routes to local supernatural powers (via certain rituals, such as kava spitting) are known, and known to work, the routes leading to America are presently blocked. As a consequence, a bigman can sometimes augment his status by claiming to have discovered a new road to America. For example, the leaders at Sulphur Bay currently use a telephone device (constructed out of datura flowers) by which they talk to a U.S. Army leader named Master Wol (or "World").

In addition, islanders link themselves to America by means of an integratory mythology. This mythology, shared by all factions on the island, incorporates America and Tanna into a special unity. The knowledge powers of America echo those of island spirits and ancestors. The land of the spirits—traditionally the mountains, caves, or the horizon—is now sometimes said to be America itself. John Frum is at home there, and other traditional figures are too. For example, the refrain of one John Frum hymn asserts:

Semsemu imwai America	Semsemu, his place is America
Hawaii Honolulu	Hawaii Honolulu
Hawaii Honolulu	Hawaii Honolulu
Semsemu imwai America	Semsemu, his place is America
Oririaue, oririaue	Oririaue [nonsense words]

Like everyone else, Tannese spirits are moving to Hawaii. Following the supply routes of World War II, people know that Hawaii is a station along the road to America. It is also now the new home of Semsemu, a traditional figure who is half ogre, half culture hero.[3]

Islanders realize that in America scientists are the people who really control powerful knowledge. Here they draw a parallel between American scientists and local spirit mediums, or "clevers" as these are called in Bislama. Just as scientists can see through glass without themselves being seen by using a one-way mirror, so can clevers discover lost objects and make themselves invisible with spiritual assistance.

A popular war story focuses on a contest between American scientific power and the spiritual power of the dead. American scientists, in this case, won the day, defeating meddlesome local ancestors.

When people went up to help America during the war everything was good. One day, however, a man from north Tanna who worked at the fuel dump was carried off by an ancestor. He was working for the Army. Everyone knows that the Army's fashion is to make you hurry through the whole day. This is why we preferred to work for the Navy. It let you rest. This man was tired of working and he sneaked away to a place in the forest where two overhanging rocks meet. But this is a place of ancestors, and one came upon him and carried him away. The man disappeared for two months. If an ancestor catches you, no one sees you go. You are powerless to escape or call out. Finally, one day, the man was spied at the top of a tall banyan tree near Vila town. We ran and called to him, but the ancestor still held him and he didn't answer. So we went to find the Americans. Our bosses, Tom Navy and Tom Army, along with a powerful doctor, arrived. They stopped all the military trucks passing along the roads and they stopped all the planes flying in the air. Then they located the man in the tree with *stil* (radar).[4] They climbed the tree and brought him down and took him away in a truck to their hospital. There he died, but the Americans brought him back to life by injecting him with their medicines, which are very strong. It was then we truly understood the power of America.

All of these parallels, this mythology, assert the right of the Tannese to the power of America, and the duty of America to provide for Tanna. Alas, despite the years of hard effort, the access roads still remain blocked.[5] As an American, I am perceived and my actions are interpreted in terms of this integratory mythology. It also structures the ethnographic information I am given. People are always prompting me to confirm their faith in a Tanna:America special relationship. I have tried to escape some of the more disturbing aspects of the myth by claiming that I am only a student, an underling sent to scout around—that only the *big* bigmen of America control its resources and powers. This is certainly true. My dodge is substantiated by the fact that my arrival on Tanna did not herald the advent of a new fleet of cargo ships, or the light of a new wisdom. I do serve, though, as a minor conduit to the goods (if not the powers) of America, and people use me as such. Through me, they have access to wristwatches, dungarees, army blankets, and boxing gloves—treasure recalled from the golden age. Tannese realize perfectly that American exchange custom is governed by money and they are quite willing to pay for the goods I import.[6] What they want is access—a road. The one thing I am always asked for is my home address in America.

NOTES

1. This story was written during my first year on Tanna. I would like to thank Fulbright-Hays; the English-Speaking Union of the United States, San Francisco Branch; the Department of Anthropology of the University of California; the National Science Foundation; and the Department of Anthropology, Research School of Pacific Studies, Australian National University.

2. To my best knowledge, the others were C. B. Humphreys (in 1925), J. Guiart (in 1951), and Ron Bruntin, Julia Wilkinson, Robert and Janet Gregory, Ron Bastin, and Soren Lund, all in the 1970s.

3. Those familiar with Tannese mythology will recognize the malefic Semsemu (see Humphreys, 1926:95–97).

4. In Pidgin English, *stil* refers, among other things, to radar and fingerprinting. This power allows Americans to "see" planes and submarines that cannot otherwise be seen, to discover the identity of thieves, and so forth.

5. There are competing mythologies that integrate Tanna with other Western powers. One of these declares that Prince Philip of Great Britain is descended from a spirit of Mt. Tukosmera. The British Resident Commissioner is apparently actively encouraging this incipient cult. He recently presented the bigmen involved with a signed portrait of Philip and five clay pipes. These prestigious trade pipes have long been

unavailable on Tanna. This political move counteracts strong French influence with the John Frum cultists at Sulphur Bay.

6. I take payment in kava root.

REFERENCES

GUIART, JEAN

1956   Un siecle et demi de contacts culturels à Tanna (Publications de la Societe des Oceanistes no. 5). Paris: Musée de l'Homme.

HUMPHREYS, C. B.

1926   The Southern New Hebrides: An Ethnological Record. Cambridge, MA: Cambridge University Press.

RECOMMENDED READINGS

GREGORY, ROBERT J., AND JANET E. GREGORY

1984   John Frum: An Indigenous Strategy of Reaction to Mission Rule and Colonial Order. Pacific Studies 7:68–90.

LINDSTROM, LAMONT

1989   Working Encounters: Oral Histories of World War II Labor Corps from Tanna, Vanuata. *In* The Pacific Theater: Island Recollections of World War II. G. White and L. Lindstrom, eds. Honolulu: University of Hawaii Press.

1981   Cult and Culture: American Dreams in Vanuatu. Pacific Studies 4:101–123.

FOURTEEN

'Pigs of the Forest' and Other Unwritten Papers

TERENCE E. HAYS
Rhode Island College

The smoke stung my eyes, I was tired and hot in the midday sun, and boredom had reached its high point. Though the occasion differed, the earth oven feast was just like all of the others I had attended in Ndumba, a Highlands community in Papua New Guinea.[1] The pit had been opened in the morning, stones were heated on gigantic fires and then placed in the bottom, grass and leaf coverings were placed over the stones, vegetable food was dumped in unceremoniously, and the whole was covered with more banana leaves and finally a high mound of dirt. Now we waited— usually about three or four hours—until the steamed food could be removed and distributed for the eating.

A feast should be exciting, but obviously *feast* was a misleading way of labeling such an event. Small groups of women sat around talking or performing mundane tasks such as weaving string bags, while most men and youths had wandered off to while away the waiting period in some other—any other—way. As dutiful observer and note taker, I sat off to one side bored to distraction, which I hoped would come soon.

There were always children to play with, of course. My wife and I were the first "red people" these children (and adults as well) had ever come to know on a daily basis, and the novelty of just looking at us and delightedly responding to any attention we gave them was still compelling. Among the children hovering about on that day was Foringa, a young boy I had not seen around the hamlets for some time. One look at him suggested the reason, as he clearly was not feeling well.

In the past, children in the New Guinea Highlands were almost inevitable sufferers from yaws. Now that scourge is gone, but skin diseases and tropical ulcers continue to be common sources of discomfort and systemic infection. Foringa, his body virtually covered with festering, fly-blown sores, was the most pitiful-looking case that I had ever seen. He managed a small smile but continually grimaced and squinted at me through crusted, swollen eyelids. I tried to speak pleasantly to him, imagining his pain and wondering whether he might usefully go to the nearby mission medical aid post for treatment. They would certainly wash his lesions, probably daub them with the purple liquid used for nearly every skin condition, and then send him back home.

As I speculated and sympathized, I caught a glimpse of his father, Haangguma, who had just arrived at the feast ground. I approached him and, after the requisite greetings and small talk, asked about his son: What was Foringa's problem, and how was he having it treated? His response was both startling and intoxicating, smacking of impending revelation of ethnographic treasure. Haangguma told me that he was treating his son's condition by no longer hunting in Maatarera, a section of primary forest claimed by his patriclan.

Haangguma went on: His wife had, some months before, given birth to a new brother for Foringa. Ndumba birth customs required that a successful birth be followed by a "coming-out party" for the mother and child, at which scores of smoke-dried game animals (*kapul,* in New Guinea Tok Pisin) would be distributed to all of her patriclan members. This entailed considerable effort on the part of the father and his kinsmen and friends, as they scoured the forest during the months of birth confinement to hunt and trap the needed possums and other marsupials that abounded in the high forest.

It seemed, according to Haangguma, that he had overdone it this time. He had obtained the number of *kapul* he needed, but all from one part of the forest. Large though it was, as he appreciated upon having to go increasingly higher to find prey, the section was now depleted of game through his and his fellows' activities. This was why his son was now suffering.

At this point I expressed my confusion. Had Foringa been with his father on these trips to the forest? Had he caught the sickness there? Was that the problem?

Haangguma, like other Ndumba adults, had learned to accept the profound ignorance of "anthropologists" (whatever that might mean, that was what we said we were), and patiently filled in the necessary background, as he might with a small child.

I knew about *faana,* right? The spirit beings that inhabit the forest, especially in its upper reaches?

Well, the *faana* of the upper forest are like people in many respects, including a having a taste for meat. Since they are unable to raise pigs, as people do, the *kapul* are their "pigs." That is, *faana* look after the game animals and regard them as their property, just as people do with their pigs. Now, *faana* realize that men will hunt and trap these "pigs" of theirs, and up to a point they tolerate that situation, though when in the high forest Ndumba men try to avoid excessive noise or anything else that might draw the attention of *faana* to their presence.

But, he stressed, if one takes too many *kapul* from the *faana,* they become angry. (What he meant by "too many" was left vague, but clearly Haangguma's haul of over a hundred animals was judged, ex post factor, as qualifying.) This anger gets expressed in various ways. Disturbed *faana* might follow a hunter home and interfere with his sleep; they might only cause bad luck on future expeditions; or, in extreme cases, they might make the wife or children of a hunter sick as a message. Clearly, in Haangguma's mind, this last had been his fate. His first-born son was now suffering from the condition I had observed. Nothing could really be done except to avoid the section of forest where the transgression had occurred, hoping that with a long enough cooling-off period, the local *faana* would forgive him or forget about the incident. Then Foringa would recover and Haangguma could resume his exploitation of Maatarera.

I scribbled furiously in my notebook—this was wonderful stuff! Visions of Ballantine labels danced in my head! Venn diagrams! "Institutions," "customs," and "beliefs" all interlocked in a tight whole—hunting, medical beliefs, and religion inextricably intertwined, the way I had learned they must be for a society to function. What was more, these customs and beliefs were *adaptive!* Avoidance of a section of forest would give the game population a chance to recover; the area would become a buffer zone, allowing the environment to restore its intricate balance with the demands of its human inhabitants. I had discovered a link between seemingly nonrational Ndumba beliefs and the practical world!

As my head swam with the possibilities, Haangguma slipped away. The earth oven was being opened, and for him the appeal of freshly cooked food and intelligent conversation with his peers could not be compared with dealing any further with my silly questions.

No matter. Details could be followed up later. I was already drafting in my mind the articles that would make my career and render the doctoral dissertation I was supposed to write almost irrelevant. Or perhaps that could be my dissertation topic as well! "Pigs of the Forest: Natural Conservationists in the New Guinea Highlands," "Spirit Beliefs and the Conservation of Resources in Ndumba," and other titles for the papers I would write buzzed around in my brain and gave rise to mental outlines until I could bear the tension no longer. Hot sweet potatoes could wait; further details could wait; I hurried back to our house to begin work on my ethnographic masterpiece.

After the initial excited discussion with my wife, of course, further details were needed. It happened that another man, Waanggusa, stopped by our house to visit that evening. Anytime we attended a feast there were sure to be visitors later—particularly those who hadn't attended it but who might benefit from a secondary food distribution from the generous portions we usually received. I seized the opportunity and pumped Waanggusa for more information about the "pigs of the forest."

As things developed, my linguistic clumsiness was not the only reason for the confused look on his face as my tale unfolded. Without identifying who specifically had told me about the *faana*–skin disease connection, as we generally tried to avoid the risk of confounding interpersonal conflicts with "ethnographic truth," I indicated that I had just learned of all this, but still had some questions. For example, how many *kapul* were "too many"?

First, Waanggusa asserted that it was possible to overhunt a given section of the forest. This led him to go on at some length about another area of bush where concern had arisen recently over birds of paradise. Some people were afraid, he reported, that the introduction of shotguns (a dreamed-of and often discussed prospect, but still not a reality in Ndumba at that time, or even as late as 1985) would mean the rapid extinction of these birds with their highly prized plumes, and . . .

I interrupted him to get back to the questions at hand. Digressions certainly have their place, and we all owe a great deal to the serendipity of chance remarks and conversational meanderings—indeed, that day's wondrous revelation was just such a case. But at the moment I had bigger fish to fry.

Unfortunately, my attempts to get Waanggusa back on the track continued to lead only to more digressions and confusion. What about skin diseases and lesions? Well, Waanggusa knew a story about the origin of skin diseases—did I want to hear it? Aha! Of course I did, and so he told me. As it turned out (when would I learn?), it wasn't a story about the origin of such conditions at all, but about how trading partnerships with the Baruya Anga to the south developed, in the "time of the ancestors," when a man from there miraculously cured a Ndumba man whose skin resembled the lichen-covered bark of a beech tree. Good stuff, this, but *not* what I was so singlemindedly, even obsessively, after at the time.

Tell me about the "pigs of the forest," I insisted. Did all *faana* have them? Did female *faana* feed them, the way human women tended real pigs?

Seemingly impatient now, Waanggusa wanted to know where I ever got the idea that *faana* kept pigs. He had never heard of such a thing! I explained that of course I wasn't referring to actual pigs, but to *kapul* that were analogous to pigs as far as *faana* were concerned.

Waanggusa chuckled at the thought of such an arrangement. It was preposterous, he said (or words to that effect). Yes, there were *faana* that lived in the forest, and yes, they sometimes punished men for various transgressions, but hunting, or overhunting, wasn't one of them. Like a member of the Ndumba Chamber of Commerce, he reminded me of the vast tracts of forest claimed by Ndumba, especially in contrast to the grassland peoples to the north, and the local abundance of game. In any case, *kapul* were not looked after by *faana,* who had rather loftier matters to occupy their attention.

What about skin diseases, then? What caused them? Why did some children seem to suffer so badly—Foringa, for instance (I sneaked in)?

Waanggusa couldn't say for sure about Foringa, but severe cases were, like most ailments and misfortunes, caused by sorcery. Knowledge of such magic was possessed by people downriver to the west. Living at a slightly lower elevation—in "hot country" by Ndumba standards, though still a mile above sea level—many of them were said to suffer from skin diseases and to be especially proficient at causing them. If someone from here angered someone from there, Waanggusa opined, he or his wife or children might experience such a form of revenge. "Look to strained interpersonal relationships," Professor Waanggusa might have phrased it, "rather than to *faana* for an explanation."

My ethnographer's heart was sinking. Had Haangguma made up this whole thing? Was he covering himself by blaming spirits instead of his own problems with neighbors? Had I been duped? Or was Waanggusa the culprit? Was he, for some reason, trying to snatch away my Nobel Prize? Or was he simply ignorant? Could a mature adult man *not know about* "Mystical Illness Causation and Ecological Balance"?

I was still foundering as Waanggusa left our house, shaking his head and snickering over my silly notions. I had met Two Crows.

I remember being rather shocked than pleased when in my student days I came across such statements in J. O. Dorsey's "Omaha Sociology" as "Two Crows denies this." This looked a little as though the writer had not squarely met the challenge of assaying his source material and giving us the kind of data that we, as respectable anthropologists, could live on.

Thus Edward Sapir (1938:7) voiced his dismay when faced with Dorsey's (1884) particular resolution of a major dilemma of ethnography—the one I had to wrestle with in Ndumba and one which cannot be avoided. We go to the field, equipped with the concepts of *society* and *culture,* in search of groups with beliefs, customs, and institutions. But what we confront, as did Dorsey before us, is "a finite, though indefinite, number of human beings, who [give] themselves the privilege of differing from each other" (Sapir 1938:7).

As A. L. Kroeber is reported to have said, "Cultures don't paint their toenails." The ethnographer in the field is set down in the midst of a Heraclitean world where some informants paint their toenails, while others do not; some did previously, but have given up the practice; others begin to do it, having been stimulated by the posing of the question; and Two Crows, perhaps thinking of particular persons, says that no one—or that everyone—does it. How, then, is this reality of variation and disagreement to be abstracted into the kind of data that anthropologists can live on? For the ethnographer seeking authoritative statements about Omaha culture, Two Crows must be absorbed into, or even become, the Omaha.

What was I to do with the conflicting statements of Haangguma and Waanggusa? How could they be accommodated in my descriptions of Ndumba culture?

Perhaps one of them was simply wrong. Maybe Haangguma was making it all up—to divert attention from his sorcery troubles, to play a trick on me, or just to entertain me (I clearly manifested excitement at what he was telling me at the time). After all, I had seen little evidence of a conservation ethic elsewhere in Ndumba behavior. Children happily robbed birds' nests of fledglings and eggs—for amusement, not food—carelessly destroying the nests in the process, and no one seemed distressed except me. The grassland that covered much of Ndumba territory was "created" by their burning activities. Burning secondary growth was an essential part of their gardening pattern, but I had also witnessed huge areas set alight out of casual mischief or curiosity as to how far a grass fire would burn before extinguishing itself. Amid such waste (from my point of view, at least) Haangguma's story had been all the more remarkable, suggesting concerns for the conservation of resources—however they might be rationalized—that were inconsistent with my experiences to that point.

But maybe it was just Waanggusa who was wrong, or simply uninformed about the *faana* of the forest and their "pigs." Yet this was not an immediately persuasive conclusion, except that reaching it would enable me to get on with my career more quickly. After all, the two men were of about the same age and comparable standing in the community. Moreover, as father of several children by two wives and veteran of many childbirth *kapul* feasts, Waanggusa had taken countless numbers of game animals from the high forest. How could this aspect of his fellows' belief system never have come to his attention?

Apart from questions about the distribution of the *"faana*'s revenge" belief in the community, what about its supposed effects on the environment? If, in the most extreme scenario, the belief was held only by Haangguma, then surely his abstention from hunting in Maatarera would have little effect as long as others hunted there. Similarly, if some others shared his belief but it was not universally held and followed, or if even a sizable minority was not influenced by such notions, again it would be difficult to presume that the ecological balance was maintained by this aspect of Ndumba cosmology.

As I pondered these complications and felt my Nobel Prize slipping from my grasp, I had to wonder where the culture I had come so far to study was. Having grown up in schools and libraries, I had come to view the world as consisting of things to be known and populated by people who knew them and people who didn't, with the latter needing only to turn to the ones who did to fill the void. Yet here were my authorities disagreeing with each other, obstructing my attempts to identify and describe the system.

The trap I had fallen into was one to which scholars may be especially prone, but one that awaits any who would reify belief systems that are continually being negotiated by their users. Living in a world of *Robert's Rules of Order,* instruction manuals, and encyclopedias, it is easy to lose sight of the fact that culture is neither static nor fully shared, even among those who enshrine "authorities" in seemingly timeless printed forms. In a nonliterate society the situation is no different, even though it would be easier for the analyst if there were analogues to reference works and card catalogues, waiting to be tapped by identifying and questioning the "right informant" who retains "the culture" in his or her head. Like consensus, culture has to be built up, though never seamlessly, from the individual and various versions of it. As Sapir (1938:11) advised, the starting point is "to operate as though we knew nothing about culture but were interested in analyzing as well as we could what a given number of human beings accustomed to live with each other actually think and do in their day to day relationships."

Two Crows, in one of his many guises, will always be there to frustrate attempts to abstract simple and clear cultural rules from the actions and statements of people who live in worlds of contingencies. Yet contingencies need not result in chaos, but in life as it is lived. Some beliefs, one will find, are held by virtually all members of a community; others are only shared by some; and still others—the ones that give us delight more often than not, when you think about it—may be unique to specific individuals, such as Haangguma (or was it Waanggusa?). The process of discovering that *patterned diversity* is the real system—and that some differences need to be resolved, others are just tolerated, and still others may only surface with an outsider's probings—is what keeps us all alive. That realization, and the new *kinds* of questions it raises, have brought me more understanding than ever could have come from the papers Waanggusa and others kept me from writing.

NOTE

1. A degree of literary license has been taken with this account, though possibly no more than is common in the classroom. The conflicting statements and explanations reported are faithfully rendered, but reattributed (pseudonymously) for narrative purposes, and are representative of quandaries that plagued me during fieldwork in the Eastern Highlands Province of Papua New Guinea in 1971–72, 1981, and 1985. Despite all of that I am grateful to my mentors in Ndumba and to those who have supported my research there: the National Institutes of Health, the Institute of Papua New Guinea Studies, the National Endowment for the Humanities, Rhode Island College, the Australian-American Eduational Foundation, and the Australian National University, Research School of Pacific Studies.

REFERENCES CITED

DORSEY, J. OWEN
1884 Omaha Sociology. Smithsonian Institution 3rd Annual Report (1881–1882), pp. 205–370. Washington, DC: Government Printing Office.

SAPIR, EDWARD

1938   Why Cultural Anthropology Needs the Psychiatrist. Psychiatry 1:7–12.

SUGGESTED READINGS

HAYS, TERRENCE E.

1987   Initiation as Experience: The Management of Emotional Responses to Ndumba Novices. *In* Anthropology in the High Valleys: Essays on the New Guinea Highlands in Honor of Kenneth E. Read. L. L. Langness and Terrence E. Hays, eds. Pp. 185–235. Novato, CA: Chandler & Sharp.

1979   Plant Classification and Nomenclature in Ndumba, Papua New Guinea Highlands. Ethnology 18:253–270.

HAYS, TERRENCE E., AND PATRICIA H. HAYS

1982   Opposition and Complementarity of the Sexes in Ndumba Initiation Ceremonies. *In* Rituals of Manhood: Male Initiation in New Guinea. Gilbert H. Herdt, ed. Pp. 201–238. Berkeley: University of California Press.

FIFTEEN

To Die on Ambae: On the Possibility of Doing Fieldwork Forever

WILLIAM L. RODMAN
McMaster University

MARGARET C. RODMAN
York University

December 7, 1985:
LATE SATURDAY NIGHT, OUR HOUSE,
AMBAE — BEDSIDE

Bill

And then I said:

An anthropologist gets sick and dies while conducting fieldwork on the small South Pacific island of Ambae. Suddenly, there she is, standing in front of these big gates beside a man with a long beard and a scroll. "Hello," says the man, "I'm St. Peter and these are the Pearly Gates. I have some good news and some bad news for you. Which do you want first?"

"The good news," says the anthropologist.

"Okay," says St. Peter, "the good news is that you have been admitted to Heaven."

"That's just great," she says, "if I've been admitted to Heaven, then what could possibly be the bad news?"

"Well," says St. Peter, "Heaven consists of little worlds. People spend eternity in the same place where they drop. You planned a few months fieldwork on Ambae, but now it looks like you'll be doing fieldwork there forever."

It was a bad joke and I knew it. Still Margy managed a weak smile: "That's not very funny," she said. She thought for a moment and her expression became more serious: "You don't suppose . . ."

"No," I told her, "of course not. Dumb joke. Sorry."

Since last night she had run a fever and endured severe chills and worse sweats. She hadn't been able to keep down a thing—not medicine, not food, not even water. We kept thinking the fever would break, but it didn't, and she was getting weaker. She had been a trooper, but now I could see in her eyes she was getting scared.

"Bill," she said, "you've got to get me out of here."

I wanted to, God knows, but there was just no way, at least not for another few days.

Friday, December 6, 1985:

THE WAR MUSEUM IN THE RAIN FOREST

Margy

On our first field trip to Ambae in 1969 we discovered that the island was, for us, a place where the days last longer and time slows down. Back in Canada, we yearned to reset our mental clocks to Ambae time, and indeed we've returned to the island for three more field trips over the years. Our most recent trip, in 1985, provided both a respite from a demanding period of fieldwork elsewhere in Vanuatu and a chance to fill in some gaps in our material.

By early December, we were ready to leave the field. My last scheduled interview was with an old man named Charlie Siu, a collector and connoisseur of World War II memorabilia. Charlie lives in an isolated hamlet near the coast with his wife, Betty, a healer who likes to seem mysterious. For years I paid more attention to her than to him. I recorded her songs, photographed her medicinal plants, learned from her the sexual facts of life that she thought every Ambae woman should know. Charlie had wanted to tell me of his wartime experiences working for the Americans on Espiritu Santo, a huge medical and supply base for the Battle of the Coral Sea. It was a topic that interested our son Sean, then thirteen, so he decided to come along with me and help by taking pictures.

We set off early on Friday morning, exactly a week before we were due to bring the field trip to an end. I had a headache and hiking to Charlie's hamlet seemed an immense effort, but perhaps the weather was to blame. It had rained in the night and then again at dawn, a windless rain that left the air so damp I could see my breath. The rain forest steamed as we followed the path down the hill, our flipflops slipping and slapping a gritty spray of dark volcanic mud up the backs of our legs. We crossed a pile of mossy stones, once a garden wall, into Charlie and Betty's plantation, a raggedy stand of old coconut palms from which they earned a little money making copra—smoke-dried coconut meat, the "palm" part of Palmolive soap, and an ingredient in coffee whitener. Copra is the main cash crop in Vanuatu and it provides the only source of income for most people on Ambae.

Their hamlet occupies a clearing in the plantation. Sean and I stood on the plaza at the center of the settlement, looking down at the bare earth,

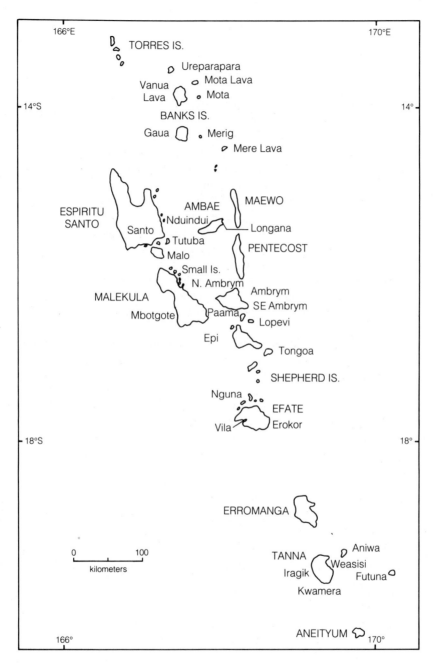

Vanuatu

shuffling our feet and clearing our throats, politely signaling our hosts that we had arrived. Sean picked up a piece of paper in the mud. "Mom, it's a pay slip from the U.S. Navy!" It was a blank, undated, unsigned, but the Navy hasn't been in the area since 1944. We knew we were in for a treat.

Charlie led us into a bamboo house where we sat on new copra sacks that smelled like freshly mown hay. He sang, his soft, whining old man's voice recalling the war as the islanders experienced it. The traditional melodic forms of Ambae warriors' songs contrasted with the sounds of a white man's war—*boom, ratatat, whirr*—and with songs he learned from soldiers: "God Save America Wan Gudfala Ples." Betty joined us and took charge of presenting Charlie's World War II collection for our inspection: forty-seven American dimes with dates ranging from 1928 to 1944, shell casings, bullets, blankets, dinner plates from Los Angeles, and forks marked USN.

"And see that big cooking pot in the corner? That's from the watime, too," Betty said. I nodded, and suddenly I felt my enthusiasm run out of me like water. I wasn't feeling well; my head still hurt and my bones ached, perhaps from the damp, hard earth beneath the copra sack.

Before we left, Charlie posed in front of a red hibiscus bush. Sean snapped a picture of him wearing a U.S. Navy cap, long-sleeved shirt, and fatigues with cuffs rolled several times to keep them above his bare feet and the muddy ground.

Sean and I climbed slowly through a soft rain to the hill village of Waileni, our field site during our three visits to the island since 1978. We walked past a fallen banyan that lay on the edge of the village like a great wooden whale beached in the last hurricane. We continued on to our compound, which consisted of a bamboo house, a separate kitchen, and a privy concealed in the bush. Our compound was part of a satellite hamlet just out of sight of the village plaza. It was the chief's hamlet: Chief Mathias Tariundu, a leader of the highest rank in the *hungwe,* an association in which men kill tusked boars in order to gain prestige. I was Chief Mathias's "daughter-in-law" because, in 1978, he adopted Bill as his "son." Since then, we have spent about twenty months living in his village.

Channing, our five-year-old daughter, hurtled down the path to greet us, village playmates in her wake. Sean ducked into the cool, dark kitchen in search of something for lunch and Channing followed, chattering, her eyes on the small ripe bananas hanging from the rafters. I wasn't hungry. I thought I'd lie down for a while.

It was a week before I got up again.

Bill

I, too, conducted my last scheduled interview that Friday morning. When I returned to our compound, I asked Sean where his mother was. "Mom isn't feeling well," he said. "She went inside to lie down." No big deal, I thought, and I left her alone to take what I thought was a nap.

I had mixed feelings about leaving the island. I was pleased that our field trip was almost over and sad for the same reason. Pleased that it had gone so well—Margy and I had gathered good data, and we'd renewed old friendships, some of sixteen years' duration. The kids had readjusted to village life and the family had remained in good health. I was sad mostly because I was leaving Mathias, my second father, almost certainly for the last time.

Once, Mathias told me he was as old as the century: I think he believed the birth date he assigned himself and thought of himself as not doing badly for an "olfala" of eighty five. He'd slowed down a bit, but not much: He mediated fewer disputes in the village but he still attended just about every rank-taking in the area, the art of killing tusked boars being his particular passion. He'd raised me to my first rank in 1978; on this field trip, I'd taken a second rank. Most days, we spent hours together in the shade of the canarium almond tree near his clubhouse. I'd heard most of his stories before but just being with him gave me pleasure. Most nights we drank kava together, he and I, and felt the sweet communion of the slightly stoned.

Toward nightfall Mathias came by our house. He leaned through an open window and I stopped typing the morning's interview. We talked for a moment in Bislama about the man I had visited, then he asked, "Where's Margaret?"

"Lying down. She's not feeling well," I said.

"Fever?" What he meant was, does she have malaria.

"I think so."

"Too bad." He paused, and then, with a smile, "Some men are coming over. Do you want to drink kava with us?"

"No, not tonight. I have to make dinner for the kids."

"Too bad," he said, and wandered off.

Saturday, Decemer 7:

AT HOME AT THE END OF THE LINE

Bill

Margy and I have always thought of malaria as a kind of dues. Everybody who works in northern Vanuatu gets it: It's part of the price you pay to conduct fieldwork there. We take antimalaria pills whenever we are in the field, chloroquine in the 1970s, newer and more sophisticated drugs in the 1980s, but still we've both contracted the disease twice. On one occasion, my fever went high enough—and stayed high long enough—that I heard two little village dogs talking to each other across the plaza from where I sat propped against a tree. That they were holding a conversation didn't surprise me at the time; however, I remember being impressed that dogs on the island speak English.

Most often, in my experience, the course of a bad case of malaria runs like this: You get a splitting headache, followed by a high fever, and then you become very cold, even though the weather is warm. Your teeth begin to chatter uncontrollably and you cover yourself with blankets. You have a miserable time out there on the ice floe, and then your personal thermostat swings into turnaround and you throw the blankets off because the room you are in has become a sauna and your sheets are soaked with sweat. By this point, you should have taken a "curative" dose of antimalaria pills, roughly three times the weekly suppressive dose, and after a while your temperature begins to fall as rapidly as it rose only hours earlier. You feel enormous relief, then you sleep, then you feel wrecked for about four days.

That's malaria as we knew it, awful but not lethal. In the late 1970s, new strains of the disease appeared in northern Vanuatu. The most recent types of malaria don't respond to chloroquin or any other medication an anthropologist might have in his pack. Left untreated, the disease can be deadly.

We worried about our children contracting malaria, so we took all the precautions we could. We chose a field site high in the hills of the island. There are no mosquitoes at night in Waileni: it's too cold for them. Sunday was pill day. Every Sunday, without fail, our whole family took the bitter-tasting pills that suppress the most common strains of malaria. One of the smells I associate most vividly with fieldwork is the smoky scent of mosquito coils made from pyrethrum, the dried flower heads of chrysanthemums; we burned a coil anytime we were in the house during the day. Deep-Woods Off was as much a part of our interviewing kit as a tape recorder and spare batteries. For all our precautions, Margy had every symptom of malaria with which we were familiar from experience, plus a few more. Her illness didn't respond to the initial dose of chloroquine; her fever remained constant. Starting late Friday night, she began to vomit and could hold nothing down. Medicine came up immediately; so did as much as a mouthful of water. My main concern was that she might have contracted cerebral malaria, an especially dangerous form of the disease, but I was almost equally concerned about the possibility that she might become severely dehydrated. How long can a person with a fever last without water? Three days? Less? A bit more, perhaps? I wasn't sure, but I knew that it wasn't very long.

On Saturday, the seriousness of our situation struck me with full force. Not only was Margy a very sick woman, but we were isolated, temporarily unable to leave our field site. Margy was in no shape to walk anywhere and the single motor vehicle in the village, an old, battered Toyota truck, belonged to a leader of the area's small population of Seventh Day Adventists. Saturday is the Adventist day of worship: They maintain a strict prohibition against work of any sort on Saturday, their Sabbath, and they count driving a truck as work. Even if we had transport, our options were limited. A truck could drive us to the cow pasture that served as a landing strip on that part of the island, but no plane was due until Monday or possibly Tuesday. A truck also could take us an hour over rough road to a small hospital located on the southeastern tip of the island. The hospital was staffed by two "doctors" whose titles were honorific: one held a degree in hospital administration while the other, "Dr." David, had received training roughly equivalent to a North American paramedic. Regardless of their qualifications, we perceived the hospital as our best hope for obtaining medical aid. But we had no way to get there.

All day Saturday I stayed in our compound. I transcribed interviews and every so often checked on Margy, remaining with her for as long as she wanted company, which was never very long. She was pale and her eyes had become dull and sunken. Her skin was hot, as if she had a furnace casting off heat inside her body. She couldn't read (a side effect of the malarial headache) and she couldn't sleep either. So she spent most of her time staring at four photographs of horses I'd torn from a Minolta calendar and taped to the bamboo wall of our room.

The village was quiet: all the kids, including our own, were off in the bush, hunting for crayfish or pigeons, gathering nuts, playing games. Around noon, Mathias came to check on Margy's condition. He leaned through the big open window in the bamboo wall of the house and rested his forearms on the sill. He looked very old and his eyes were troubled.

"How is she?" he asked.

"Not so good. About the same. She still has the fever."

He exhaled slowly, audibly, his eyes fixed on the floor. Then he looked up, directly at me.

"What do you think she has?"

I told him I still thought she had malaria.

"Did you give her the medicine?"

"Yes. But it won't stay down."

He thought about this for a moment and then shook his head. "You say it's malaria but if it is, then your medicine should help her." His statement didn't surprise me. I'd heard many times his view that Western medicine was made for white people; hospital medicine (as opposed to bush medicine) always helped restore white people to good health. Modern medicine sometimes worked with islanders; other times, bush medicine worked better.

"Well," I said, "I think it's a *different* kind of malaria."

He raised and lowered his eyebrows. It was an ambiguous gesture that could signify agreement or a withholding of judgment or even disagreement, but with a desire to avoid confrontation. He left abruptly, without saying another word, and retreated to the cool semidarkness of his men's house. I didn't see him again for the rest of the day.

Sunday, December 8:
THE FAREWELL FEAST

Bill

In the January before our August arrival in Vanuatu, Hurricane Nigel devastated most of the northern islands of the archipelago. On Ambae, only one person lost his life in the hurricane but damage to property was immense: According to the government newspaper, over 90 percent of the houses on the island were flattened. When we heard the news in Canada, we wanted to do something to help the relief effort on Ambae, especially that part of the island with which we had long-standing ties. We conduct our fieldwork in the Anglican sector of Ambae and at that time Margy attended the Anglican church in our neighborhood in Canada. She received permission from the minister of the church to give a Sunday sermon concerning the plight of the people in Vanuatu. Part of the collection was set aside for hurricane relief. A few weeks later, she showed slides and gave a talk to a church woman's group. They too made a generous contribution to the small relief fund we were accumulating.

Margy had planned to present part of the money she had collected to Waileni in church on our final Sunday in the village. She was too sick to attend the service, so I acted in her stead. I explained the origin of the donation and gave the treasurer of the village council the funds she had collected. Mathias stood up and made a short, graceful speech thanking us on behalf of the community. After church, I went immediately to find the man with the truck to take my wife to the hospital.

Margy

The very complexity of a passage that I had always performed simply and without thought brought home to me, and to our neighbors, how quickly I had become as weak as the oldest, feeblest widow in the village. To walk from our house to a waiting Toyota Landcruiser, pull open its heavy, squeaky door, clamber into the passenger seat, and close the door behind me was much more than I could accomplish on my own. I leaned heavily on Bill's arm as he led me across the few yards that separated our house from the truck. I tried to smile but the eyes that gazed back solemnly reflected my own discovery that, try as I might, I could not even create an illusion of being less sick than everyone feared. This scared me. And I could see that it scared Sean and Channing. Bill helped me into the passenger seat, closed the door, boosted himself into the truckbed, and signaled the driver that we were ready. The children waved as we drove off, Channing almost, but not quite, in tears and our teenage son beside her, dry-eyed and tall. Two brave kids, I thought.

I rode with my eyes closed as the Landcruiser lurched through potholes and ruts. The driver was proud that he had maintained this truck for nine years; he eased it carefully through washouts and down hills. Time slowed to walking speed, and I remember the journey mostly as a sequence of scents—the smell of gardens, the damp earth of the forest, woodsmoke from cooking fires, the rancid bacon odor of drying copra. When at last the driver shifted into third gear, I could smell cattle manure mixed with sea salt and I knew we had reached the flat coastal plantations. The hospital was nearby, just over the lip of an extinct volcanic crater that had blown open to the sea.

A local nurse in a crisp blue uniform and bare feet greeted us, seated me on the veranda which served as the waiting room of the colonial-style hospital, and took my temperature. She was young and shy; long thick lashes protected her downcast eyes from the intrusive gaze of outsiders. Her sympathetic bedside manner depended entirely on softly sibilant intakes of breath combined with clicks of the tongue. Nurses in Vanuatu all seem to be experts at producing this consoling sound, somewhere between that of a purring cat and a sitting hen.

Lulled by the nurse's care, I began to think everything would be all right. Then "Dr." David appeared, dressed in Sunday shorts and a Foster's Lager T-shirt. He was proprietary about my illness. I remembered his Australian predecessor haranguing us in 1970 when we complained of loose teeth: "No one on *my* island gets scurvy," he bellowed as he treated our vitamin deficiency. I don't know if the old doctor was really David's role model, but it was quite clear that no sick person would be evacuated from *his* island if he could help it. Go back to the village, take more antimalarial drugs and rest, he prescribed. He had seen more serious cases. Why, one man from a remote settlement came down with resistant malaria and had been unconscious for two days by the time his friends carted him to the hospital. He survived and so will you, David assured me. Turning to Bill, he signaled the end of our consultation with a cheerful "No worries, mate!"

Bill

In fieldwork, as in show business, there are times when the show must go on. Our farewell feast was one such occasion. The village had planned the feast for weeks. By Sunday, the event had a momentum of its own, an inevitability quite independent of the moods and wishes of its guests or even its planners. Some invited guests lived in the deep bush of a neighboring district. There was no way to contact them quickly in their own communities; in any case, by Sunday morning, they were on their way to our village. During the past few days, our neighbors and friends in Waileni had brought taro and yams from their gardens. They had grated and processed the tubers into the principal feast food in Vanuatu, lap-lap, a starchy pudding. In small compounds all around Waileni, lap-lap had been cooking in earth ovens since early Sunday morning.

Upon our return from the hospital, I was told to remain in our compound until preparations for the feast were complete in the main village. Sean posted himself at the window of our house overlooking the dirt track connecting our compound with the village. Around four P.M., he saw a small group of men leave the main village and walk down the road toward our house. He turned to me. "Better lighten up, Dad," he said. "It's party time!"

My mother's brother gave me a head of kava to take with me to the feast. He gave Sean and Channing each a small bundle of *lap-lap*. Then he led us to the meeting house, located on a small rise overlooking the plaza and fallen banyan in the village. When we arrived, the meeting house was filled with people. It had been decorated for the occasion with flowers and ornamental shrubs, gardenias shaped like ivory pinwheels, hibiscus as red as heart's blood, crotons with corkscrew leaves that look like a thermal map, splashes of sea green on a base of vivid canary yellow. The three of us were seated on a wooden bench. Facing us were ten heads of kava and twenty-six bundles of *lap-lap* wrapped in banana leaves, each weighing from ten to fifteen pounds—a lifetime supply unless you know the rules for disposing of it. Channing's friend, Ndiu, ten years old, placed an artificial lei around her neck. This was an honor indeed: In Waileni, real flowers are commonplace but plastic flowers (which bridesmaids carry in all church weddings) cost money and last indefinitely. Sean and I received wreaths of real frangipani. In fact, Ndiu placed two leis around my neck, one for the absent Margy.

There were speeches of welcome and thanksgiving, of friendship and the sorrows of distance, and then ten half coconut shells of kava were set out in front of the bench where I was sitting, and I drank the gray-colored, bitter liquid with all the chiefs, a kind of "kastom" communion. According to one local myth, kava first grew from the decomposing genitalia of a murdered woman and everyone agrees it tastes terrible. It is acceptable, even polite, to make loud phlegm-summoning noises and then spit after drinking kava. So the chiefs and I all rushed outside the meeting house as soon as we had drained our shells. There we all stood, lined up on the grass in front of the meeting house, spitting over the edge of the small rise, and at that precise moment the sun broke through the clouds, bathing the fallen banyan across the plaza in golden light.

It was the last light of late afternoon. Night fell quickly and I distributed the bundles of taro and yam pudding with the help of my adoptive kinsmen. Women and children began to leave the area of the meeting house for their own compounds. Most of the men stayed behind to drink more kava. The wife of my mother's brother sent one of her children to tell me that I was to remain with the men, that she would look after Margy and would summon me if I was needed. I trusted her and gratefully I accepted her offer. As I waited for my second shell of kava, some of the men asked me about Margy's condition. I told them she had malaria and they said "ahhhh" or "sori" or else they drew in their breath sharply through their teeth in an expression of sympathy. I had no idea at the time how thoroughly the villagers rejected my diagnosis in favor of their own judgment.

I returned home after my second shell of kava. As soon as I stepped through the door of our house, I wondered if I was hallucinating. Margy was sitting up in bed. By the light of a single kerosene lantern at her bedside, I could see that she was grinning. That struck me as odd, but odder still was the way she smelled. She smelled smoky, funky, as if she had spent the last few hours putting out a brush fire in a coconut plantation. "You'll never guess what happened while you were away," she said.

Margy

As I lay in my bed, drifting with the fever, I became aware that not everyone was at the feast. The corrugated iron roof creaked as it expanded to absorb the heat of the day; but the bamboo floor also creaked, and for no apparent reason. From time to time, I saw worried brown faces peeking through the open window above my bed or watching me from the darkness of a doorway as I staggered to the privy. By evening, the worried faces had settled down at the foot of my bed to stay.

Woibani, the local kindergarten teacher who lived next door, acted as the spokesperson for the other women. I should realize, she explained, that while I might be ill with malaria, I was clearly suffering from something more serious.

"Like what?" I asked.

"Well, like spirits," she said, her dark eyes shining with excitement and concern.

"Oh," I said.

"The women—my mother and the others—want to do something to help you."

It soon became evident to me that I was being made an offer I couldn't refuse. "No" was not an acceptable response; what I didn't have was a choice. Looking back, I realize that the village women had no choice either. To fail to give me the appropriate customary treatment would have been like a doctor withholding a tetanus shot from someone who had rolled through a barnyard full of rusty barbed wire.

Woibani's mother inched forward from where she had been standing at the foot of the bed. She held a tiny green coconut in one hand and in the other a fistful of crustlike fibers of dry coconut husk. I felt the round smoothness of the coconut move down my right side from my cheeks to my thights, while the coarse, scratchy fibers followed the same course on my left side. Then she took the coconut and the husk away and faded into the outer dark. Woibani explained to me that she was taking the implements to Eva, a local healer. Eva would say a spell over the coconut and the husk and that would begin my cure.

Eva must have been nearby. In a few minutes I heard voices ouside the house: "Woibani, *pssst!*" Woibani slid off my bed and conversed softly with her mother through the slats in the thin wall. As she listened to her mother, Woibani looked down at the dry woven bamboo floor of the bedroom, shook her head, and said, "No, Mother, I think I'd better do it in the kitchen." I began to be apprehensive about what was going to happen next.

Soon I found myself, unsteady but upright, standing in our kitchen, surrounded by Woibani's younger sisters. They drew back as Woibani carefully put a match to the crusts of coconut husks. First she held the burning husks and solemnly wafted the smoke around my body like a priest with a censer. The sisters cringed from the smoke, which was meant for me alone. Then she placed the little fire right between my feet. I was relieved that Woibani had the good sense to suggest the coral floor of the kitchen for this event.

Someone handed me the small green coconut and said, "Here! Drink this in one swallow!" I did, and promptly threw up. That didn't seem to matter. Woibani helped me back to bed, and I lay there, reeking of smoke, feeling that—in a small way—I had given my body for science.

Monday, December 9, 1985:
DENYING THE RIVER SPIRITS

Bill

The night passed. Margy seemed to sleep well enough—sheer exhaustion will do that—but when we took her temperature first thing on Monday morning, I became alarmed. During the last few days she had a relatively low fever in the morning, and then her temperature had risen gradually during the day, reaching a peak at night. Today she was starting out close to 103 degrees Fahrenheit. I tried again to give her some food and medicine; none of it stayed down. I decided that I had to get her out— today.

Mathias came to our house at about six A.M., as soon as he saw we were awake. He looked grim. His eyes were serious and his mouth was set in a deep frown. I had assumed that he agreed with my diagnosis that Margy had malaria, even if he didn't understand the technicalities of chloroquine-resistant strains. I had further assumed that he would be relieved if I put her on the plane to Espiritu Santo, where Western doctors could treat her. He listened to me in silence as I tried to reassure him that proper medical care could cure her and told him my plan to get her to Santo. I expected agreement, sympathy, and relief. Instead he wore a curious expression on his face, one I had never seen before. There was something about the set of his eyes and a certain tightness around the edges of his mouth. Then I knew: I recognized with a shock that he disbelieved and discounted what I was saying. But there was something else, too, in his expression, something more than mere disbelief, an emotion closer to contempt. What was the matter? Why was he looking at me like that? Then he told me, his voice cold and harsh:

"You white men think you know everything," he said. "You may *think* this illness is malaria, but that's just not right. If you take Margaret to Santo right now, you will kill her. She must stay here in the village."

"What are you talking about?" I asked him angrily. I felt confused and defensive and not fully awake.

"I'm talking about *wande,* river spirits, the ones that killed Elsie a few years ago. When your medicine had no effect on Margaret's illness, we knew it couldn't be malaria. We began to consider other possibilities, other ways of explaining why she is so sick. I thought it might be *wande* because I know she went swimming at Waisala last week. That's their place, you know; that's where they live. Last night Eva took the young coconut that the women rubbed over Margaret's body and she dreamed on it. Early this morning—before dawn—she came to see me. She told me her dream. She said she saw rows of little houses on the banks of the Waisala, dwellings just like our own but much smaller. As Margaret swam with her friends, the *wande* watched her from the other side of the river. They liked her and they decided she must come live with them. They lined the riverbank and waved at her, but she couldn't see them. She couldn't hear them either, but they were calling to her: 'Come live with us. Come live with us.'

Mathias's voice became melodic, almost pleading as he imitated the *wande*. "Come live with us" was a bush-siren's call, entrancing, irresistible.

He continued: "Eva spoke to them in her dream. She told them that Margaret couldn't come to live with them, that they must release her. The *wande* agreed, but now Margaret must take the medicine that will cure her."

"What medicine?" I asked.

"It's *our* medicine," he said, "special leaves. Eva prepared some to give to Margaret. She must take it."

"No," I said sharply, and knew immediately that our relationship had been altered forever. With one word, I had shown him the limits of my trust in him and the boundary of my belief in his world. Damn it, life has its bottom lines: Mosquitoes, not bush spirits, made Margy sick; proper medical care would cure her, not concoctions made to guard against invisible enemies. I had known Mathias for sixteen years. I had spent almost two of the last eight years living with him, much more time than I spent with my own kinsmen during the same period. During all the time we had known each other, we played our roles well: He was my teacher and I was his eager student, he was a warm father and I tried to be his loving son; he was the chief and I was his follower, bound to respect his word. Suddenly it all seemed like play-acting. If the stakes were high enough, and I thought they were, then I was willing to take off my mask called "anthropologist" and kiss cultural relationships good-bye. What I didn't consider at the time was that he thought the stakes were high too, and he too was willing to take off his mask.

"She *must* take the medicine," he said.

Margy

Bill didn't know that Mathias's will had already been done. While the old leader confronted Bill in the front yard, Woibani slipped through the bushes and came silently in the side door. She stood by my bed, breathless for a moment, holding another little coconut and a green leaf folded as if something was wrapped inside of it.

"You have to drink this. Drink it all at once," she said handing me the coconut. "And here, you must eat this medicine. Eva made it for you."

She opened the leaf wrapper, revealing a paste made of chopped greens. Mixed with the greens were dark brown chunky bits, like dry cat food in pureed spinach.

"It's useless, Woibani. I'll just throw up."

"That doesn't matter," she said reassuringly. "Just eat it and see what happens!"

"See what happens, eh? What if I take a bite of that stuff and grow so big I fill this entire house? Or would I find myself tiny as a mouse, swimming in a pool of tears?" I really didn't say that, except in my mind. In fact, I said nothing at all as I reached out for the medicine. I heard Mathias's and Bill's voices outside, in front of the house, and I wondered what they were arguing about. I envied them their strength to argue and knew I was too tired to do likewise. The simplest thing was just to do as I was told. How could a few leaves make much difference to my poor body?

Later, Bill asked me what the leaves tasted like. They tasted green, that's all I remember. What did strike me as remarkable at the time was that they were the first thing I'd eaten since Friday that stayed down. Woibani smiled the smile of the vindicated. *She* knew the leaves would help me. Before she left, she told me with something like pride in her voice that she would bring me another round of medicine in only a few hours.

I didn't want to be around for that. Not that I felt the medicine was harmful. I simply had no faith that herbal cures could prove effective against a new strain of malaria. The women meant well—they really cared about me—but I'd had enough.

And so I left the village. It was a visit cut short and not properly ended. The women stood at the edge of the clearing in front of our house; they did not approach the truck that came to take me to the airport. I wanted to assure them that I would be all right, but for them to really believe me, I would have had to stay in Waileni. Anyway, I was having difficulty putting words together coherently. My head had begun to buzz. I felt as if I were underwater listening to people speak on the surface. As the truck pulled out of the village and headed for the airfield, what had been ordinary daylight began to pulse and flare.

Bill

Semiconscious and still smelling strongly of smoke, Margy must have been quite a sight to the young French pilot of the Britten-Norman "Islander" that landed on the airstrip on Ambae. He helped me carry her to the plane and settle her in the copilot's seat. I kissed her on the cheek and whispered to her that I loved her. Then, when the pilot got ready to close the door of the aircraft, I let go of her hand and walked back to the bush shelter at the end of the runway. A few minutes later the plane raced down the cow pasture that served as an airstrip, gathered speed, lifted, and then headed out over the coconut plantations, toward the sea. Santo was only thirty miles away but it might as well have been on another planet. My separation from Margy was complete, as complete as if she had been in the *Voyager* passing the dark side of the moon.

That afternoon I packed our bags. Getting ready to leave Waileni was lonely work. Except for Mathias, the compound was empty of people: No kids played under the almond tree, no women clustered around our kitchen, no men squatted on the bare packed earth in front of the club-house. It was an ordinary Monday in an average week. Children were in school and, for their parents, there was work to be done in the gardens, copra to be made, pigs to be tended. Mathias often remained behind when others set off to work; he was an old man, entitled to an old man's rest. Every so often he would come to my house and sit in the place where he always sat, just inside the door, on the bamboo floor. Neither of us felt like talking. Silently he watched me pack, and then, as silently, he would leave, only to return a little while later. His anger at me was gone but I could still feel his concern and his sadness. He *knew* I'd made a terrible mistake in sending Margy to Santo before her cure was complete. He'd done what he could, but in the end I had acted just like the white man I was. There was nothing else to say.

Tuesday, December 10, 1985:
FINAL ACTS

Bill

Getting out of the field is simple in concept (pack only two suitcases; everything else stays) but difficult in practice (you must dispose of the rest of the stuff). I arose at three A.M. and went into the kitchen, my storeroom and staging area. I lit a kerosene lamp and looked around me: There, on tables and on the coral floor, was the detritus of our stay in Waileni—plastic buckets, gray trade-store blankets, a machete, bright blue calico curtains, spare flipflops, a half-empty sack of rice, a can of shaving cream, a case of corned beef, an unopened bottle of French champagne Margy and I had planned to open on our last night in the village, and more, much more. My problem was how to distribute our belongings fairly—that is, how to give everybody in the village *something,* with special gifts for special friends. I made myself a cup of coffee and sat down at a table with two pads of Scotch Post-its.

By dawn, every item in the kitchen bore a little yellow sticker with someone's name on it. I woke up the children.

Outside the house, people were gathering—under the almond tree, in the clubhouse, on the road. I could hear men's quiet laughter and women shushing noisy children. I carried the first bundles outside. It was like Christmas morning, two weeks early. Mathias received the lion's share, as was his due. He sat apart from the rest of the men and received my gifts without comment. To Eva, I gave our very best lengths of calico; to my mother's brother's wife, a silver-plated necklace I had brought from Canada for just this occasion; to Woibani, many small gifts, including Margy's favorite brush and comb. And so it continued, the final act, with everybody on stage except Margy.

Then the stage emptied: I'd given my last gift, shaken everyone's hand, said my good-byes. For the people of Waileni, it was the beginning of another ordinary day and there was work to do. Only Mathias stayed behind, waiting for the truck that would take us to the airfield. When it arrived, I slung our suitcases up to Sean, who had clambered into the back of the truck. I lifted Channing into the Toyota's cabin beside the driver and shut the door. I stood beside the truck on the road with Mathias, not knowing how to end it, what to do or say.

"I don't know when I'll see you again," I said awkwardly, "maybe soon, though. You never know."

He just stood there.

"Good-bye," I said, and stuck out my hand.

He just looked at it. Slowly his gaze returned to my face, and he said loudly "Awwww, *buggerit!*" which is not a local word at all. He smiled and put his arms around me in a short, strong embrace and then let go of me forever.

The Australian doctor's wife in Santo is the only woman in town with freckles and long red hair. As we landed, before we disembarked, I saw her standing behind the wire fence bordering the airstrip. We had become close friends, and with dreadful certainty I knew she'd come to the airfield to meet me. My God, I thought as the plane rolled to a standstill, what's happened to Margy? I raced across the tarmac toward her, my mind a broth of nightmares: Margy flown out to a larger hospital, Margy in coma, Margy dead. "She's going to be all right," I heard the red-haired woman say. "I thought you'd want to know immediately."

RECOVERY TIME

Margy

"You *ate* those leaves!" The young, bearded Australian doctor at the Santo hospital looked appalled. He was my friend, and one reason we had become friends is that we seemed to share so much in common. He had visited us in the village, drunk kava with the men, and gone swimming (without ill effects) in the Waisala. I had assumed that his attitude toward customary medicine would be rather like my own: It can't do any harm and it might do some good . . . *they* take leaf potions themselves when they are sick . . . and anyway, who knows, maybe the cure for cancer grows wild in the rain forests of Ambae.

There's a certain expression that humans reserve for friends who have acted foolishly. The doctor wore that expression—incredulous, bemused, embarrassed *for* me—as he stood by my bedside. He didn't want to tell me he thought my views on customary medicine were naive and romantic, but that's what he let me know. As he took my temperature, he said he had seen many patients arrive at the hospital unconscious and half dead from the effects of "bush cures." Indigestible leaves sometimes caused intestinal blockages. In any case, he said gently when he finished taking my pulse, "the medicine probably *did* have an active agent. From your symptoms, I imagine they were trying to ward off the spirits with leaves that contain atropine."

My recollections of the first few days in Santo are vague. I lay in bed in the doctor's house, my jaws and every muscle in my body clenched tight, a side effect of the massive doses of quinine the doctor gave me. He also gave me medicine to inhibit the vomiting, which had resumed some hours after Eva's treatment.

We left Santo on Thursday, four days after I'd arrived, but before I was really well enough to travel. According to the hospital scales I had lost fifteen pounds: I weighed less than when I was fourteen years old. I still couldn't walk steadily. Both my vision and hearing were impaired from the malaria or the quinine or the leaf medicine, or all three.

In Port Vila, the capital, we stayed on the outskirts of the town in a house more suited to the plantations of Mississippi than those of Vanuatu. It was a mansion in a state of genteel decay, redolent of rotting flowers and the sea breezes and mildew. We were houseguests of a British public servant who spent early evenings and weekends whacking away at decorative shrubbery gone wild. Hibiscus flowers, purple bougainvillea vines, avocado trees, all fell to his machete and left a swath like a firebreak between the house and the jungle. I lay in bed looking out the window, listening to the hum of tropical fields and to the slap of the knife, growing stronger, and gaining distance from what had happened on Ambae.

"THAT WHICH DOES NOT KILL ME (GETS NO SECOND CHANCE)": CONCLUSIONS FROM EXPERIENCE

Margy

Would I go back to Ambae? Certainly. In part, I want to return so that I can make a proper leavetaking. I want Woibani and the others to see that I have regained good health. I've written letters but I'm sure some people in the village wonder if I'm telling the whole truth. Maybe I'm shaving the edges of the truth to save them worry or maybe I'm unaware of some lasting effects of my brush with the spirits: Maybe the *wande* are not so easily denied. Peoples' residual doubts will be stilled only when they see me. That's the way things are on Ambae. Seeing is believing.

When I return to Ambae, there's one thing I *won't* do: I won't swim in the Waisala. *Wande* may exist only in people's minds, but I am not brave enough to mock them or fool enough to risk another invitation to come live with them. Fieldwork is the most tempting of fates for an anthropologist, but in doing fieldwork you don't tempt fate, not unless you're willing to do fieldwork forever.

Bill

Nietzsche said, "That which does not kill me makes me stronger," and Hemingway believed him. Me, I'm not so sure. I think experience makes us wiser, wilier, sometimes sadder, but seldom stronger. If anything, a crisis such as the one we experienced is more apt to introduce new hesitancies to the human soul than build character. To do fieldwork in a remote area, an anthropologist needs self-confidence, a sense of being able to cope with the islandness of islands, the secret ways of jungles, or the emptiness of deserts. This can lead—easily—to a soldierly illusion of invulnerability, a fiction that the slithergadee (which comes out of the sea) "will get all the others, but won't get me." It is not the mere fact of isolation that makes us vulnerable. Nor is it a lack of caution or preparation that is most apt to get us into trouble. What renders us helpless most often is circumstance. Even where there are planes, there always is a last flight out. If you need to be on it and you are not, then—for you—there might as well be no flights at all.

Another thing I learned from the events surrounding Margy's illness concerns a hidden element in the economics of fieldwork. Anthropologists never view themselves as being a burden on their hosts; we all try to repay the many kindnesses of the people we study in whatever ways we can. It's true that there is a sense in which our exchange with our host communities always is imbalanced: Without fieldwork, we would have no careers as anthropologists. We never repay the people we study for the benefits we receive in our own societies from our fieldwork. But it's also true that reciprocity always underlies a good relationship between a fieldworker and a host community—we exchange goods for glimpses into lives, the rewards of learning for the pleasures of teaching, big gifts for oceans of story and a host of intangibles. Everyday exchange and mutual generosity come to feel natural, balanced, value given for value received, a relationship between equals who like each other. What I learned during our last fieldwork was that some people had been giving us gifts that we hadn't even recognized, let alone repaid. Margy's illness cast into bold relief the degree to which our presence in the village was a burden to Mathias. We chose to live with him because we respected his knowledge and liked his personality. It was easy for us to choose him; it was an added burden for him to accept us. He likes us, of that I'm sure, but he also felt very, very responsible for our well-being. We were babes in the woods and as such a source of worry for him. He knew about hazards to our well-being (river spirits, bush spirits, God knows what else) of which we were either unaware or else did not take seriously as threats. He loved us, I think, and I also think he must have counted the days until our departure. When we left him, we were sad; he may have been sad too, but he also was relieved. It couldn't have been otherwise. Looking back, I am a bit mystified that he managed to tolerate us for so long with such apparent ease and good humor.

The final lesson I learned was the hardest of all, and it has to do with the *real* politics of fieldwork. In most places, at most times, anthropologists conduct fieldwork in an atmosphere of political relativism: We observe but do not interfere; the people we study tolerate our observation and do not attempt to exercise authority over us. A crisis can change all that. During our final days in Waileni, Margy and I became key participants in a small-scale drama involving the politics of curing, and by so doing we became less innocent about the political realities of fieldwork. I had always thought that my relationship with Mathias was based on rough and ready equality and bonds of mutual goodwill. After all, he adopted me; I interpreted that as having to do with kinship and amity, not politics. But Mathias understood something I did not: Ordinary sentiments of friendship and affection are inappropriate to extraordinary times. He is the chief of a territory—we were in his territory at the point at which Margy became ill. I assumed (incorrectly) that he would never try to impose his will on us. He assumed (incorrectly) that I would not challenge his decision in a time of crisis. Being in conflict with each other was a learning experience for us both. We both learned something about ourselves, about each other, and about each other's culture.

There are other lessons I learned that are less cautionary and more personal; they are implicit in the story we have told and need no underlining. The lessons we learn breed lessons we continue learning. Even when anthropologists return from the field, they continue to do fieldwork as they remember and interpret their experiences and learn from them. In that sense, for as long as we care, we do fieldwork forever.

ACKNOWLEDGMENTS

Sharon Tiffany, Isabel Brymer, and Richard Brymer provided us with valuable comments on earlier drafts of this story. We are grateful for their editorial advice and for their insights into the experiences we de scribe.

SUGGESTED READINGS

ALLEN, MICHAEL

1981   Vanuatu: Politics, Economics, and Ritual in Island Melanesia. Sydney: Academic Press. The only major collection of articles on Vanuatu.

FITZGERALD, FRANCES

1986   Vanuatu: The Original Bali-h'ai. Islands 6:34–53. The author of this travel article (which has beautiful photographs) is a Pulitzer Prize winner. And Ambae, our fieldsite, is the island James Michener used as a model for *Bali-h'ai.*

HARRISON, TOM

1937   Savage Civilization. New York: Knopf. A lively and very readable early ethnography of the New Hebrides. He describes a cannibal feast on Malekula but his title is ironic: The British and French colonialists, not the native people, are the "savage" civilization.

RODMAN, MARGARET

1988   Deep Water: Development and Change in Pacific Village Fisheries. Boulder, CO: Westview Press. Looks at development from the point of view of the participants—both developers and islanders—and how and why it works (or doesn't work), focusing on the interaction of the island culture, the culture of North American volunteers, and the outside impetus for development.

RODMAN, WILLIAM

1985   'A Law Unto Themselves': Legal Innovation in Ambae, Vanuatu. American Ethnologist 12:603–624. This article describes what happened when colonial rule ended on Ambae. When the state withdrew from participation in local legal affairs, the people reorganized their villages, codified their laws, set up their own courts, and became—for more than eight years—"a law unto themselves."

SIXTEEN

🌀 A Letter from the Field

MARTY ZELENIETZ
Saint Mary's University, Halifax

November 14, 1977
Ongaia, Kilenge
West New Britain
Papua, New Guinea

Dear Joel,

Can't remember when I last wrote you—months ago, as I recall. We're head over heels into our research, pushing ourselves about as hard as we can in this heat and humidity. I'm glad that my advisor, Dave Counts, steered us to this field site. We couldn't have conjured up a better group of people to work with. The people of Ongaia tolerate our strange ways and incessant questioning, look after our welfare, and support us and our work every way imaginable. They've even stopped calling us "Masta" and "Missus" (the usual appellations for white people) and have pulled us into the village system by giving us local names.

Jill and I make a good team. Asking her to come was the smartest move I've ever made. I'm sure I'd go stark raving bonkers without a sympathetic soul to speak my own language, to share my own cultural background. Bush living offers the ultimate challenge to our relationship—if we make it through the next few months without loathing each other, I guess we'll get married.

Early on we gave up trying to run our own separate research projects. It just didn't work. Now we cover the same topics from different angles. I handle the male perspective, and Jill discovers the female view. This saves us both agony and frustration, and fills in otherwise inevitable gaps. By myself, I'd never find out what women think and say. Married women and single girls generally avoid me. I could never sit down for personal or confidential interviews with them, for the Kilenge *know* what a man and a woman do alone together. Now if Jill came to the village alone, she would have to "unsex" herself, become some sort of nonwoman, in order to gain access to male gossip, rituals, and secrets. So I work with the men, and Jill with the women. Our gender identities secure, we sit down together to work with families and couples. I think we get the broadest perspective possible.

Jill picked up a bit of Male'u (the local language) in the last few months, while I basically work in Tok Pisin (the lingua franca spoken by nearly all Ongaians) Her knowledge allows us to cross-check what our informants tell us. Most men (but not the women) don't credit her with understanding Male'u, so they frequently use Male'u to discuss their answers to our questions before giving an answer in Tok Pisin. Usually we get the same answers in both languages, but not always. Differing responses give us clues to questions we should ask, issues we should pursue.

It's not all work and no play for us. We took a quick trip to Lae in September. Lae, ah, lovely Lae—my vision of the perfect tropical town. Lush flowers, tree-lined streets, relaxed pace of life, all that you could want. After five months in the bush, Jill and I flipped out: take-out food, white tile bathrooms, showers, flush toilets (quite a contrast with our current "facilities"), paperback novels galore, and booze that we didn't have to ration by the thimble full. We dropped a fortune on supplies and gifts for friends in the village. I think economists call this the "trickle-down" effect.

The only disconcerting note of the trip came at a party on our last night in town. A loudmouthed overseas volunteer claimed that five days in a village gave her *total understanding* of life in the bush. Worse yet, given the opportunity, she would convert that village to her worldview—cultural missionaries we don't need! What a contrast to Jill and me: After five months in Ongaia, we only began to learn of the depth of our ignorance about village life, organization, and customs.

As I wrote to you earlier, in our first months here I hadn't made much headway trying to study sorcery. I thought sorcery might tie in to my work on political and social change, but people just didn't want to discuss it. Villagers responded to my pointed questions with vague generalities and closed the topic by saying that they banished sorcery long ago. Either sorcery had disappeared or people didn't want to talk about it, so I dropped that line of investigation and moved on to other things. Rule number one in this business: Don't push anything people don't want pushed.

But surprise, surprise! We found a dramatically different situation when we returned from Lae. In our absence, somebody announced his sus-picions: An unknown sorcerer had attacked him. With a sorcery accusation out in the open, with the threat of sorcery exposed in the village, people not only talk about sorcery now, they're preoccupied with it. The pre-occupation transcends mere discussion—someone actually gave me the chance to learn some potent homicidal sorcery spells and techniques! I might use that kind of knowledge to work wonders on my supervisory committee when I get back, but meanwhile having that knowledge would blow my fieldwork by compromising my position in the village, so I declined. Let me tell you the story. . . .

We only left Ongaia for a week in September, but returned to find a prominent man in the village deathly ill with a mysterious ailment that no one (mission hospital or local healers) could seem to cure. The people at the mission hospital, just up the hill from the village, think that Herman has a form of TB, but the poor man believes someone sorcerized him. Herman's talk of sorcery opened a floodgate of fear, information, and debate. The Kilenge see sorcery as we do nuclear armaments: If you don't think or talk about it, fine, but once it hits your consciousness, the consequences horrify and overwhelm you. A hidden, latent fear of sorcery and its destructive potential lurks beneath the surface of village life. With sorcery now a public affair, with gossip buzzing about the validity of the sorcery diagnosis and the identity of the assailant (and people wondering who would next fall victim), our friends and informants have inundated us with detailed cases from the not-so-distant past. And my guess panned out. Much to my relief, a lot of the sorcery stuff ties in with my research on leadership and social control.

To pick up the narrative, in the beginning of October, we heard that a famous sorcerer, Tangis, would come from a Lolo (mountain people) village to attempt a cure of the afflicted Herman. I'd never met Tangis, but his reputation preceded him—a real man of "power," a suspected homicidal sorcerer. Just the way people whisper about Tangis echoes their fear and respect for the man. Mind you, the Kilenge regard all Lolo with suspicion, see all Lolo as potential sorcerers, but they hold Tangis in special awe.

On October 5, Tangis (who villagers describe as the Number One Doctor) showed up at the mission hospital. Assisted by another Lolo man of power, Akone, Tangis performed a curing ceremony on Herman. We got lucky: some friends alerted us, so we grabbed our notebooks and camera and charged up the hill. Receiving permission to attend, I witnessed the ceremony and documented the event. Jill commiserated with Herman's female kin gathered outside the room. No one minded our presence; in fact, they made us feel welcome. As he performed the cure, Tangis explained each stage to the onlookers. He rubbed leaves on the patient to locate and neutralize pain, spat ginger to "heat things up," and chanted spells and songs.

Later, my adopted father Steamship formally introduced me to Tangis and Akone. (You probably think that no one could *really* have the name "Steamship," but here people often take a "death name" when a close relative dies. My adopted father's son died while on board a ship—hence the name Steamship.) Steamship explained that since Tangis called him "big brother," I could cell Tangis "smol papa," or junior father. Such instant relationships derive from the Kilenge notion of cognatic descent and a kind of Hawaiian kinship terminology. Don't let the anthropological jargon get to you. Translated into plain English, it means that if you're related to anyone, you're probably related to everyone.

I felt a little awed meeting Tangis. He carries such a heavy reputation and commands such respect. Oddly enough, he's a quiet, unassuming man, short even by local standards, and not at all fierce—not my mental picture of a killer sorcerer. After we met Tangis, we headed back for the village and spent the rest of the day and night recording villagers' views of why someone attacked Herman and who they thought did it. No matter how I looked at the episode, no matter whose interpretation of events I examined, people generally agreed that some unknown sorcerer had targeted Herman. Somehow the sorcery attack on Herman tied into local power struggles for social standing and leadership status. Many villagers felt that Herman had moved too far, too fast, in his bid for leadership status.

A few days later, the evening of the eighth, Tangis and Akone came to our house for a chat, accompanied by a man from the village next to Ongaia. As a general rule I don't tape interviews; I usually take extensive notes and then write up the material the following morning. But I taped the session with Tangis and Akone, partly for accuracy, partly because they enjoyed listening to themselves talking on the tape, and partly, I guess, because I hoped for some bit of esoteric knowledge too precious to lose. So the five of us crowded around the tape recorder, with only one hurricane lamp for light, as Tangis talked about Herman's case. He described how he and Akone diagnosed the malady, how they located the "infection," and the steps they took to draw the sorcery out of Herman's body. Tangis then talked in general terms of his life as a man of power, of his father's instructing him in various spells, rituals, and techniques for the communal good. His teachers enjoined him never to use his powers to hurt others, unless others tried to hurt someone in his group.

In talking about defending family and kin, Tangis digressed to describe how to sorcerize a person, how to make them sicken and die. He discussed the procedures and actions for sorcerizing (with Akone adding a comment here and there). He carefully avoided telling us what spells to use, what powers to invoke. (Okay, Joel, I know this must sound strange as you read it in the relatively civilized surroundings of Chicago, but remember I came here to study these things, and in the still of the night, wedged in a creaking hut between the ocean and the jungle, this stuff is not only believable, it's reality! And no, I'm not suffering malarial hallucinations!) Tangis said he couldn't tell us the spells, not here in the village, and he could never say them in front of Jill (some things women may never know). In essence, Tangis gave us an empty gun which was useless without the ammunition.

What Tangis said next really caught me by surprise. He casually offered to take me into the bush, up the mountain, for a few days of instruction on the proper spells to cure people of various kinds of sorcery. On the surface an innocuous offer, but the way sorcery works here, if you can remove a spell or illness from someone, then you can (so common belief and knowledge goes) also put that spell or illness on somebody. One implies the other: Those who cure can kill, and vice versa. Tangis, so it seemed, invited me to join the ranks of homicidal sorcerers. After presenting his offer, my "smol papa" and his assistant gave us a couple of spells for making the new gardens grow better—our consolation prize of esoteric knowledge for the night. Shortly thereafter, they left.

Jill and I talked long into the night about Tangis's offer. Honestly, I felt ambivalent, a bit frightened, a bit intrigued. Days and nights in the mountain bush could drag me out physically. Then again, gaining that priceless knowledge might more than offset the discomfort. But knowledge for what ends? Do I want to know *how* to do sorcery, or does my real interest lie in what people believe about sorcery, and the *impact* of sorcery beliefs on life in the village? I worried about the effect that my learning sorcery would have on my neighbors, the people with whom I lived and worked. I mean, how would you feel if a man feared for his homicidal potential lived next door to you?

The next day decided things for me. Word travels fast in the village where gossip and information exchange provide a major form of entertainment for the two hundred fifty inhabitants. Besides, who can keep secrets through flimsy woven bamboo walls? I sneeze, and everyone within a twenty-five-meter radius catches a cold. Anyway, two people came separately to me that day to tell me the fate of fledgling sorcerers. "Marty," I heard twice that day, "do you know what happens to men who have just learned homicidal sorcery? All the established sorcerers get together, and they send powerful spells his way. It's a sort of test. If the new one commands true power, he can deflect those spells and survive. If not, if he has weak command, well . . . they plant what's left of him in the cemetary afterward."

I got my answer. The people of Ongaia didn't want another sorcerer, another man with power, living in their midst. Such a man can threaten community stability—an ever-present potential danger upsetting peoples' lives. The Ongaians don't want me hiking up the mountain to learn how to handle power. If I insist, if I discover how to "down" people, I'd cut myself off from the community. I'd become a pariah and blow my fieldwork. Building solid rapport with the people of Ongaia took a long time, and I'm not going to endanger those relationships and my academic future (and maybe even my chances of getting out of here in one piece) in search of esoteric knowledge. I'll stay here on the beach and be a good boy, the "white skin" providing occasional entertainment and valued goods to people.

I'm glad I read the signs and made my decision, because the villagers here sure want to keep me from Tangis. A couple of nights after the Tangis interview, Steamship came to the house to say that Tangis had wanted to see me during the day, to witness the final curing ceremony for Herman (similar, I understand, to the final ceremony I saw). Steamship said he had told Tangis we had important work and couldn't come. I could have strangled Steamship, because we spent that day in the village looking for something to do. Fathers can be so difficult at times.

After Herman's cure, life returned to normal and people showed no apparent concern about sorcery and sorcerers. Out of sight, out of mind. Then, about a week ago, Herman, still sick but a little more mobile, got embroiled in an incident involving a marauding pig. His big pig allegedly destroyed a garden, a major catastrophe for subsistence horticulturalists. Sorcery accusations bubbled to the surface again. Two days later, on November 10, Tangis showed up in the village, ostensibly to tell people about the provincial fair in Kimbe. Few, if any, believe that story. Tangis came over to our house that night. No sooner had he settled down with coffee and a smoke than our best friend and key informant, Paul, just happened to stop by. I felt chaperoned: Obviously, no one intended to leave us alone with Tangis. Tangis wanted to tell me some legends about the creator/trickster hero, Namor, but said he couldn't finish them in one night. He invited me to visit his village for a couple of days. If I would bring a jar of instant coffee, some rice, and some meat, we could "story" for hours on end. Paul promised him I would come and added that I would bring a load of nails for Tangis's new house. I thought Paul seemed rather generous with my possessions, but I guess he would promise anything to get Tangis away from me. We'll see what happens. I suspect I'll never get to Tangis's place.

The sorcery scare generated more positive fallout for my research. For months I'd tried getting Steamship to "story" about his career as a *tultul,* a government-appointed assistant village headman. I figured Steamship's tales would help me understand the colonial era here, the relationship between the villagers and the Australian administration. But Steamship would tell me *nothing*. His standard response: "Oh, I didn't have to do anything. The people were good, the government was good, everything was good, so I did nothing." To listen to Steamship, no one ever got upset or involved in disputes in the village. The government behaved benevolently, and people harkened to the *kiap*'s (patrol officer's) call. Harmony ruled. Sure! Then, some time after sorcery became an "approved" topic for our research, Steamship told me he owned a simple little spell, using a feather hidden under his tongue. This spell gave the user great oratorical abilities while simultaneously tongue-tying the opposition. Steamship said he used it often as *tultul,* when making peace in the village and for deceiving the *kiap*. I asked him about how he used it, and he began to answer the questions I'd asked months earlier. Once started, he didn't stop: Steamship spent the next three days relating his adventures during those halcyon years! I'd tried so hard for that information before, and then it all flew in through the backdoor.

So much of our information *does* come through the back door. Most often we get open and forthright answers to our questions, but occasionally we hit a topic that villagers don't want to discuss. Rather than push things, we just sit back and wait, keeping our ears open to what people say. Days, maybe weeks later we'll hear a stray remark on the topic and then jump on it. When villagers themselves mention the previously ignored topic, when they acknowledge its existence, they'll gladly discuss it and patiently answer our questions. Funny, Ongaians willingly answer specific questions, but often don't respond if they think we are "fishing." If we go into an inteview cold, with no prior information, we often end up no better off than when we started. But our slightest hint that we know something—anything—about the issue usually generates informative answers. The more we know, the more we can learn. That's where Jill's knowledge of Male'u comes in handy, and where patience, detailed notes, and a memory stuffed full of seeming trivia pays off. I've learned to slow down, to realize I can't do it all in one day. I play by Ongaia rules. Here, patience is the game. Wait long enough, don't push things, and we'll get most of the data we want. Before this simple fact dawned on us, we often felt frustrated with our lack of progress and suspicious of the way people responded to us. Frustration seldom bothers us now. If things don't come today, then maybe tomorrow—a true tropical attitude.

And speaking of tomorrow, it promises to be a busy day, so I'll end this here and get some rest in our tropical paradise. Right now the volcano groans and spits ash and smoke, and the sea breeze carries the promise of a storm. Real tranquility, eh? With luck I might get this letter onto a plane or a boat in a few days. Jill sends her regards. Take care, and write soon. Stuck here as we are beyond the edge of the world, mail is our main link with home.

Marty

SUGGESTED READINGS

Jill and I have, individually and collectively, written extensively on our Kilenge fieldwork. Our work covers the gamut from traditional ethnography to aspects of social change. Some examples are:

GRANT, J., H. SAITO, AND M. ZELENIETZ

1986   Where Development Never Comes: Business Activities in Kilenge, Papua New Guinea. Journal of the Polynesian Society 95(2):195–219.

ZELENIETZ, M.

1981   One Step Too Far: Sorcery and Social Change in Kilenge. In Sorcery and Social Change in Melanesia. M. Zelenietz and S. Lindenbaum, eds. Pp. 101–118. Social Analysis #8 (Special Issue).

ZELENIETZ, M., AND J. GRANT

1980   Kilenge Narogo: Ceremonies, Resources, and Prestige in a West New Britain Society. Oceania 51(2):98–117.

1986   The Problem with *Pisins:* An Alternate View of Social Organization in West New Britain (Parts 1 and 2). Oceania 56(3, 4):199–214, 264–274.

For a rather different view of the Kilenge, see:

DARK, P. J. C.
1974   Kilenge Art and Life: A Look at a New Guinea People. London: Academy Editions.

SEVENTEEN

❦ The Sorcerer's Rainstone

JAMES B. WATSON
University of Washington

One afternoon, during a short stay at Arogara, a neighbor told me how to make rain. What then followed makes quite a tale. Whether the hearer's disbelief will exceed the teller's may matter less than whether they can agree on what to disbelieve. As for the main events, it is not at all difficult to relate what I saw and did. The full story doubless goes beyond that, however. It concerns appearances and interpretations as much as visible events, and it concerns what people think happened and how they felt about it. In attempting to keep things in focus, therefore, I will be as circumstantial as I can, simply recounting what took place at Arogara on the day in question, during the night, and the following day. I will then express what sense I am able to make of it all today, and you can reach your own conclusion.

To set the scene in 1955 I will use the present tense, describing things as they were then. The Arogara are a Tairora-speaking people, one of many hereabouts who speak some dialect of that language. The Arogara themselves number about two hundred. They live, hunt, and make gardens in the forested foothills of the Kratke Range, in what was still at the time the Eastern Highlands District of the Territory of New Guinea. Here the Arogara still live today, although their remembered ancestors hail from various other locations within the region. To locate Arogara on the map you would now look for Papua New Guinea, an independent nation since 1975, and you would find that the Eastern Highlands is now a province. Arogara is about ten miles southwest of Kainantu, the nearest town large enough to find except on a very large-scale map.

All around them, at distances of a few miles or so, and especially in the grasslands below them to the northeast, are other peoples who, like the Arogara, still consider themselves separate and distinct. This is the reason for referring to each of these, including the Arogara, as a "people": Each has its own territory, name, ancestors, and traditions—in short, its own character and identity; and each acts politically in its own behalf, fostering friendships or harassing enemies according to what leading men decide is best.

No people lack power in various magical forms. It would be a sorry group who were bereft of such vital knowledge and capability. In fact, it would be unthinkable, like trying to cope in the world with no idea of what the world is or how the things that matter can be controlled, protected, promoted, impaired, or prevented, according to need. Since different peoples share most of the same broad coping concerns, it is no surprise that certain kinds of magic are widely recognized and practiced. Among peoples speaking the same language—Tairora, for instance—common practices are likely to be called by a common name. It was in an attempt to learn how widespread one particular form of magic is that I consulted a small group of Arogara men the afternoon this story begins.

My meeting with these particular neighbors began casually. Pausing on the path to their various errands in the garden or bush, they had happened to meet and now stood talking by my house as I came out the door. There I joined them. We discussed this and that for a while until it struck me that this might be a good chance to ask a question that had been on my mind for some time.

My question concerned an alleged sorcery packet that I had been given, some months before coming to Arogara, in a distant village of another language. Ever since getting the packet, I had wondered about its authenticity. It was small, wrapped in a scrap of faded red cloth, about an inch and a half or so long, perhaps half an inch in diameter, and bound in the familiar yellow fiber of a tree orchid. From my pick-up panel of presumed experts, so to speak, I hoped I might get an independent opinion. If I needed to show them the packet, I could easily fetch it from the house.

The man who gave me the packet was not himself a sorcerer, but he nevertheless insisted on its lethal power. His demand for secrecy and his refusal to say how the packet had reached his hands, however, left me wanting to know what others might say of it. Yet I could not ask other people in his own community without betraying a confidence. Arogara was safely distant, however, and if their lethal sorcery resembled that of the people I'd lived among in the past, the group in front of my house could probably settle the question. I gave my panel a rough description, offering to show them the packet if they wished. To my surprise, however, the spokesman of the group abruptly dismissed my keepsake, sight unseen. It was, he said, almost certainly a fake.

The Rainmaker, as I shall call him, had meanwhile joined the group, but like the rest he acquiesced in the spokesman's judgment. Since my sorcery packet seemed to lack interest, I let the question drop and the talk turned to other matters. Very soon, in any case, the group showed signs of breaking up, its original members understandably wanting to be about their business. At the last moment, however, ostensibly as an afterthought, the spokesman returned once more to the sorcery packet. Did I actually have this thing? Since they were here, he suggested, they could all take a look at it, if that was what I wanted, before going on their way. By now I was wondering whether Arogara men could recognize the packet, whatever its real nature, given their apparent skepticism and the possibility that their own sorcery was quite different. But I brought out the matchbox in which I kept the packet.

Sliding the box open, I showed the group its contents. As one, the startled men shrank back from me. From across his distance the husky-voiced spokesman told me how dangerous it was to keep such a thing around, urging me to throw it away. He noted that my infant daughter, Anne, was living in the same house with this lethal power. Clearly he spoke for all of them, and I could see no choice but to indicate that I would take their advice at the first opportunity. One could not after all simply toss such a thing into the bushes.

By now the men were ready to be on their way. Seeing the fearful packet, I suspect, simply made it easier for them to depart. Only Rainmaker remained. An older man who lived quietly nearby, he had probably seen us through his doorway before approaching the group and he had joined us not because we were on his way somewhere but simply to learn what we were talking about. In any case he seemed to have no pressing business. Remaining behind, he asked if I would be interested in knowing how to make rain. I sensed that this would be a good time to learn.

At first it was Rainmaker's casual offer of magic that I found curious. Though prevalent everywhere in the region, a specialist's magic is no commonplace practice to be casually volunteered to women, children, or strangers. We had been at Arogara for only a few weeks and would be there only a few weeks more, though people had doubtless heard something about us before we came. I can only guess that the sorcery packet had in some sense established my credentials, probably not as an insider or a knowledgeable colleague, but at least as one who was interested, respected magic, and took it seriously. But if that explained the offer of magical instruction, what explained the rain?

Rainmaking sorcery at Arogara—*rainy* Arogara? What could be the point? In their forested foothills, beneath the Kratke Mountains, as their neighbors knew for miles around, the Arogara received much more rainfall than any of the peoples of the grassland below them to the north. In the rainy season dark days and lowering skies were frequent if not constant here. This fact was called to our attention before we left Haparira, a drier, grassland village some miles to the north. From Haparira in the rainy months one could often see a magnificent afternoon buildup of cumulus clouds towering high above the Kratkes and nighttime skies rent by brilliant chains of lightning, sometimes lasting for hours. It made a gorgeous spectacle. "The source of rain," the Haparira would sometimes say, contrasting their own bright grassland to the mist and gloom of forested Arogara. In the mid-fifties precipitation readings were still in their infancy throughout much of the Eastern Highlands. I doubt there was a rain gauge within ten miles of Arogara. For what it may be worth, however, ninety-plus annual inches was sometimes suggested as the probable norm for this stretch of foothill country. I can believe it.

Evidently taking no offense at my surprise, Rainmaker denied that his magic was used for calling down rain to water gardens in the dry season. At Arogara, understandably, this was not a pressing problem. What then was the purpose? By way of answer he gave me an illustration. Suppose you have been drying firewood in your garden in the bush, he said, obviously referring to the trees one fells in making the garden clearing. While still green, this wood is too heavy for any sensible man or woman to carry back to the village, and besides it is of little use yet for cooking or heating. Among other things, then, the Arogara garden is a place for seasoning firewood. Others will consequently know that firewood is seasoning in your garden. Once it is dry someone less provident than you but with a need for dry firewood may decide to help himself to yours. Such a need recurs. It arises every time pit ovens must be fired and used, as when pigs and feast food are steam-cooked for visitors and guests. Thus it may now and then occur that when you go to collect your firewood, you find it gone. Then you make it rain on their feast.

So rainmaking was a spoiler's technique, a threat to would-be thieves, an answer to the arrogant. Was this all? Rainmaker's example seemed to leave room for expansion, but he showed no interest in discussing the rationale of rainmaking or pointing to further applications. The practical side of his knowledge—how the magic is performed—was of course what he had proposed to talk about, and this in fact proved to be his real interest. Perhaps for him this was the difference between a dull or obvious question and an interesting one: Everybody knows or thinks he knows what sorcerers do with magic, but only sorcerers can tell you how they do it.

Narrow and limited as it was, in any case, Rainmaker's hypothetical(?) case nevertheless had one clear implication: He did not see rainmaking as a technique for promoting food production. This he readily confirmed. It was not, in other words, a means for correcting or overcoming a shortage of seasonal maldistribution of rainfall. From the first mention of rainmaking, you may recall, that had seemed an improbable concern at Arogaga. Rainmaker's work, then, matched modern cloud-seeding not in aim but only in being a specialist's practice. It resembled community-wide rainmaking rituals among arid-land farmers neither in aim nor in practice. According to what he said that afternoon, Rainmaker performed his magic privately and for a private purpose, viewing it in a frankly defensive/punitive light. Rain magic was not deployed for the benefit of crops, game, or livestock but to control people. Taking his own example at face value, this meant controlling fellow villagers.

Turning directly to the actual procedures for making rain, Rainmaker left no opening for further reflections. He began to describe a remarkable stone he had found some time ago in digging a garden. He was obviously proud of owning this stone, which he saw as fundamental to his magic.

Without it, rainmaking as he knew it would be quite impossible. The stone had a hollow in one face, a shallow concavity that could hold water, and this was basic to the procedures he went on to relate. His hands described a round or oval stone, perhaps several inches thick and a foot or so in diameter. The description suggested a prehistoric mortar, but Rainmaker himself evidently did not recognize the stone as an artifact, let alone one that might have served earlier humans for some purpose more domestic than his. For practical tasks like grinding pigment or pounding food, mortars of either stone or wood are virtually unknown today in the Eastern Highlands. This alone probably makes it unlikely that the people of the region would recognize as ordinary human artifacts the stone mortars they occasionally find. Ground or polished stone objects, furthermore, frequently become keepsakes or heirlooms, often being considered as possible sources of power, though by no means necessarily rainmaking power. Whether or not it was in fact a mortar, then, Rainmaker stood on firm cultural ground in seeing his stone as singular. For him of course it became his rainstone.

Rainmaker would have seen no need to explain the importance of stone heirlooms. In order to make clear what for him was simply obvious, however, let me interrupt my report of his afternoon's presentation. Beyond what was just said about heirlooms, two further points may be useful. The first concerns the rainstone as a container for water. Like the peoples around them, the Arogara have various sorts of water vessels. These include bamboo tubes, clay pots, and gourds. In a pinch they can use the wooden bowls in which steamed food is served. Since any of these vessels can hold water better than a shallow concavity in a piece of stone, it follows that Rainmaker saw his singular stone as something more than a receptacle for water.

The second point concerns stone heirlooms and their keeping. Rainmaker kept the rainstone in his garden, thus treating it in the way peoples of this vicinity treat other singular stone objects. Most if not all of these well-kept objects are ground stone artifacts, no few of which, indeed, are recognized as such. Notable among them are polished axes and adzes. In the original sense of *heirloom* such former tools are disused today but, unlike mortars, are well remembered for their recent use, even sometimes for their users. Keeping axes and adzes in a garden is widely said to benefit the garden. If like these stone heirlooms the rainstone were also an artifact, it nevertheless differed from them of course in its distinctive power as well as in being unrecognized as an artifact. One thinks here of the thunderstones of ancient and medieval Europe, before these objects were recognized as former tools.

Besides filling the concavity of the rainstone with water, Rainmaker's magic called for the use of an eagle's wing. Wing in hand, the sorcerer follows a ritual sequence in which he places the wing across the concavity of the stone. The wing is then raised and moved in a precise manner above the water, all of this in conjunction with words and other prescribed materials and accompanied by additional placements and manipulations. In fact, Rainmaker distinguished more than one ritual sequence. One by one he detailed alternative sequences, pointing out what was peculiar to each, what particular substitutions of paraphernalia or procedure it involved. Each of the several rituals was evidently thought complete, however, its efficacy equivalent to that of any other. In causing rain, that is, Rainmaker appeared to see no one ritual as more valid or authentic than others, none as unambiguously the best, and none as better suited to some purposes or circumstances than to others. To an outsider, at least, the several rituals Rainmaker described differed so slightly one from another that they could easily be considered close variants of a single central pattern of rainmaking. In every procedure, for instance, filling the rainstone with water and manipulating the eagle's wing both figured as essential.

The sketch I've just given belies the time it took to record what Rainmaker considered basic information, in addition to the further clarifications I needed. He proceeded slowly with the details, taking pains to leave out nothing vital. Even with a simpler subject, moreover, note taking can be slow, with frequent queries and confirmations, as well as recurrent pauses for the pencil to catch up when the speaker gets too far ahead. The lesson in rainmaking in fact was closing out the day. It was well into the afternoon when we first sat down. By the time Rainmaker was going over his final magical sequence, the shadow of the nearby forest had begun to darken the village, leaving little light for legible pages. In the gathering dusk, at last, he said we had exhausted our subject. Thanking him profusely, I stood up and stretched. It was more than mere ceremony to express admiration for an account that had in fact been comprehensive yet, perhaps thanks to its emphasis on technique and sequence, orderly and generally easy to follow. I felt I was deeply in his debt and said as much, which he would surely understand to mean that in due course my debt would be materially acknowledged. Already I was beginning to wonder what gift would be right to match the one just given.

Even as I turned to go, however, Rainmaker brought me back with a further thought. Now that I knew how to use it, would I like to have the rainstone? At least that is what I thought he asked. I replied I couldn't possibly accept such a gift. What would he do without it? He might never find another. But I had misunderstood him. He reminded me once more that he always kept the rainstone just inside his garden near the fence. A while ago, while he was firing the trash for new planting, flames had reached the edge of the garden and cracked the rainstone in two. But these were not two broken, useless halves, he reassured me, since each would still hold water. Evidently the amount of water was not crucial. In fact, he himself had simply gone on using one of the broken halves for making rain, and thus he was sure of its power. He was convinced the other half would serve as well. The point was that now, with two rainstones, he could keep the one he was using and give me the other.

From a gift I could not accept, this had now become one I could not refuse. I said I'd be pleased to have a rainstone, would proudly take it with me to my country when I left Arogara. Rainmaker thereupon insisted on holding me a little longer while he went to fetch the stone from his garden nearby. In fact, it wasn't long before he reappeared and handed me a fairly hefty stone. Holding it in my own hands made it easy to see, as suspected, that my rainstone was indeed the broken half of a mortar. Broken roughly in the middle, it appeared, the remaining concavity would still be capable of holding water, perhaps as much as half a cup. Even as I thanked him once again, a new question came to mind. Here I was now in possession of this considerable gift; but I was therefore also responsible for an object its giver knew to be potent. How should I keep it, or where should I put it until leaving the village some weeks hence?

"As I now know from you," I said, "a garden is the proper place for keeping a rainstone. But since I have no garden, where do you think I should keep this rainstone you have given me?" In the gathering darkness his look was unreadable. It might mean that the very question took him unawares or only that it was not for him to say. I knew I was holding up supper. On the other hand I was frankly concerned, wanting neither to make too much of where to put the rainstone nor, on the other hand, to treat this gift too lightly. There was also, I thought, a responsibility in having such a stone.

Evidently I would get no help from my tutor. The leads my own limited knowledge of local magic then afforded were ambiguous at best. Much of the most dramatic power in this region is explicitly hot and dry. It belongs to the same domain, that is, as the sun, the dry season, fire, fighting, anger, and maleness. The magical antitheses thus include the moon, the rainy season, water, peace, and femaleness. Wetness has such negative valence, it is sometimes claimed, that by merely pouring water on the site the sorcerers or their paraphernalia can nullify their magic. Being washed by rain is said to have the same effect. So what to do with a magical object whose very aim is rain and whose use requires filling it with water? All these thoughts were only mine, I should say, for while I was thinking furiously, I was not thinking aloud. Whatever Rainmaker's thoughts at this point, he kept them to himself, leaving me to my own decision. In fairness to him, the problem—if it actually was one—had presumably not been faced before. Like Rainmaker himself, everyone he knew of course had a garden. He may thus have produced that evening the first person ever to have a rainstone without a garden to keep it in!

For me, in any case, the ultimate ambiguity was how big a problem I truly faced. Demurring, I might well be making too much of where to keep the rainstone. Had it come to appear an issue, after all, only because I brought it up as one? Had I simply slid the rainstone under the bed, would it have mattered? Ethnographers in New Guinea, as they themselves recognize, sometimes see more rule and rigidity than the people observed and written about. Any or all of this might be true, of course, but it seemed too late now to casually walk away and leave the matter hanging. Whether or not I had invented the question, I was stuck with having to answer it. In consulting Rainmaker, that is, I had led him to anticipate my resolution.

More to cut a Gordian knot than from any firm belief, I decided to go with cold. Nominally the antithesis of power and efficacy, cold at least struck me as more unlikely to activate the rainstone's magic. At the back of our cookhouse we stored taro, yams, and sweet potatoes. (Garden stuff! it now occurs to me.) Windowless and dark, this spot was on downward-sloping ground below and behind the cooking fire. Did that seem a reasonable place? I asked Rainmaker. If not, could he suggest a better one? Whether out of conviction, politeness, or simple unconcern, he did not dissent. With his knowledge, then, the back of the cookhouse is where I left the rainstone before going in to supper.

At supper there was always catching up to do. My wife, Virginia, could fill me in on her day's adventures. Small daughter Anne's activities also needed daily updating. I related that the sorcery packet was recognizable to Arogara men and hence was judged authentic, and of course I reported the still surprising practice of rainmaking and its ostensibly narrow use in rainy Arogara. Virginia thus soon knew about the afternoon with Rainmaker and his culminating gift. I cautioned her that the rainstone should not be mistaken for a common piece of rock when discovered at the back of the cookhouse.

We were already finishing instant coffee when a spatter of rain on the thatch overhead gave the conversation a fresh if entirely predictable impetus. There was naturally a joking accusation and a mock-serious admission of responsibility. Even in the dry season, however, a spatter of rain hardly threatens the laws of chance, certainly not here in the shadow of the Kratkes. The joke staled as the sprinkle remained unconvincing—as much rain as a mere beginner could manage, no doubt.

The shower seemed unlikely to last, and in fact it didn't. The patter on the roof ceased well before bedtime, leaving the village to its nightly quiet, broken only by the occasional voice from some house nearby, a child's sleepy cry, or the grunting and snuffling of pigs in search of food along the path. I was half asleep when suddenly, more insistant than before, the rain began again. This time it was heavy rain whose sound alone normally signals a full-scale tropical downpour. Drumming relentlessly against the thatch, splashing the ground, and splattering the leaves of the adjacent garden, the rain now drowned out almost every other sound, dominating the senses in its sheer audible presence.

Despite the unmistakable violence of a tropical rain, I still assumed this unseasonable storm was a fluke. Surely it would not set in for the night like rain in the midst of the wet season. So I made a point of staying awake till I could hear it stop. To keep from falling asleep I remembered hearing a story from Ralph Linton several years before, a story concerning an unseasonable storm in the Marquesas. The story was roughly as follows.

On the island where he worked Linton learned of a disused *marae* (stone temple platform) in the mountains. Upon visiting the place, he was excited to find two Marquesan gods, wooden idols in surprisingly good condition. Hoping to collect these irreplaceable objects and thus preserve them from inevitable deterioration, Linton broached the idea to several villagers. No one in the village still professed the old religion. No one even went near the *marae*. But everyone he asked warned him against moving the gods. Despite their certain decay, they must be left alone.

Failing to sway the villagers, Linton eventually decided that the interest of both science and posterity compelled him to disregard their caution. Choosing a strategic moment, he spirited the idols from the *marae*, furtively bringing them to the beach. He hid them in the top of a palm, there to stay until some ship should call to start them on their way to a museum overseas.

So far the plan had worked, but long before a ship arrived heavy and unseasonable rains set in. All too soon a flood threatened to wash away parts of the village, which stood athwart a normally gentle stream never before known to flood. As the water rose, Linton feared the worst. Having flouted the caution of the villagers in removing the idols, he knew his predicament. The deed discovered, he might be blamed for the rain and thus for bringing on the flood. As soon as possible, therefore, he secretly returned the gods to the *marae*. Now he might at least hope to escape responsibility for the impending disaster. To Linton's amazement, however, the rains soon stopped and the flood subsided, relieving all concerned. The gods were left to rot in the *marae*.

That night at Arogara, listening for the rain to stop, my initial ambivalence concerning Linton's story came back to me. The uncanny storm following the removal of the gods, I had felt, had to be accepted on grounds of chance. The margin of credibility narrowed, however, when the impending flood was promptly quelled with the restoration of the gods. This seemed too pat, I remembered thinking, and one could not wholly dismiss the possibility that Linton might have enhanced the story to heighten its appeal. Though perhaps pedantic in any case I recalled this as my original reservation.

Rainbound now as I lay there musing, I could see another side: My original case could be turned around. Suppose that story had unfolded just as Linton said. Relating those same events, however, a different storyteller might be more anxious than Linton to allay a listener's doubt and he might thus temper or even suppress the story's tidy outcome, lest it strain belief. But that would no less be enhancement than exaggerating the uncanny outcome. I could not remember weighing that possibility when I first heard the story. If the storm at Arogara made this dilemma more real, however, it left too little time for resolution. After perhaps a half an hour, as abruptly as it had begun the pounding rain stopped. Seemingly vindicated, I put the dilemma on hold and quickly fell asleep.

Sleep was some time later interrupted and the quiet of the village once more canceled by a new assault on the roof. Once more awake, I decided to wait it out before sleeping again, and once more I think I may have succeeded. But not for long, as successive short lulls in the storm were each in turn followed by a continuation of the downpour, and I gave up my vigil, allowing the steady sound to serve as a soporific. This worked as long as the rain continued to beat on everything it its way; but after each storm passed and until the next one came, the sound was broken by silence and sleep was accordingly fitful. Storms alternating with briefer intervals of silence, I vaguely now conceded, would probably last out the night.

At some point in the early morning hours a different sound aroused me, but I could not make out what it was. It was still raining steadily but the new sound could now and then be heard above the beating rain. In my stupor I thought of falling trees. I even thought I could hear the rush of wind through the leaves, the cracking of branches, and the muffled thud as trees toppled into the mud. To my turgid mind this seemed a solid deduction, and I concluded that the heavy rain must have turned the forest ground to soup in which the roots of trees could no longer hold the heavy tops aloft. Later I would realize that in my scenario no forest could ever reach full height. But at that point sleep meant more than flawless reasoning. In a while the new sounds ceased, leaving only the steady downpour. Satisfied with my falling trees, I lapsed once more into sleep.

Daylight brought the reckoning. Just outside the door shrill women's voices revealed that several gardens had slid down the mountain during the night—parts or all of four of them. The sound of falling trees had been mudslides! Excitedly briefing each other, the women stood there during a lull in the storm, taking stock of the damage. My anxiety began to rise.

Yesterday evening at the first hint of rain, it had been amusing to imagine fiddling with fate. One could pretend to see the rain as the sorcerous sequel to Rainmaker's instructions, the outcome sealed by his gift of the very stone required for this magic. Not only good fun, it was welcome relief from the stresses of fieldwork. But what might be only fantasy for a foreigner could be reality itself for the villagers. For them, certainly, a connection could hardly be denied between the magical rehearsal and its magical outcome in this otherwise improbable storm. Hurting innocent people as a consequence of recording their culture was surely a cruel inversion of intent. To be sure, I could only be *seen* as hurting people. But what was the use of knowing I had not hurt them? Or, accepting Arogara premises, of knowing that I had not done so with foreknowledge? There was little reason to expect exemption on either count. There might in fact be slim hope of persuading the Arogara—or Rainmaker himself—that I had not been tempted to use the rainstone— especially after learning precisely how to use it. Here the Linton option was unavailable. Where there were no gods to restore I could not thereby deflect the accusing finger. Besides, the calamity was not merely impending. It had already taken a toll.

The women quickly left for shelter as the rain began again. The cycle of intermittent lulls and downpours that had held through the night continued into the morning. I wondered if I would see Rainmaker and what he would have to say. Breakfast over, my family and I kept to the house, stepping out of doors only at the following lull. Soon we noticed that now, with morning light, each break in the storm produced a movement of people about the village. Back and forth among the houses they went, exchanging remarks as they passed one another, on their way home or on their way to spend the ensuing downpour in someone else's house. I doubt that every lull meant a change of house for every villager, but one could easily get that impression. I regret not making an actual tally. For a sociometrician the moment was made to order! The children and younger adults were most visible, as for them these rounds were accompanied by high spirits, laughter, and merriment; but even the elders seemed to enjoy the enforced suspension of normal work in the garden or bush, by nature often solitary, in sharp contrast to the conviviality prevailing this morning. From some of the houses the animation of the people crowded inside could be heard from quite a distance beyond the dooryard.

My own anxiety, needless to say, was quite at odds with the mood of the village. It is useless now to think of the pleasure and the opportunities probably missed that day, but I could not dismiss the thought that sooner or later some role in making this storm would find its way to me, casting a shadow over our remaining few weeks in the village and jeopardizing the comparisons we hoped to complete between Arogara and the two other villages where we had earlier lived. That is not to mention souring relations with people we liked and had no wish to alienate. In the intimacy of one small village there are so many ways for such a thing to happen. Life in these circumstances, just as the cliché has it, is life in a goldfish bowl. Suspicion thrives and paranoia is another name for simple prudence.

I had barely known Rainmaker before yesterday afternoon. Would he prove to be boastful, spreading the word of what he—or we—had done? Or was Rainmaker perhaps now fearful on account of the garden destruction? Would he be concerned therefore to deflect suspicion from himself? Would he be ready to concede to fellow villagers some purpose and involvement of his or mine quite beyond merely wanting to know about rainmaking magic? Indeed, for Rainmaker as for other Arogara, what sense could it make for a full-grown man merely to want to know? From the village point of view, compared to the well-understood intervention of men in the world, that could seem a truly idle and unintelligible purpose, making it difficult for people to believe in innocence, neutrality, or lack of intent, let alone uninvolvement. Or was Rainmaker, to the contrary, a quiet man, a prudent man, quite able to keep his own council while waiting to see what might happen next? But there is no need to go on. If it is clear how I saw my situation at that moment, the possible faces of anxiety will suggest themselves. I could only wait for what might happen next.

In my mind, needless to say, much seemed to hinge on Rainmaker. Yet I wasn't sure I wanted to see him that day. When he passed our door during a midmorning lull, I must have appeared very tentative in greeting him. For his part he was also difficult to read. Neither smiling nor frowning, his expression was something in between. Nothing in his face clearly suggested anxiety or concern. His words almost ring in my ears, three full decades later, as I recall them today. "A lot of rain," he said, to which I could only assent. "Not the time of year for rain," he added, to which I assented again. Our exchange closed with that, and he moved off up the path. If life at that moment had demanded some reading of Rainmaker, however, wrong it might be, I would have said he had a "knowing" look, that his words were "noncommittal." Not that that was much help!

Some time later that morning, in another lull, of course, Rainmaker passed our house again and spoke. Absolutely nothing was different! The same look and practically the same words! "Lots of rain," he said. "It's not the time of year for rain." To me at the time the man seemed inscrutable. Nothing angry or accusatory. Nothing conspiratorial either, like a wink, raised eyebrows, or a sideways glance. Nothing apprehensive—no lowered voice, no downcast eyes, no hurried speech. In short, nothing to dissolve my doubts about his thoughts or state of mind. Nevertheless, he was apparently calm and in control of himself. Another would perhaps have found in that all the reassurance needed. Perhaps I would, too, in other circumstances. All the more since there was as yet no outward sign of disquiet in the village, no hint of an impending storm. The storm above, however, continued monotonously throughout the day. But no more gardens slid down the mountain, or if they did we didn't hear of it.

There was ample opening for wry humor, though I don't recall exploiting it. In any case, I was not joking in announcing that, if the rain continued through the night, I would ask Tubi to take the rainstone with him when he went to Kainantu for mail in the morning. He could leave it in our house at Haparira, where he would certainly be stopping in any case, to visit his people there. I asked Tubi if he thought there would be concern about the risk of unseasonable rain. He agreed that any extra rain would do no harm there in the grasslands if it came; the country is so much drier than Arogara anyway. The only other concern about this contingency plan was the rainstone itself, which was heavy and awkward to carry. But Tubi said he didn't mind. It helped that he didn't see this as a fool's errand.

It rained and stopped all night again, much as it had been doing. It may have rained as hard as ever during the downpours, but the truth is I can't be sure. Possibly the storm was losing some of its violence, or we may simply have been getting used to it. After a night and a day, even the unusual becomes routine. In any case it rained. Tubi made a late start for Kainantu—about half past eight in the morning. It was still raining when he left, but he had waited as long as he felt he could for a lull in which to leave the village. Since Kainantu and back in the same day is quite a walk, he finally chose getting wet over getting back late. Of course he took the rainstone with him.

By nine o'clock it stopped raining altogether.

The coincidence escaped neither my wife nor I, and we told Tubi when he got back at dusk. For him, I suspect, it clinched the purpose of carrying the rainstone all the way to Haparira.

REFLECTIONS

The storm's quiet aftermath settled one anxious question: There would be no confrontation over the mudslide damage to gardens. But in settling that, Arogara's silence raised another question: How could the injured parties accept their losses with no open protest. What did they really think had taken place and who, if anyone did they hold responsible? Or were storms and mudslides, even if manmade and out of season, simply a fact of life with responsibility in doubt? A confrontation might have provided answers.

Despite several peaceful weeks longer at Arogara, without challenge or ostracism, I can cite no villagers directly concerning their reactions to the rain, the magic, or the magician. This leaves some interesting questions hanging. The silence of the village is not the only reason. Whether or not people would have been willing to speak up if asked, I felt my hands were tied. I did not feel free to ask villagers about the storm, much less about their thoughts concerning Rainmaker and his or my involvement. This reluctance of course arose from what might seem, if not complicity in the magic, at any rate an involvement with Rainmaker. Even if I were unconcerned for my own part, I had no right to draw him in where he might not choose to be drawn. In short, I continued to believe that in some degree or manner the community must hold us or him accountable for what had happened. If neither of us was in fact compromised by this outcome, in any case, I had no way then to know it. I therefore deliberately left questions unasked and villagers unqueried concerning the storm or its perpetrator(s). Rainmaker's thoughts, however, are another matter.

My uncertainty concerning Rainmaker is surely obvious—how he viewed his role and, seemingly a part of the same question, what he thought about mine. Since he was the key to my ostensible participation, and thus the key to how that participation might be perceived, I continued to wonder about him. But I could reach no conclusion, either in our remaining weeks at Arogara or for a long time afterward. Today, however, several things seem clearer, particularly (1) whether Rainmaker saw our afternoon's discussion of rainmaking as a direct cause of the rain, (2) why he was aloof and noncommittal during and after the storm, and (3) how he could calmly accept the damage the mudslides caused his fellow villagers. As for the reflex of Rainmaker's own role, I think I have a better idea of (4) how he saw mine. Right or wrong, then, I close with the following hindsight.

More than ever, I am convinced that Rainmaker recognized a direct connection between the afternoon's discussion of magic and the subsequent rain. To reject such a connection would be to see the storm as mere coincidence. In the face of almost ideal proof of the magic's potency, in other words, indifference on his part would make his magic irrelevant. Apart from the possible recriminations of mudslide victims, moreover, he could take positive pleasure in this proof. Does that imply that, without rain, Rainmaker would have been dismayed, obliged to doubt his magic? Certainly not. In Arogara as also elsewhere, magical thinking is guided by common sense. If something happens for which a plausible cause is known, convention strongly favors accepting that cause. A deliberate act without the anticipated outcome, on the other hand, can often convincingly be explained by countervailing magic or some mistake in execution. Had fair weather followed our discussion, there was a perfect explanation: We had none of the key paraphernalia at hand, no rainstone to fill with water, no eagle's wing. But Event B, a spectacular rainstorm, had nevertheless followed Event A, our rainmaking tutorial. Not to connect Event B with Event A would probably seem perverse to an Arogara. It would in any case concede so much to chance or accident as to challenge any consistent magical viewpoint. If even in the presence of appropriate magic something can happen purely by accident, in other words, why seek causes?

The nature of magical power has an undeniable if only general bearing on the case. Magical power is refractory. Often only partly understood, it is sometimes difficult to control. Like radiation, moreover, particular forms of magical power are present in the world and can be activated without knowingly being summoned. Not all powers are known, moreover, and even known powers can unknowingly be summoned. On a revisit to the region some years after leaving Arogara, for example, I would hear people in another village complain of a widespread sickness among their pigs. Some pig owners ascribed the outbreak to the imminence of "too much magic." To them, in other words, the sickened pigs were not themselves intended targets. So far as the sorcerers were concerned, their sickness might be wholly inadvertent. This suggests that, in attempting to wield it, sorcerers may sometimes have less than a full understanding of the power they are using. They may consequently underestimate its range or fallout. They may fail to recognize other triggers to the power. Magic is remarkably open-ended, and magical knowledge is heavily empirical. Present knowledge and practice are not exhaustive and new discoveries are thus reported from time to time—sometimes momentous discoveries.

I think my point is clear. Rainmaker more than likely assumed that telling me how to make rain would simply be an exercise—a dry run, let us say. When a storm nevertheless ensued, it may well have surprised him, revealing his magic in a new, possibly even astonishing light. All the same, he need not openly profess his surprise, and he could heartily accept the outcome, considering it, inadvertent or not, his own accomplishment.

As to Rainmaker's behavior in the wake of the storm, he would have good reason to be aloof and noncommittal. As a competent magician his reputation for rainmaking would neither depend on nor would it be enhanced by boasting or self-advertisement. He was already known within the village and probably well beyond. He certainly had no need to boast to me.

Some of what I know today, it is only fair to point out, I did not know at Arogara. Ten years later I would be working at Abiera, a grassland village laying to the north, downstream from the Kratke foothills. Abiera is thus one of those grassland villages that look south to the forested Kratkes, to their evident and perpetual canopy of clouds. Like other grassland villagers, the Abiera speak of these mountains and likewise of their inhabitants as "the source of rain." As I have mentioned earlier, I had already heard that phrase applied to the Kratke people even before going to Arogara. But I did not grasp the full depth of its meaning.

One afternoon, from the ridge on which the main Abiera settlement sits, I heard an unfamiliar sound. It was a kind of low roar, faint at first but progressively growing louder. Rushing from the house to see what the sound might be, I found clusters of Abiera people standing and watching a torrent inexorably approach along the valley below, cresting as it came, and then, in an instant, passing by, scouring the valley bottom and sweeping away the best of the village's gardens. The loss was great for those with gardens in the choicest bottom land. Even as the Abiera stared mute and helpless at the oncoming wall of water, they already silently blamed the people of the mountains to the south for calling down the rains that started this destructive torrent. I only know they blamed the peoples at the source of rain because I asked. Several of the Abiera standing nearby answered me spontaneously and without an instant's thought. Only for an outsider were spoken words needed.

"Why do the people of the rainy mountains do it?" I asked and was given an answer I had heard in other instances of sorcery. They do it because it is what they do. It is usually pointless to try to recall some specific offense of Abiera in accounting for such a flood. Who knows? Whoever the rainmakers were, in a given case they may not even have been aiming at Abiera but rather at someone upstream or downstream. Or they may have been aiming at no one in particular. This is simply their kind of magic. Controlling it is a part of them. They have the rainmaking power and they use it if they wish. In short, they are rainmaking people, proud makers of rain.

Fair enough. Peoples from afar, especially downstream victims of flooding, might reasonably believe what they did. They had to believe something. They might believe, for examaple, in the wanton rainmaking of upstream enemies like the Arogara who, living at the source of rain, therefore possess rainmaking power. And as I would later understand better than I had while living there, the Arogara in turn could comfortably acknowledge their rainmaking reputation among outsiders, affirming the power ascribed to them, along with the blame for wanton damage. For what more convincing testimony to their power could there be, after all, than being blamed for using it? Being blamed was therefore beneficial, the damage inflicted a measure of the power. After all, magic is power and uniquely held magic is unique power; and where many a potential friend is also a potential enemy and vice versa, counts.

If you sense a change in how I see the rainstorm today, you are right. I can now recognize how much my understanding of the rainmaking episode was limited at the time to one particular scenario, as if no other scenario were logically possible and possibly more logical. In the midst of the storm I had fixed on a worst-case scenario roughly like Linton's theft of the Marquesan gods. But the Marquesan scenario—causing rains that hurt one's hosts and having to answer for it—has at best a fairly superficial resemblance to what happened at Arogara. From an Arogara point of view, in fact, it is a largely alien scenario. Let me explain. For the Marquesans their former gods were moribund. While their power was not denied, the validation of godly power could hardly have a positive value for people already by then committed to other—missionary—sources of power and authenticity. If the gods were to demonstrate their power, in short, it would be as revenge, for the people no surprise but nevertheless quite likely ominous.

The Arogara case is almost diametrically opposite. The contrast between power-wielding gods and power-wielding people is one part of the difference, of course, but in the foreground is another point. Although Arogara beliefs had been impugned by foreigners—government and missions— the Arogara had yet to renounce their traditional intimacy with certain unique sources of power. Even if already beginning to wonder about their own powers, they had not generally acclaimed missionary beliefs as an alternative source of identity or power. The ability to produce rain, in short, was still a vital source of strength and validation for them. To risk success in rainmaking would not be to invite the revenge of resentful gods but to produce a stunning reaffirmation of belief and commitment still current among them, even if under fire. Reserved though he might have been about the untimely rainstorm, therefore, Rainmaker could hardly be dismayed by it. In such a triumph, quite possibly, the loss of several gardens was but a small defect.

My role? For all of my anxious concern at the time, I am not convinced it was anything but secondary. I don't think I caused the rainstorm. So far as I can now see, I probably didn't hasten, intensify, or prolong the rain. The only tangible reason for exception that I can identify seems remote. It is that I was writing down all that Rainmaker said and his answers to my questions. The act of writing—making little marks—admittedly has a semblance of magic, and its very strangeness might suggest a possible source of power or enhancement. Our very conversation, being both prolonged and intensely concentrated on the subject of making rain, seems the more likely catalyst, but here, as with the writing, I am in the realm of speculation. That is probably just where Rainmaker himself would be, indeed, had he been moved to discuss these possibilities. It is at least pertinent here to point out once more that the world of magaic is in principle vast, with boundaries not yet reached, boundaries that may never be reached.

There is one more thing, and this is not strictly hindsight. My uncertainty regarding Rainmaker, as I have all along known, had its counterpart in his uncertainty about me. This reciprocal uncertainty was at the heart of my anxiety and it was precisely what created the impasse between us. I could never bring myself to ask him outright if, in instructing me, he had all along meant to make rain, fully expecting and intending it. And evidently he never cared to ask me if, in learning from him, I had meant to make rain, had perhaps therefore tried my hand at doing it the night the storm struck Arogara. For me this means I do not know how much of the rainmaking credit Rainmaker claims for himself. For Rainmaker it means he does not know how much of the credit I might claim. Neither of us, in short, knew or knows the other's mind—what the other meant to do, or did, or may have done. Rainmaker could well believe I made immediate use of his lessons in rain magic. In retrospect, I can see, my very elaborateness in deciding where to keep the rainstone, rather than forestalling his suspicion, could have fueled it.

Assuming I did at once put his teaching to use, would I deserve the major credit for the storm? Technically this could follow because of my being able to use the proper paraphernalia, especially the rainstone. There is also the fact that, whether or not I brought on the rain, I may have made it stop. Sending the rainstone out of the village, after all, had that consequence.

One cannot escape the fact, of course, that Rainmaker was ultimately the key to the whole episode. His was the knowledge and power, his the offer to impart his knowledge to me, and his the gift of the rainstone. Either way, then, whether Rainmaker made the rain or thinks I did it, he cannot be disappointed. It is the sorcerer's own magic even if this time the apprentice filled the rainstone.

What the apprentice will never know, moreover, is whether that same evening the sorcerer filled his own rainstone.

EIGHTEEN

Amgoi: Entrepreneurial Muck-up

EDWIN A. COOK

SUSAN M. PFLANZ-COOK
Florida Department of Community Affairs

Amgoi was probably born about 1942 or perhaps a year or two later, the youngest of his mother's five children. Both his parents died while he was still quite young and his care devolved upon his immediately elder brother, Tsapinde, and to a lesser extent upon his eldest half-brother, Wando. There is no reason to suspect that his early childhood differed significantly from that of other children placed in similar circumstances. Very little is known of this formative period in his life. In 1953 the group of which he is a member, the Manga of the Jimi River Subdistrict, Western Highlands District, Papua New Guinea, were initially contacted by a patrol originating in Minj, the Jimi River area being at that time an uncontrolled area.

In late 1955 and into 1956 a number of serious wars in the Jimi came to the attention of the Australian administration. In particular, the Manga had been routed in warfare by their neighbors the Yuomban and a patrol from Minj was sent to quell the disturbances. The patrol was successful; several Yuomban wre killed when they attempted to ambush the patrol and the Manga were reestablished in their traditional territory.

At this time, one man accompanying this partrol from Minj named Nopnop, said to have been an interpreter, told Amgoi that Amgoi was to accompany him on the return to Minj. Nopnop is alleged to have said that this was at the request of the patrol officer. There is reason to believe this, since it is true that the patrol officer did take two other Manga adolescents (Mai and TsiNe) with him on the return to Minj, the purpose being to place them in school or utilize them around the patrol post as informal "cargo" boys in order to familiarize them with European ways and to teach them Neo-Melanesian. At any rate, Amgoi accompanied Nopnop to Minj, where he was put to work on Nopnop's private coffee holdings. He continued in this occupation for approximately two years and then returned to Kwiop, the government-established census point for the Manga, in either late 1958 or early 1959. In the interim, a patrol post had been established at Tabibuga in the Jimi, a half day's walk from Kwiop, and the airstrip that had been completed in 1959. From these activities Amgoi had undoubtedly acquired some knowledge of the more sophisticated practices of the Wahgi Valley indigenes.

In early 1961, the Anglican mission, operating out of its base at Simbai under the direction of Father Peter Robin, placed two indigenous lay catechists at Kwiop. Amgoi immediately attached himself to their enterprise, since at that time he was the only resident Manga with any command of Neo-Melanesian, though it must be noted that this command was extremely limited. In fact, we feel it would not be an exaggeration to state that his low level of competence made him essentially a functional non-Neo-Melanesian speaker. Toward the end of 1961, I selected Kwiop as the site of initial field investigations for a study in minimal acculturation, this site to be compared later with investigations conducted among the Morokai located at Warames, a short fifteen-minute walk from the patrol post at Tabibuga. At the suggestion of other ethnographers who had worked in the Highlands, I brought with me to Kwiop a young man from another village located close to the patrol post to act as my "head of household" (*manki masta* in Neo-Melanesian). Within two weeks this individual successfully courted and ran off in the night with two of the local belles (taking one for a friend) and I found myself with no assistant. Amgoi immediately presented himself for employment and I acceded to his request. He claimed competency in Neo-Melanesian, cooking and domestic skills, carpentry, and other esoteric Western lore. I was soon to learn that all these claims were spurious. Nevertheless, he did *attempt* all of these various activities at one time or another, though as it developed he much preferred to tell others what should be done than do it himself.

At this point in time, late 1961 into early 1962, the Manga were within a few weeks of uprooting the ceremonial plants (/om/ and /ndama/) as a part of the pig festival cycle after which dancing would be permitted. This was to culminate in December 1962 with the slaughter of a great number of pigs and the subsequent distribution of large quantities of pork and wealth to previous war allies, kinsmen, and others to whom they were indebted for various earlier activities. During this phase of the pig festival cycle, men decorate themselves elaborately and a part of this decoration includes the wearing of green beetle headbands lashed together with yellow orchid fibers. Amgoi immediately set about purchasing all of the green beetles he could acquire and in almost no time had hundreds of them; in short, he cornered the green beetle market. It was his plan to manufacture these headbands and sell them to other pig festival celebrants.

After the beetles had dried out sufficiently, he collected the yellow fibers and sat down one evening to commence his project. In no short time it became apparent, not only to me but also to Amgoi, that he simply lacked the technical skills requisite to the task. In short, he didn't know how to *make* green beetle headbands. Within a few days he subcontracted with an older male kinsman, a coresident cross-cousin, to manufacture the headbands while he would supervise the project in terms of distribution and sales. Unfortunately, the kinsman only showed up sporadically at Amgoi's headband "factory" and over a period of several weeks only made two or three of them, and not too well at that, which Amgoi was unable to sell. In the meantime, the green beetle bodies commenced decaying until even Amgoi could smell the failure of his project.

A few weeks after this he was offered a young cassowary and he subsequently purchased it. Now, the cassowary figures significantly in certain rituals at the conclusion of the pig festival and a measure of prestige is usually accorded those who slaughter one. However, this effort was also unsuccessful, since the cassowary was too young to attain full growth before the end of the festival and Amgoi was also subjected to some mild ridicule because he had paid approximately twice what the going price was for cassowary chicks.

A couple months later I went on a walk to the Simbai patrol post, stopping at each census point I passed through to collect Swadesh word lists. After arriving at Simbai I elected to return to the Jimi via airplane to Tabibuga and then a half day's walk back to Kwiop. Since the size of the plan prohibited taking other than immediate effects, I gave Amgoi a quantity of salt which, at the request of the administration, was then used to purchase indigenous food products in the Jimi, so that he and the cargo carriers might purchase food on their return walk to Kwiop. I later learned that Amgoi initiated the following modus operandi: Upon entering a native village he would speak only Neo-Melanesian, remain somewhat apart from those carrying cargo boxes, and assuming an air of importance, would require that his requests in Neo-Melanesian for food be translated by one of the cargo carriers into the local language. When food was brought he would then supervise the distribution of salt.

On another occasion, Amgoi had made the necessary arrangements to purchase his own shovel, the only shovels owned by the Manga at that time being of government issue. He walked to Tabibuga and bought his shovel. Having some money left over, he then walked on down to the Nazarene Mission Station at Tsingoropa to shop at the mission trade store. After concluding his transactions at the store he began his return to Tabibuga (a one- to two-hour walk) only to realize halfway back that he had forgotten his shovel at the store. He immediately returned to the store and, as you might suspect, the shovel was not only not there but all denied ever having seen it. Amgoi then walked over to the Reverend William Bromley's house (the Nazarene missionary at Tsingoropa) and told Mr. Bromley that the patrol officer at Tabibuga had told Amgoi to tell him that his presence, along with that of all the indigenous population located at Tsingoropa, was immediately requested at the patrol post in order to investigate, and subsequently incarcerate, those responsible for the theft of the shovel. Mr. Bromley immediately sent one of his own employees to the patrol officer with a note stating his somewhat amazed disbelief at this request and asking for clarification. This, of course, was the first the patrol officer had heard of the incident. The patrol officer sent a policeman to apprehend Amgoi. Amgoi was returned to the patrol post, a court was held, and he was jailed for two weeks for behavior tending to incite others to riot.

During the second week of Amgoi's detention, a group of men of the Okona phratry into whom his elder sister (then deceased) had married, arrived at the patrol post and informed the patrol officer that they had come as the patrol officer had requested. After a somewhat lengthy and convoluted discussion it developed that while Amgoi was in jail he had told another detained indigene of the Okona phratry that upon the latter's release from jail he was to inform his deceased sister's husband's group that the patrol officer had personally told Amgoi to tell them that they must now pay his sister's death payment and that it must be brought to the patrol post immediately. Since she had died prior to administration contact in the valley, and since traditional transactions of this sort were legally to be honored by the administration, the patrol officer directed that the payment be made to Amgoi and the proper notations were made in the Okona census books.

Upon Amgoi's release from jail he attempted to return to Kwiop with the wealth he had thus acquired, but unfortunately both his elder full brother and his elder half-brother forbade him to bring any of the wealth items home. Their grounds for denying him the opportunity to manipulate this wealth were that an unresolved state of enmity existed between the Okona and the Manga and therefore the wealth objects were contaminated and would probably cause sickness and death if brought into the home territory. As a result, Amgoi was compelled to deposit them with distantly related affinal kinsmen in another village where they were, in effect, impounded.

During the several months in which these events occurred, Amgoi also successfully courted and entered into a marital relationship with a girl named Kum. As was traditional, she was at first housed with his elder brother's wife, Mitsi, in her woman's house. This precipitated some additional conflict primarily for two reasons. First, Kum and Mitsi both originated in the same-named minimal segment of the Manga segmentary organization and their exists a mild prohibition against "brothers" marrying "sisters" when those brothers and sisters belong respectively to minimal named segments of intermarrying clans. Second, Mitsi saw the presence of Kum as a threat to the payment of her own bride-price. This eventually resulted in certain behaviors by Mitsi which culminated in her husband having to prematurely pay her bride-price. Since the administration had entered the Jimi they had been promoting the policy that bride-prices should be paid at the commencement of cohabitation by the couple. This is quite counter to local custom, in which it is usually the case that a bride-price is not paid until there are two living children both past the age of weaning. Mitsi had only one child.

Shortly after this Amgoi made an unceremonious (other than it being public) presentation of wealth to Kum's parents. The amount, acquired

principally through his employment by the anthropologists, was approximately one-third of what was then considered an adequate bride-price;
nevertheless, after having made this payment Amgoi maintained that he
had now paid his bride-price and that Kum no longer had the option of
returning to her natal home. At the payment, none of the preliminary
ceremonies were attended to, there was no singing and dancing, and other
than Amgoi's there were no presentation speeches. Amgoi made the
payment dressed in shorts and a shirt, something no one else had ever
done. (During the various dances held as part of the pig festival cycle,
Amgoi was the only person who consistently wore European apparel in his
self-decoration.)

The pig festival ended in December 1962, and shortly thereafter I
moved to the second site of my field investigation. For a variety of reasons,
I dismissed Amgoi from my employ, preferring to employ members of the
community in which I was residing.

A few months before to the end of the festival at Kwiop, the eight men
who were the first from Kwiop to go to the coast as plantation laborers in
the Highland Labour Scheme returned. Their impact was significant in a
number of senses, but principally in demonstrating to other young men
the wealth and goods that could be obtained through this form of employment. As a result, when the festival was finished a number of Manga
decided to walk out of the Jimi to Mt. Hagen and sign on as laborers.
Amgoi was in this group, stating before his departure that he would
become a truck driver, as had one of the Manga who had just returned.
However, during the night the group spent on top of the Wahgi-Sepik
Divide, just before entering the Wahgi Valley, Amgoi became fearful that
evil ghosts and spirits would attack him on the coast and as a result he
alone returned to Kwiop. A few months later, in late 1963, I left the Jimi
and at that time planned to return in about five years. Amgoi knew this.

Before I left Kwiop, Amgoi brought a handful of coffee beans to me one
day. He explained that this was the second time he had had such beans but
that rats had eaten the earlier batch. He told me that some men at Warames
had planted coffee and when the patrol officer came through and noticed
it he beat the responsible parties. At this time Amgoi did not understand
the necessity for planting the beans along with shade trees. I explained
also that the beans were inedible and that it would take several years for
the trees to bear. Upon hearing of the amount of time and effort necessary
to the project, he declared that it would not be good for him to plant the
beans and as a result get beaten and end up in jail (in Neo-Melanesian, "*No
gut mi planim nau kiap kam kalabusim mi.*")

Later, sometime in 1964 of 1965, the administration did make coffee
beans available for planting in the middle Jimi, the area in which the
Manga are located. Four important Manga elders informed the administration officials that the Manga did not wish to plant coffee, as they were
uncertain of the impact this would have and desired instead to wait and

see what happened to other groups who planted coffee. Three of the younger men—Amgoi, Mai, and one of the sons of the Luluai, KipuNga— were disturbed by this decision of the elders, all appointed local officials. While Mai and KipuNga actually did nothing to overthrow this decision, Amgoi went to Tabibuga, had an audience with the patrol officer, and said that the decision of the elders was not representative of the thinking of most of the Manga, who actually wanted to plant coffee. The patrol officer gave Amgoi a bag of beans to plant and Amgoi returned to Kwiop. Amgoi, Mai, and KipuNga prepared the beds, planted the beans, and when the seedlings were large enough to transplant, Mai distributed them to those individuals who wanted them. It is recognized by all the Manga that it was Amgoi who "brought the coffee to Kwiop."

Meanwhile, Amgoi waited for my return until sometime in 1966. I was told by some missionaries and others that he would periodically turn up at the patrol post inquiring as to whether I had returned or not. In late 1966, he departed for a rubber plantation outside of Port Moresby. But he had left not in company with other Manga, but rather with a number of men from a place further upriver in the Jimi, with whom he has some tenuous affinal relations. Amgoi claims that he actually worked on the labor line but only for a short time, and that instead he became the head cook and houseboy of the plantation manager. Extensive questioning of Amgoi and others, however, revealed that this was not exactly the truth. Amgoi began his first month on the rubber plantation as a *boss boi* supervising his fellow Jimi River laborers, who were employed to cut the grass around the rubber trees. At this time Amgoi was heard bragging of his extensive experience as a cook and *manki masta*. This information was ultimately communicated to the plantation manager, who hired Amgoi as a laundry boy and dishwasher to assist his houseboy, who did the actual cooking and serving. Amgoi worked in this capacity for only five months. Whether he was fired or whether he resigned is open to question. He was then given the job of picking up full rubber buckets and riding with them on a truck to the scales for weighing. He maintains that the truck driver was a good friend of his and that he taught Amgoi how to drive the vehicle. Amgoi claims that he then asked to be hired as a driver but was told that men on Highland labor contracts were not allowed to be drivers.

Amgoi returned to the Jimi sometime in 1968. Shortly after that, Kennecott Copper Corporation exercised their copper exploration lease in the lower Jimi. Kennecott had several exploration teams in the area which were supplied from a series of helicopter pads they had cleared in the bush. Amgoi attached himself to this organization as an occasional laborer and cook. When Kennecott had completed its survey and testing it departed, having found no commercially valuable sources of copper. After the company's departure, Amgoi traveled around in the lower Jimi telling other groups that Kennecott had said that it would return shortly and that it had placed him in charge of constructing additional helicopter landing sites. Over a period of several months Amgoi claims that he actually succeeded in building three additional landing pads using the labor of those whom he talked into this scheme. As of mid-1972, Kennecott had not returned to the area.

After this, Amgoi then worked for an indigenous carpenter who had been retained by the administration to erect a prefabricated house at the patrol post. He had this job for three weeks. He was subsequently hired for four months as houseboy for a European storekeeper who had been employed by a Tabibuga store licensee. After the European storekeeper left, he was hired as an assistant storeboy in the same store for one month. Amgoi says he was fired after being accused of giving away store goods to young girls. He self-righteously points out that his accuser was the same fellow who subsequently embezzled several hundred dollars from this store.

Shortly after these events, his marriage dissolved. In fact, he had mal-treated his wife so severely that the local government councillor for Kwiop, Mai (who was the first to hold this office when elections were initiated in 1966 and has been returned to office in the elections of 1967, 1969, and 1971), had him jailed and Amgoi was unable to gather any support from his consanguineal kinsmen to help him in retaining his wife. His ex-wife married another man and Amgoi received no return on any part of the bride-price he had paid to her parents.

In May 1971, Amgoi was again jailed by the local government councillor, Mai. A few years earlier, the first trade store had been built at Kwiop by Councillor Mai and a classificatory brother of his, Men. This store was later torn down, the capitalization base was extended by subscription, and a larger store was built. A controversy arose over the nonrepayment of the invested shares in the second store. Amgoi, though not a contributor, joined in the arguments. All of the potential plaintiffs were summarily ordered to be jailed by Councillor Mai. (We should note that this occurred immediately prior to the 1971 councillor elections; that of the four clan-moieties, or subclans, at Kwiop three were represented among those jailed; and that no one from Mai's clan-moiety, which was also the clan-moiety of his opponent in this election, was jailed.) While in jail, one of Amgoi's occasional duties was to fill up the water tanks of the assistant district commissioner's house and to cut firewood for his stove. (On June 19, 1970, the Jimi River patrol post was elevated to subdistrict status and an assistant district commissioner was posted to Tabibuga.) Amgoi sub-sequently claimed he had not actually been in jail but had instead been employed as domestic help by the assistant district commissioner.

On the very day I arrived back in the Jimi in June 1971, Amgoi was released from jail. Less than two hours after my arrival, Amgoi sought me out and greeted me in a highly emotional manner. To say that he was overjoyed at my return would be to understate his reaction. Consequently, I once again employed Amgoi as my principal domestic help, paying him the sum of $A7.00 per week, regarded as a fair wage in the Jimi for that type of work.

After leaving the patrol post at Tabibuga and arriving back at Kwiop, Amgoi besought me to hire an employee for him. I agreed to this but made it his responsibility to select this employee. His first and second selections were inefficient at the tasks Amgoi assigned them and were released from employment. His third choice turned out to be a hard-working and, for Amgoi, appropriately subservient employee. He was retained. All three were men younger than Amgoi and affiliated with Amgoi's own minimal named segment of the social organization. Amgoi then initiated a rotating credit union among three of my employees, one person to receive the wages of all three at the end of one week, another person at the end of the second week, and the third at the end of the third week and then the cycle was to begin again. Amgoi, of course, was the first to be paid on this system, and he appointed me as recordkeeper since he could neither read nor write. In subsequent weeks, when other members of the rotating system received the total amount, Amgoi would borrow money from them, promising to repay them when his turn came around again. The system suffered internal collapse when, on the second go-around, Amgoi did not repay those from whom he had borrowed in previous weeks. As a result, the union was disbanded.

Where was the money going? It soon became readily apparent that Amgoi was a chronic card game gambler and that he very rarely won. Over the next few weeks it had become known that I had returned to the area and that Amgoi was employed and earning money. It was thereafter not unusual that at least once a week a creditor would turn up requesting payment of Amgoi's debts. In only one case was a creditor successful in causing Amgoi to part with any money. Usually, Amgoi had no money no matter what day of the week, except for a period of a few hours after being paid on payday, Friday afternoon.

Within a few days of our arrival, Amgoi began talking of building his own trade store. Capitalization of this store was originally to have come from his ex-father-in-law, who according to Amgoi owed him approximately $A50.00 for a cassowary. Amgoi had also hoped to enlist the aid of others by soliciting capitalization subscriptions. We encouraged this activity and provided time off from his household duties so that he might cut the posts and make the walls, doors, and window for the store. He was unable to enlist the monetary support of any kinsmen and he realized he would need money in order to purchase the three sheets of corrugated iron (in Neo-Melanesian these are referred to as *coppers*) he would need for a roof and for his initial inventory. Since he was losing his wages at gambling, I took it upon myself to place a "taboo" (in the local language, Narak, /*kats mab1A*/, *kats* being Neo-Melanesian for English "cards"). upon his playing any cards. I also withheld a portion of his wages, so that by the time he was ready to purchase the roof pieces he would have funds for them and for his initial inventory. The roof pieces would cost him $A3.50 to $A4.50, depending on where they were purchased, the higher price at Tabibuga and the lower at Minj. By September 1971 he had finished the store except for the roof.

I accompanied him to Tabibuga, where for $A6.00 I purchased a license as a trade store operator for Amgoi from the local government council. Since no roof pieces were then available at Tabibuga, Amgoi elected to walk to Minj to buy them and his initial store inventory. He intended to return on one of the itinerant coffee buyer trucks coming into the Jimi. He had $A50.00 with him. The amount was more than sufficient for his aims. When he got to Minj, however, he first purchased a new set of clothes, including a hat, tennis shoes, and long white stockings of the style worn by Europeans in the Highlands. He then played several card games and lost the remainder of his money. As he was returning to the Jimi, walking, an old woman spotted him and, deciding that he was a man of some obvious substance, gave him one of her marriageable-age daughters. Amgoi promised the girl's parents $A200.00 (the maximum amount of cash to be included in a bride-price as established by the Jimi River local government council) and ten pigs and they had shaken hands over this arrangement. He returned to Kwiop with the girl who was initially placed in his elder brother's woman's house, but Amgoi failed to take proper care of her. He rarely brought her extra food, store-bought delicacies, or other goods expected by her under the circumstances. She complained, in writing, several times to the councillor at Kwiop and he eventually held a minor court hearing which Amgoi confessed that he really didn't want to marry. Amgoi said he had tried marriage before and it was too much work. He then agreed to her assignment to one of his kinsmen. That arrangement didn't work out and she subsequently cohabitated with a third man. When this man then acquired the widow of a recently deceased brother the girl protested, saying she had been baptized and therefore could not be part of a polygynous union. The local government councillor held another hearing, a small amount of money was paid to her by the third "husband," and she was returned to Minj. The councillor told her that Amgoi was recognized throughout the Jimi as a terrible marriage risk and that she should spread this word in the Wahgi so that other girls would not become entrapped by him.

An additional interesting facet of Amgoi's nonexistent store was that during the entire time of his building it, his primary concern appeared to be who he was going to recruit to manage it for him. It was never his intention to run the store himself. At any rate, after this series of events Amgoi left Kwiop and was not seen there for several weeks. The store structure, built on Anglican mission land with the consent of the two resident lay catechists, was torn down by them and used as firewood sometime in October 1971.

During the period of June through September 1971 Amgoi attempted in other ways to acquire funds. On the occasion of a bride-price being paid into his group he solicited a loan of $A10.00. He promised the loan would be repaid immediately after the bride-price itself had been distributed. He eventually found a person who loaned him the money and he did in fact repay the loan within a period of days. Amgoi *has* been known to pay pressing debts but only on those occasions when he is known to have money. In this case of a publicly known bride-price there was little opportunity to deny he had the cash.

At another time he subcontracted with a male affinal kinsman of another clan who owned an unlicensed shotgun to come to Kwiop and shoot some of the lesser birds of paradise that Amgoi owned (that is, that lived on land he owned). Plumes from this bird are valued at A$10.00 in the Jimi and considerably more in the Wahgi. The Kwiop local government councillor, Mai, owned the only licensed shotgun among the Manga. Mai had, further-more, stated that it was a council law (which is not true) that nonresidents may not shoot birds of paradise on the land of others when there is a resident there who owns a shotgun. Mai's fee for use of the shotgun was $A4.00 per bird shot. Amgoi sought to circumvent this by bringing in the relative and his shotgun and promising him a portion of the sale price of any birds he got. Unfortunately, the hunt was not at all successful and no birds were shot.

I left the Jimi in September 1971 and returned in June 1972 with my wife. This third time we refused to employ Amgoi on the grounds that no matter what he did, he screwed it up. In front of an audience, I recited many of the past events (which are, in fact, common knowledge), adding that as his "father" (he has always, for the last twelve years, addressed me as "father") I had supported him in numerous endeavors, aided him in a number of enterprises, paid him a lot of money, and provided him food and shelter, and that my patience and concern with his well-being were now exhausted. During the period of June through September 1972 we did, however, continue to observe Amgoi's activities and collect additional data from and about him. It became extremely evident that he began to be even more involved in card gambling than he had been previously. He constantly asked me to provide him with numerous forms of magic that would assure his winning. On one occasion Amgoi asked for a special green- or blue-colored perfume in a gaudy bottle, which he assured me was powerful magic. This perfume is placed in the armpits or under the fingernails before playing cards and assures a winning evening. Amgoi was able to obtain some of this perfume and the second time he used it he won $A50.00. His faith was of course reaffirmed. He also explained to us how important it was to play with his own deck of cards; he maintained that he always won with his own cards. On another occasion, he asked us to get him a little bottle that had water in it. He claimed that a man from Wabag had one and had shown it to him and that it had been obtained from a person living on a secret small island somewhere off the coast from Port Moresby. If the water was high in the bottle and of a particular color, then you knew that you would win a lot of money; but if the water was low in the bottle and a different color, then you would not win very much. We think this must have been a barometer but could think of no way to explain its true functions to Amgoi in a way that would make him believe us.

Since Amgoi inevitably lost his money sooner or later, a question arose concerning his source of income. His current holdings in coffee and pigs were not significantly more or less than those of other single men dependent on male kinsmen's wives for labor. His coffee trees had not yet begun bearing so he had no income from that source. In 1971 he had only three immature pigs. In early 1972 he did, however, sell one of these pigs which had proved to be very troublesome due to a fondness for other people's gardens. He told his elder half-brother's wife, who had cared for this pig, that he was taking it downriver to trade for a cassowary, which he would then sell in the Wahgi for a large cash profit. He promised to share this with her.

He did successfully trade the pig for a cassowary and then headed for the Wahgi. On the road he met a coffee truck driver who offered him $A100.00 for the bird, $A50.00 then and $A50.00 to be paid later. Amgoi took the $A50.00 and rapidly lost it all at cards. He waited for the truck driver to return, but when he failed to show up again Amgoi traveled to the Wahgi to visit the truck driver's kinsmen. Arriving at Banz, he inquired about his cassowary and its new owner. He was told the driver had married a woman from the Southern Highlands District, had taken his pigs and the cassowary with him to live there, and was not expected back for some years. Amgoi later faced some harsh words from his half-brother's wife, who had received no compensation for her pig-raising efforts.

Also, immediately prior to our arrival in 1972, Amgoi's lineage brothers pooled their money to capitalize a trade store for themselves at Kwiop. (Trading at these small stores is most often conducted on the basis of kinship affiliation with the store owner or owners.) About this time Amgoi managed to win approximately $A20.00 at cards and attempted to invest this as his share in the new store. His lineage mates refused to let him participate. They returned his money to him, explaining that he had had his chance at his own store the previous year and that he had failed at it. They did not wish to take the risk of him causing their store to fail.

Once an old man from a neighboring clan arrived at Kwiop and inquired about the European breeding sow he had recently purchased from Amgoi, sight unseen, for $A14.00. Their dealings had occurred on one of Amgoi's gambling expeditions when his need for cash outweighed his veracity. The unfortunate fellow was told that Amgoi had never owned a European pig and that his money was lost. The old man left immediately to report the incident to the assistant district commissioner at the sub-district office at Talibuga.

Another technique Amgoi used to obtain funds rests on the following deliberate strategy. In Manga social relations, if two people are involved in a conversation or an argument and one of them verbally abuses the other, then the abuser is liable to a fine. Amgoi would approach friends, particularly close male kinsmen, and unctuously ask for a loan, just a few coins or at the most a dollar or two. He would promise and promise to repay them as soon as he won, and he was certain that he would win this time. In a number of instances, we learned he was already heavily indebted to the person to whom he was making this request and frequently that person would become quite irritated and would consequently end up verbally abusing him. As a result, later in the day or perhaps the next day, that person would simply give Amgoi $A.50 or $A1.00, apologizing for his behavior and saying he felt sorry about the way he had treated Amgoi. In short, Amgoi was exploiting his kinsmen by manipulating the conventions to his advantage.

We also noted during this period that Amgoi has taken to jocularly referring to himself as *Masta Amgoi, masta* being the Neo-Melanesian term for any European. No one else did this and everyone else thought it was quite amusing.

In sum, Amgoi's reputation as a debtor, gambler, and poor marital risk, is becoming increasingly widespread in the Jimi. His chance of gaining another wife would appear to be much reduced by his incessant gambling. He rarely finds the time to enter courting events in other villages because his interest centers more on the accompanying card games than on the girls. And because of his monetary reputation, he is finding it difficult to borrow the sums necessary to finance his ventures. It seems probable that he will eventually return to the coast as a laborer in order to find new gambling territory and new funds—that is, if he isn't already in jail for some other reason.

NINETEEN

🌀 An Anthropologist as Travel Writer

ROBERT TONKINSON
University of Western Australia

Some years ago, a friend who is a professional travel writer invited me to attempt something different from my accustomed ethnographic reporting by writing an article about the lighter side of doing fieldwork in Vanuatu. He thought that if I could put to paper some of my anecdotes about the ups and downs of immersion in a foreign culture, it would be of interest to a more general audience—*general* in this case referring to those airplane passengers who read in-flight magazines. I accepted the challenge and wrote the story I will present here. It remains substantially as written, but with some minor updating.

The story could be called ethnography in only the very broadest sense, being less a portrait of a society than a pen portrait of aspects of what it is like to conduct fieldwork in a small island in the South Pacific. The concentration is on the lighter side of doing ethnography, but there is also serious intent: acquainting the reader with what anthropology is and is not, and alluding to some of the ethical and political aspects of doing field research in a small-scale society. There is also an important parallel with the mission of anthropology in general—that is, the attempt to render our understandings about the human "other" accessible to Western society (cf. Burridge 1973).

The story was entitled "At Work in the Isles of Coral and Ash" (Tonkinson 1979). I will follow it with my thoughts on what was and was not being communicated in this attempt to address a nonanthropological audience.

"So you're an anthropologist. Oh yes, bones and stones. . . . Where do you dig?"

"Nowhere! I leave that to the archaeologists. I'm a cultural anthropologist," I reply, ready to explain further in case my questioner thinks this means I read Hegel, speak nine languages, and did a postdoctorate at the Sorbonne.

"Oh yes. You're the crazies who go and live with the natives in exotic spots at the end of the earth—escapees from the rat race. So where's your hideout?"

An immediate problem arises: whether or not to disabuse my questioner of the notion that anthropology equals the study of "the natives" in far-off places, by pointing out the fact that most students today are doing fieldwork in their own countries—and then risk a debate over the difference between anthropology and sociology—or press on regardless, eager to talk about "my people." So I opt for the latter, hoping to get back to the bigger issue of the scope of anthropology later in the conversation.

"I work in Vanuatu," I reply, and then quickly add, "Which is between Fiji and Australia," since most people don't know where this ruggedly scenic string of tropical islands hides in the vastness of the Western Pacific. They may have read something about it during the turbulence surrounding the final move toward independence, which was achieved in 1980, but more often than not Vanuatu is confused with New Caledonia, where serious problems remain between the colonizers and the now-outnumbered indigenous Melanesians, or "Kanaks."

The combination "anthropologist–South Pacific" is a surefire trigger that evokes for many a romantic vision of a long and languorous idyll beneath waving palms on remote golden sands, the epitome of getting away from it all. There is truth in this vision, but it ignores certain realities. No one who abandons the comforting familiarity of his or her own culture for a year or two's immersion in a very different one does so without some traumas of adjustment. So when the inevitable question comes—"What's it like working there?"—my usual response mirrors the ups and downs that virtually all anthropologists experience in the field: "Mostly I really love it, but never every day, and there are times when I wonder what the hell I'm doing there."

Given half a chance, I'll then regale my listener with the pros and cons of fieldwork. I sometimes feel like the Ancient Mariner with the wedding guest, except that my anecdotes generally favor the lighter side of research. For the most part I sidestep the weighty moral and ethical aspects of fieldwork with which anthropologists, as very close-range voyeurs of the lives of other peoples, must contend. In our dominant self-image we champion respect for cultural difference and rigorously oppose any forms of racism and the oppression of cultural minorities, particularly the more powerless, among whom many of us have chosen to work. But anthropologists, the askers of a million questions, have been condemned in some countries as being CIA agents. (Who else would be so nosy?) In others, the close identification of anthropology with the colonial period has rendered its practitioners suspect. And in some cases, the mistaken belief that we study only "primitive" peoples leads to rejection, in favor of those who designate their work "sociological."

I began research in Vanuatu in 1966, when colonialism was still in full swing, and the country, then called New Hebrides, was in the thrall of a unique (and seriously flawed) experiment in joint governance, the Anglo-French Condominium. Typically, the necessary permission to actually

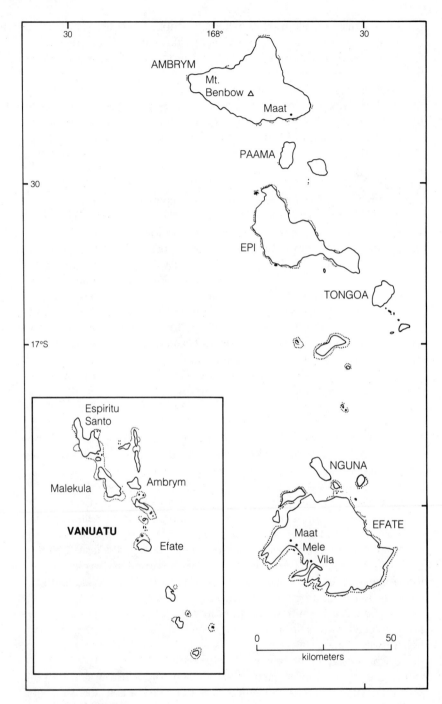

Ambrym, Epi, and Efate

carry out fieldwork had to be obtained from the colonial authorities, who had not consulted the villagers prior to my arrival—the villagers' concurrence was taken as a given, though it was left to me to carry out the actual negotiations. There were no problems, as it turned out, and since that time there have been no difficulties with my return and with continued fieldwork. My enthusiasm for the islands and their people has never weakened, and after more than twenty years the lure of Vanuatu remains undiminished.

The pace of change has quickened remarkably since independence, and greatly improved communications have opened up virtually all the islands to much greater contact with the outside world and with Western cultural influences generally. Tourism has become an important industry, but as yet not many visitors have managed to get to the southeast corner of Ambrym Island, where I do most of my fieldwork while in Vanuatu. Ambrym, in shape like a three-cornered hat, is centrally located about midway between the capital of Vila on Efate Island, and the second town, Santo, an Espirito Santo Island to the north. It measures about eighteen miles by twenty-seven and is dominated by two volcanic cones and a surrounding ash plain. The wide, flat two-thousand-foot-high plain gives Ambrym a cut-off look as one approaches it by sea. It is usually covered with a mantle of smoke and clouds that hides the pair of four-thousand-foot cones much of the time. The ash plain neatly divides the island into three habitation zones, each a distinct culture area with its own language. The volcanoes groan and rumble and glow pink some nights, but most of the time they behave. Major eruptions of lava are usually several decades apart, with periodic belches of ash emitted between times just to let the people know that the island's volcanic heart is slumbering, not dead.

About sixteen hundred people live in the southeastern part of the island, in fifteen villages and a number of small hamlets. Their lands are far from the two volcanoes, so they have little to fear from lava flows. The last one in the southeast was in 1888, spewing from a newly opened crater; it engulfed nine villages, but in leisurely fashion and apparently without fatalities. Ash-falls, however, have caused problems. The worst were in 1950–51 and resulted in the complete evacuation of the area. For ten months the southeast was blanketed with up to thirty-five feet of ash. It scorched the vegetation naked, fell as mud when mixed with rain, turned day into night, and lobbed grapefruit-sized chunks among the people from time to time. Life became quite uncomfortable and food was in short supply, but no one was killed and today people remember the funny side, such as confused chickens going to roost in the middle of the day. After the falls abated, the evacuees, unhappy at having been moved by the government to a nearby island, soon returned home to dig out, replant, and rebuild.

The people of one of the villages, Maat, did not go home. They remained on Efate Island in a new settlement they had built. Fifteen years later I went to live with them with the aim of attempting to gauge the effects of their resettlement, as part of a large Pacific Relocation Project being directed by Professor Homer Barnett out of the University of Oregon. So my initial field research was carried out in the new Maat Village, not far from the picturesque port and capital city of Vila. When I first visited Maat I had not yet mastered the country's lingua franca, Bislama, and though most villagers spoke some English, I had communication problems. I didn't realize this at the time, however, and only years later was I told the real reason some of the old women didn't want me to live in their village. The explanation I'd heard shortly after moving into Maat was the some of the older people feared that, having the "thin skin" of a European and living in a very malarial environment, I would be bitten badly by anopheles and probably die of malaria; the government would then blame the villagers and deport them to Ambrym as punishment. Such had been their limited and generally negative experience of colonial officialdom, they were bound to fear the worst.

The real reason, I later learned, stemmed from the fact that, before my first visit to Maat, I had copied a list of names (including those of deceased parents of villagers) from a census book in the Vila district agent's office. But once in the village and attempting to gain rapport by reference to the census list, I failed to make clear the source of my information. Who else but a returned spirit of the dead would know the names of the dead, reasoned the old ladies. And who would want such a *temat* (ghost) living cheek by jowl with them? Reassured by their menfolk, they later acquiesced to my request to live in the village. Fortunately, no one became ill after I moved in, so I was eventually accepted as a mere *metalo* (European) and not a potentially vengeful ancestral ghost.

The people of Maat proved to be most helpful, interested, and friendly hosts, which made the early months of settling in and language work relatively painless. Two of the community's most respected elders, Yonah Taso and Maxi Solomon, devoted much time to educating me, showing patience beyond the call of duty as I battled to assimilate a wealth of information. The villagers were very generous, and I received many gifts of food plus readily volunteered information. The kids, for every fieldworker the source of many blessings—and sometimes the odd curse—kept me, their first live-in European, under constant scrutiny. My self-appointed guides and informants reveled in the role of teacher and rarely let me out of their sight. I began to wonder who was studying whom. For a while at least, the villagers were at least as interested in me and my behavior as I was in them and theirs.

As the people of Maat on Efate had maintained close links with their homeland and most still continued to visit the old village from time to time, it was necessary for me to conduct part of my research in Ambrym. I needed to see how people's lives there compared with those of the resettled community in Efate. I went easily in 1967, accompanied by my two guardians, Yonah and Maxi. Ambrym had no airfields then but still looked like an easy place to reach. This is true of the sheltered western coast, but the southeast lies open to the full force of the prevailing trade winds, so getting ashore is a struggle most of the year.

The journey up from Vila is one of contrasts. Little interisland vessels (in times past, often of dubious seaworthiness and overloaded with cargo and passengers) peacefully cleave the calm waters in the lee of the islands en route, then fight what too often appears to be a losing battle with heavy seas in open waters. There is nowhere comfortable to sit, nothing much to hold on to, and the spray is drenching. I was always too preoccupied with thoughts of mortality to get seasick, but there is also an exhilaration as the boat rough-rides its way out of the hollow and crests the next big wave. The final half hour from Paama Island to Ambrym is across a wild stretch of water. Ahead is the low profile of southeast Ambrym, with its dense green forests and beaches of jet-black soil; to the east as you clear Paama towers the majestic, smoking cone of Lopevi, rising five thousand feet straight out of the ocean and capable of mounting spectactular eruptive displays for its Ambrymese audience a scant dozen miles to the north.

It was too rough that first time to allow our vessel to navigate the narrow, dangerous passage through the fringing reef, so we were put ashore in a dinghy—a wild, very scary wide as we almost surfed through the passage into the calmer waters near the beach. I scrambled ashore with shaking knees and great relief to be on terra firma with ourselves and my precious gear (swaddled in plastic bags, as is our custom) all safe. Cheery introductions followed, and there was embarrassment for me when some of the locals began talking rapidly to me in their language. They had taken my confident greeting in the vernacular to mean that I was a fluent speaker. I beat a hasty retreat into Bislama and we set off toward the old village of Maat, an hour's walk away and less than a mile inland from the coast. Many gardens were visible en route, as were the groves of coconut palms, which supply the raw material for copra, the area's only cash crop.

Excited to be home again, Yonah and Maxi gave me an impromptu botany lesson en route: "This is *nanggalat,* the stinging nettle; touch the top side of the leaves, go on! See, it's okay—only the underside stings, but better to keep right away. Over there, those nuts are called *tavu* . . . you can't stop eating them once you start; you'll see." We left the ocean and walked on the "main road"—a rough, black-sand track—through more groves interspersed with patches of thick jungle, from which much of the sun was blotted out. Suddenly, a fork in the road, a couple of huge mango trees, a clearing and an oval of blue sky, a cluster of decaying huts all overgrown, and another cluster of newer dwellings, surrounded by neatly cut grass. This was Maat, and one of its thatched-roofed, bamboo-walled huts would be my home for the next few months.

Yonah and Maxi took me on a guided tour of the entire southeast region and made my entry into the society an enjoyable and relaxed one. After more than six months in the country I was much less anxious about my situation and felt that I already knew a great deal about the home island of the Maat villagers with whom I'd been working near Vila. News of my presence in the Efate village had long since reached Ambrym, and the people knew I was coming. My mentors undertook to explain my work and my research objectives, thus relieving me of a very difficult task. Few anthropologists are so lucky, and many have a hard time establishing themselves in the field. They are fortunate that in so many cases the local people give up trying to work out why the fieldworker is *really* there. Instead, they take them as they find them and make judgments on the basis of their behavior as individuals.

Ambrymese still ask me if I'm there on vacation, since nothing I do fits their notion of work. (As academics, we have these same credibility problems with sections of our own society!) What are the locals to make of someone who wanders from village to village, always questioning, scribbling notes, counting things, clicking a camera, recording stories, measuring garden plots, gossiping, and watching the world of the village go by? This outsider of insatiable curiosity stays for months at a time, not like the few government officials who drop in very infrequently and usually for only a day or two. The anthropologist appears to be harmless, though small children flee in terror on first encounter; he or she must be the white man their parents are always warning will "get" them if they're naughty.

Unless they are given good reason not to, the villagers treat the few outsiders who visit with unfailing courtesy and hospitality. I was accorded the same treatment but was regarded as different because I had learned some of their language. Also, I maintained contact with several people through letters while away from Vanuatu and kept on returning regularly. These things were taken as indications of a serious interest in Ambrym and in continuing my relationships with its people.

For anthropologists it is essential to join in the lives of the people studied and to observe as faithfully as possible the local customs and rules of etiquette. But this does not mean "going native" and attempting to do everything the locals do. I have brown thumbs, not green, for a start, so gardening would have been a lost cause. My early attempts to wield a machete—say, when opening a green coconut for a drink of its delicious water—usually resulted in a small child relieving me of the knife and deftly showing how it should be done. I think many anthropologists provide the people among whom they live with a measure of reassurance by demonstrating what hopeless incompetents Westerners can be. Have you ever tried to paddle an outrigger canoe in a straight line? Or hit a fleeing chicken at forty paces with an arrow? Or spear a fish when your far point of clear vision without glasses is about a foot? Some day soon "my" Ambrymese are going to have a comic best-seller on their hands by telling about "their" anthropologist's search for knowledge in the tricky shoals of another culture.

Southeast Ambrymese, like many other peoples, tend to judge foreign visitors to a large extent on how well they take to the local diet. Ash-falls and the occasional hurricane aside, Ambrym is very well served by Mother Nature. A combination of high rainfall and very fertile soil ensures an abundance of tropical fruits, nuts, and wild bush foods to supplement the highly productive gardens. The fresh meat staple is chicken, and every family feeds a large flock on coconuts and food scraps. There are also a lot of cattle and pigs, usually reserved for special occasions, such as wedding feasts. Men sometimes hunt, with rifles and bows and arrows, for wild pigs, birds, flying fox, and for wild cattle up on the ash-plain. The ocean and fringing reefs are a convenient source of protein, and fishing is a popular leisure-time activity that also provides food.

Getting used to the likes of mangoes, papayas, an array of delicious nuts, fresh fish, lobster, and chicken was really no effort. Some of the staple root crops took me longer to develop a liking for, especially when boiled or roasted in large chunks. Fortunately tubers such as yam, taro, manioc, and sweet potato are often cooked as *lap-lap* puddings, some varieties of which are very tasty. The vegetables are peeled, grated, mixed with coconut milk, perhaps garnished with "bush cabbage" and fresh meat or shellfish, wrapped in leaves, and steamed slowly in an earth oven over hot stones. Manioc *lap-lap* topped with coconut cream is excellent, especially when baked with octopus fresh from the reef. Another mouth-watering seasonal staple is *huhu,* a bright yellow paste of pounded breadfruit. The preparation of *huhu* involves much effort and many workers, so it is often prepared in a communal kitchen and the whole affair can take on the aura of a happening. An addict, I listen for the rhythmic pounding of the freshly roasted fruit on huge oval platters. The rolling pin is a green coconut, and when the pastrylike ball is flattened to cover the board in a half-inch-thick layer, thickened coconut cream is splashed over it. A sliver of bamboo is used to cut the pastry on the diagonal, producing diamond-shaped pieces. Everyone then sits around the board and within minutes reduces it to an empty, cream-spattered expanse.

Some local foods such as flying fox, edible grubs, green bananas, *lap-lap,* and porkfat will not appeal to most foreigners. I heard protests from the French about flying fox, since *rousettes au vin rouge* is a delicacy they aver. Personally, I can live without the simple pan-fried version.

As in many parts of the Pacific, some of the foods favored by the Ambrymese are not at all exotic: white rice and canned meat and fish! Even where local foods abound, these imports are often preferred, largely because they are convenient and easily prepared. Many people have gardens quite a walk from the village, so after a hard day cutting copra the cooks prefer something quick and easy. As to why children, especially, adore plain boiled white rice, I have no idea; but I do know that it was a source of amazement to the villagers that a five-year-old child could eat much more of it than I ever could.

There are no fast-food joints on Ambrym. And one look at the stock in the local village stores would send a suburban shopper into a tizzy. The wise Ambrymese have never been bitten by the consumerism bug, and their shops reflect this disinterest. Tea, sugar, tobacco, kerosene, batteries, matches, cloth, and clothing are among the important basics. On the island there is very little else to spend their money on, so people who want luxury items such as radios must go to the towns or else wait for trading vessels with on-board stores.

When people need cash they make copra, especially when its price on the world market is high. The villagers like to organize work parties. Tackling the coconuts communally allows people to socialize as they work and lessens the boredom of repetitive activity out in the groves. The Ambrymese are their own bosses, free to work when they choose and at their own pace. Some of their gardening chores are arduous and their slash-and-burn technique requires that new areas be cleared and planted each year, but there are times when the gardens need very little attention. Every village has communal workdays devoted to keeping the site clean and tidy, or to some project such as repairing the church or digging a well, but there is still plenty of time for people to pursue a variety of different activities, ranging from visits to kin and friends in distant villages, to building a new kitchen, to preparing and drinking kava (a man-only pastime that has swept the nation since independence).

By anyone's standards it's a good life, and the people of southeast Ambrym appreciate its leisurely pace. Listening on their radios to the woes of the rest of the planet, they often remark to me about how lucky they are. Their society is remarkably peaceful and tranquil. There has not been a homicide in decades, and an easygoing politeness, devoid of aggression, dominates people's interaction. Until the 1970s, however, the good life was marred by a lot of anxiety. This was generated by the alleged presence of sorcery, an antisocial activity that a number of the local men were believed to practice in secret. Severe illness and sudden deaths were taken as proofs of the presence of sorcerers in the society. In Melanesian thought, volcanoes are associated with heat, and heat with magical potency. Ambrymese have always been feared as sorcerers by other non-Vanuatu, and for this reason were allegedly never employable as cooks on European-owned copra plantations because of the workers' fears of being poisoned. People of neighboring islands also avoided Ambrym because its volcanoes were said to be the homes of malevolent spirits of the dead. An outsider may begin by being quite skeptical, but a walk alone through the forest, with its black soil, eerie silences, and atmosphere of foreboding can arouse disquiet, especially at night. Twice, in exactly the same spot on a moonless evening, coconuts crashed to the ground right beside me as I was walking home from a nearby village. Coincidence, of course, but I was unnerved and came close to conversion both times. When I told my mentors, they were certain I had been attacked and forbade me to travel alone again at night.

I was fortunate to be back on Ambrym in 1973 in time to witness what happened when local church leaders declared war on sorcery. They organized an evangelical campaign, which was a spectacular success. Great euphoria followed, and people talked confidently of the victory of the Holy Spirit over the forces of evil. A lot of the old fears subsided and the change in the society was palpable: People moved about with a new confidence and talked openly about a once-secretive topic. It was too much for a cynical social scientist to expect that the change would be long-lived. Yet as recently as 1986 there still had not been any resurgence of sorcery in southeast Ambrym. Development, in the form of new schools and clinics, a water supply, a local government council, and better communications, has finally begun in this isolated and long-neglected area.

The Ambrym of today is a far cry from "uncivilized" times, and the tourist in search of the proverbial unspoiled "savage" would be disappointed. Before the Europeans came, people lived in small fortified hamlets scattered throughout the bush. Feuds and ambushes were apparently common elements in the social scene, and alliances were flimsy, uncertain things. With traders and labor recruiters came rifles to change the technology of the feud. The death rate escalated as the haves massacred the have-nots. Not everyone was a crack shot, however. A chief of the old Maat Village is said to have shot at James Taltasso and missed him at point-blank range. A fateful miss, this, because James was a west Ambrym man who arrived about the turn of the century to convert the heathen southeasterners. James was quick to attribute his miraculous escape to the power of the Christian god. At about the same time the locals refused to hand over an escaped plantation worker to his European master. The irate planter threatened the southeast Ambrymese with punishment: bombardment of their villages by a French or British warship. As the local people now relate the story, James ordered prayers, the planter died suddenly shortly after, the warship failed to arrive, and Christianity became the hit of the day.

In the twenty years that followed, the traditional society was rapidly transformed. Many of the old customs were abandoned; for instance, women no longer walked on their knees in the presence of certain male relatives. Many of the old crafts fell into disuse. The magnificent carved slit-gongs that surrounded their dancing grounds were burned and the grounds razed. People built new villages around churches and sought to please the new god by putting aside all reminders of the Time of Darkness. Today, in a still-young republic, where the need to forge a strong sense of national unity remains, leaders are searching for what is left of their traditional past. In southeast Ambrym, as elsewhere, old people are being urged to tell all they know of the old days and the old life. The Ambrymese want to revive elements of their traditional culture that are compatible with Christian values and with modern life. The new, postcolonial society is an lively amalgamation of Christian and *kastom* (tradition) elements.

There is an excitement and dynamism in the Vanuatu of today. This is part of what draws me back, as does the same anthropological curiosity that lured me there in the first place. Anthropologists everywhere study two sides of the same societal coin: continuities and change. The continuities are the essential and precious threads that give direction, purpose, and a sense of security to our lives. Changes force us to adapt continually as we must make new choices and learn to live with the consequences. So far the people of southeast Ambrym, somewhat cushioned by their isolation, have been able to balance the new and old very well.

There are by now twenty-one years since my first visit, and I have many reasons to go back to Ambrym: a great desire to be reunited with old friends, obligations to be lived up to, and a readiness to be of some assistance if I can. There are changes to be noted and make sense of, true, but it is always reassuring to see just how much the place and its people remain the same. The experience of immersing yourself in another culture is never without some pain, but the enormity of the satisfactions to be gained overwhelms the minuses of the adventure. I once asked a friend, newly returned from two years' fieldwork on a tiny Micronesian atoll, how it went. "Great!" he replied. Then he added after a thoughtful pause, "I'm still not sure how much I learned about the islanders, but I sure as hell learned a lot about myself." For many of us who are anthropologists, that is perhaps what the long journey into otherness is really all about.

No matter what the intended audience for our product, selective reporting of some kind is essential to the distillation of a mass of disparate data from the wealth of observed and reported events, both real and imagined, that constitute human social process (cf. Marcus and Fischer 1986). Given the target audience for my story, it was inevitable that I could not dwell on the heavier side of the anthropologist's role, though I was determined to allude to some of the ethnographic problems. The story was written immediately before Vanuatu's independence, and what has happened since regarding the status of foreign researchers in the country highlights the enormous difference between our privileged access in colonial times (provided we agreed not to openly foment revolution) and the bureaucratic hurdles placed before us now by indigenous governments decidedly ambivalent about the relevance of our research to their aspirations. A more serious and scholarly article would have necessarily dwelt on the debate over whether or not anthropologists have been tools of colonialism or defenders of oppressed minorities. At the least, it would be mindful that the romance and adventure of the search for the "other" never took place in an apolitical vacuum, and that at base "our people" were for us as much of a commodity as they were for the labor recruiters or missionaries we frequently criticize.

In this story I wanted to amuse, but not to amuse at the expense of the Melanesians. No, the target must be the writer, whose ignorance of the alien culture (and consequent missteps as, babylike, he attempts to master a particular task but so often discovers himself awkward and stumbling) is used to reverse the stereotype of the "ignorant native" bedeviled by Western technology. Nigel Barley (1983), in his wickedly funny book about doing fieldwork in West Africa, adopts a more evenhanded approach: Everyone gets it in the neck at some stage, including "his" people. But then, fieldwork in Vanuatu was a breeze compared to what Barley claims to have endured in the Cameroons, and for all my frustration at aspects of colonial rule, I most truly had an easy time of it. Also, unless I've totally suppressed it, I suffered no traumas at the hands of vindictive locals, either, so there was no desire whatsoever to satirize them. I was never physically threatened, or robbed, or thrown out of a village, (or a dinghy, for that matter), or openly denied access to information, and my comments about missing the island and the people while away were absolutely true.

The concentration on food was based on my experience of being asked frequently by people in my own society about this aspect of doing fieldwork. It also allowed me to give readers some idea of the range of local food resources. The brief discussions of subsistence and of cash-cropping likewise address the common question, "What do the people there do for a living?" and my exposition of the uneven rhythm of work and leisure is in implicit contrast to the vastly more regimented lives of most outsiders. Had I remembered, I would have related my chiding of islanders who wore, or wanted, wristwatches, warning them that this object is our own "god" and master, and urging them to avoid that kind of partitioning of their existence.

The discussion concerning problems with establishing my identity and motives was included for the interest value of the particulars, but also because it highlights an important aspect of entering the field in cultures unlike our own. We cannot ever know fully what "our people" are making of us when we go to live with them, and the disjunction between our motives and explanations, and their interpretations of them, are at the root of many of our difficulties in the field, at least in the early stages. The obvious (to us, as anthropologists) ethical and moral issues that surround and lie beneath our self-presentations, and vexed issues of unmeetable expectations and the constitution of "adequate" or "just" reciprocity, lie in the realm of the deep issues which cannot be part of a discourse aimed at the kind of general audience addressed in the foregoing article.

We are often accused of not writing for, and reaching, an audience beyond the social sciences and humanities. Perhaps some of the issues I've mentioned are better not given a wider airing, lest we end up with "anthropology on trial," without the opportunity to answer our critics immediately and forcefully. That said, I would still respond positively to any request to write the same kind of story for a general audience again—and not simply because there is monetary reward, but because the act of doing it heightens one's awareness of what is entailed in rendering "things anthropological" accessible to the nonspecialist reader. It turned out to be more difficult than I had envisaged, but it was also quite refreshing to write in a looser and more creative mode. The need for us to reach a much wider audience, to put our skills as cultural translators to better use in making what is alien and exotic meaningful and logical in Western cultural terms, remains as strong as ever.

SUGGESTED READINGS

BARLEY, NIGEL

1983   The Innocent Anthropologist. Baltimore: Penguin.

BURRIDGE, K. O. L.

1973   Encountering Aborigines: Anthropology and the Australian Aboriginal. New York: Pergamon.

CLIFFORD, J., AND G. E. MARCUS, EDS.

1986   Writing Culture: The Poetics and Politics of Ethnography. Berkeley: University of California Press.

JOLLY, M.

1982   Birds and Banyans of South Pentecost: *Kastom* in Anti-colonial Struggle. Mankind 13(4):338–356.

MARCUS, G. E., AND M. J. FISCHER

1986   Anthropology as Cultural Critique: An Experimental Moment in the Human Sciences. Chicago: University of Chicago Press.

TONKINSON, R.

1979   At Work in the Isles of Coral and Ash. Pacific 8(4):50–59.

1982a *Kastom* in Melanesia: Introduction. Mankind 13(4):302–305.

1982b National Identity and the Problem of *Kastom* in Vanuatu. Mankind 13(4):306–315.

 A Long Voyage

BEN FINNEY
University of Hawaii

INTRODUCTION

In 1965 I embarked on a research venture from which I have yet to extricate myself. Its genesis goes back to 1958 when I enrolled at the University of Hawaii to study for an M.A. in anthropology. One of my teachers, Katherine Luomala, gave me a recently published book to read, *Ancient Voyagers in the Pacific*. It had been written by Andrew Sharp (1956), a retired New Zealand civil servant turned historian, who argued that the islands of Polynesia had been discovered and settled accidentally by people pushed randomly around the Pacific by wind and current. He claimed that the canoes of the Polynesians were not seaworthy enough, and their noninstrument navigational methods were not accurate enough, for them to have purposefully explored and settled the Pacific. In fact, Sharp went so far as to declare that planned and navigated voyages of over three hundred miles were impossible for the Polynesians. Although many acclaimed the book as a salutory correction to an overromanticized picture of Polynesian migration and voyaging, as a longtime student of Polynesian legends, Katherine was suspicious of anyone who could so readily dismiss the many tales of searching for new islands and of sailing back and forth between known ones separated by hundreds or even thousands of miles of open sea. In giving the book to me, she wanted my opinion of Sharp's thesis, as a sailor and as a budding student of Polynesian culture.

Although I admired the wit and clarity of Sharp's rhetoric, I really did not think much of his argument from a sailing point of view. In particular, I objected to his portrayal of Polynesian sailors haplessly drifting before wind and current, unable, because of their flimsy canoes and lack of navigational instruments, to sail where they wanted to go. But as I began to read the literature on Polynesian navigation and voyaging, I realized that it was most difficult to refute Sharp. The kind of evidence a historian would demand for a refutation was scanty and contradictory. To be sure, there were legends galore of heroic voyages, and a growing body of archaeological evidence which indicated that Polynesians had purposefully colonized island after island. But firsthand accounts written by early visitors of canoe voyages, canoe performance, and navigational accuracy were rare, and those that were available were typically vague and often contradictory. Thus, Sharp would cite a few sources to the effect that the Polynesians and their canoes were not up to the task of island colonization, while his critics could cite a few other sources to the contrary. But neither could definitively prove their case.

As voyaging canoes and traditional navigators had long since disappeared from Polynesian waters, it seemed to me that only through experiment could we hope to find out how well Polynesian canoes sailed, how accurate the Polynesian navigation system was, and how hard was it to sail between distant islands. But as a impecunious M. A. student struggling to grasp what anthropology was all about, I was in no position to start building canoes to sail around Polynesia. So I filed that fantasy away in the recesses of my mind and went back to learning what E. B. Tylor, F. Boas, B. Malinowski, and other founding fathers of anthropology had talked about, and to writing my M.A. thesis, and then later, at Harvard, my Ph.D. dissertation.

Not until 1965, when I was working at the University of California at Santa Barbara, did the idea resurface. While teaching a course on the Pacific, I found myself sketching canoes on the blackboard and explaining to my students how I thought the Polynesian navigation system worked. From there I began to think seriously about reconstructing and sailing a Polynesian voyaging canoe. However, because I lacked the resources to immediately build a big canoe, and because I realized that as an untenured assistant professor I had better not put all my efforts into such an unconventional and risky project, I decided to first build a medium-sized sailing canoe and use it for controlled experiments on sailing and paddling performance. Then, if the results were encouraging, sometime later—ideally after I had received tenure—I might be able to reconstruct a large voyaging canoe and then sail it between Hawaii and Tahiti as a test of Sharp's thesis that long, purposefully navigated voyages were impossible.

Fortunately, not everybody at the university and in the Santa Barbara community thought I was crazy. Combining my own savings with gifts from private donors and the use of student helpers provided by the university during the academic year of 1965–66, I was able to build a replica of a Hawaiian double-canoe—between teaching classes and writing articles on the socioeconomic research I had undertaken in Tahiti for my Ph.D. dissertation. The canoe measured forty feet in length and had two hulls and a single mast on which we rigged a canvas copy of a traditional Hawaiian "crab-claw" sail. It was ready to sail by late spring of 1966, when fortunately a grant from the National Science Foundation came through to allow me to test its sailing abilities and the physiological parameters of paddling such a heavy sailing canoe, first offshore Santa Barbara, and then in Hawaiian waters.

In Hawaii we enlisted the help of canoe paddlers from the Waikiki Surf Club, a mostly Hawaiian group who were then the champion paddlers in the islands, and the aid of such traditional scholars as Mary Kawena Pukui who christened the canoe *Nālehia,* literally "The Skilled Ones," referring to the two hulls. From our paddling and sailing trials in Hawaii we found out what we wanted to know. Although the Hawaiian paddlers could move the canoe all day long at a pace of three to four knots, because of the high cost in terms of food and water, paddling did not appear to be an efficient mode of propulsion for long voyages. However, it was clear that *Nālehia* had a definite, if modest, ability to sail to windward—despite its long, shallow, keelless hulls and the "upside-down" Hawaiian sail. As my contribution to a volume honoring Kenneth Emory, the doyen of Polynesian ethnographers, I worte a paper in which I used the data gained from sailing *Nālehia* to propose that a double-canoe could sail across and slightly into the wind from Hawaii to Tahiti and then back, duplicating the voyages celebrated in Hawaiian legends (Finney 1967). At that point I would have loved to have gone on to build a larger voyaging canoe for that voyage, but a back injury incurred while building *Nālehia,* and again the requirements of professionalization, intervened. I loaned the canoe to the Sea Life Park oceanarium to use as a display, underwent back surgery, and upon recovery flew to Papua New Guinea to take up a Fulbright grant (the first one to Papua New Guinea) to study indigenous entrepreneurs there.

VOYAGE TO TAHITI

I did not get back to Hawaii until 1970, when I took a post as associate professor of anthropology at the University of Hawaii. While one of my motives for returning to Hawaii was to continue with my canoe experiments, for the first few years there I found myself fully occupied with developing courses, publishing research results from work in Papua New Guinea, and developing a research program on entrepreneurship in Asia and the Pacific at the East-West Center, a federally funded institution that works in cooperation with the University of Hawaii. Those duties, plus the responsibilities of a growing family and a large mortgage, as well as lingering physical problems (after two more back operations), made me hesitant about attempting to build a large canoe to sail between Hawaii and Tahiti. But in 1973, by which time I had published a couple of economic anthropology books, received tenure, stabilized my finances, and recovered from my last operation, I was ready to try.

At this propitious time, two other canoe enthusiasts approached me with a proposal to build a canoe for a voyage to Tahiti and back: Tommy Holmes, an ardent racing canoe paddler and student of Polynesian maritime culture, and an Hawaiian artist searching for his cultural roots, Herb Kane, who had recently moved back to Hawaii from the Chicago area,

where he had pursued a successful career as a commercial illustrator in
the advertising industry. Together we formed the Polynesian Voyaging
Society, drew up plans to build a large voyaging canoe, and started raising
funds. Although I did not know it at the time, that decision effectively
derailed my career as an economic anthropologist and has molded my life
ever since.

None of us fully realized the complexity of the task we had set for
ourselves. Raising funds to build a double-hulled canoe sixty feet in length
(but five times the displacement, the true measure of size, of that of
Nālehia), building the canoe, and then preparing for the five-thousand
nautical-mile round-trip voyage to Tahiti and return was difficult enough.
We made the task immensely more complicated by giving the project two
goals. In addition to carrying out a difficult experiment to shed light on
Polynesian voyaging and migration, we wanted to make our effort culturally significant. We wanted Hawaiians and other Polynesians to be fully
involved in the design, building, and sailing of the canoe, and to have the
entire effort serve to awaken an appreciation among them of the technology that made the discovery and settlement of their islands possible.

Fund-raising went well, particularly with the help of Herb Kane's
artwork, which we used to develop brochures and posters. We also had
the advantage of *Nālehia,* which we relaunched to serve as a training vessel
and also to demonstrate to skeptics that we did know something about
sailing double-canoes. By mid-1974, after receiving a handsome advance
from a New York publisher for a book about the voyage, we had enough
money to start construction.

Because we could not relearn, in any reasonable period of time, the
precise skills needed to carve keelpieces and then build up the hulls by
fitting and lashing together planks, we built the hulls out of layers of
plywood attached to frames and stringers carefully cut and laid out to
duplicate the lines of a traditional canoe. Similarly, although we lashed the
two hulls together with crossbeams modeled on traditional ones, because
we could not obtain the many miles of coconut sennit line required, we
used synthetic line. This substitution of modern materials and methods
saved time, but added to the cost. Continual fund-raising kept the construction going, and by the spring of 1975 we had fabricated all the com-
ponents, which we then trucked from our work site, a warehouse on the
Honolulu waterfront, to Kualoa, a beach park on the north shore of Oahu
for assembly and launching.

It was after the launching, and during the sea trials that followed, that
the troubles began. We named our canoe *Hōkūle'a* after the Hawaiian
word for Arcturus, the bright star that passes directly over the island of
Hawaii. The name, we felt, was apt. Literally, *Hōkūle'a* means "Star of Joy."
We thought the name fit the intended voyage, particularly the return leg to
Hawaii. A sailor returning to Hawaii from distant Tahiti would greet with
joy the sight of Arcturus arching ever higher in the sky, a sure sign that the

canoe was approaching the latitude of Hawaii. But after sailing *Hōkūle'a* around the Hawaiian Islands for six months, the troubles we were experiencing began to drown out whatever feelings of joy we had felt upon launching the canoe and in anticipation of the voyage.

Whereas before the launching we had labored in happy obscurity, once the canoe had been ritually presented to the sea and the public, divisions arose. The planned sequence of first a period of rigorous sea trials to test the canoe and improve our seamanship, then to sail to Tahiti and back in as authentic a manner as possible, followed by the use of the canoe in Hawaiian waters as a "floating classroom" to teach Hawaii's children about their Polynesian maritime heritage, was challenged again and again. Some wanted to put the cart before the horse by sailing boastfully from one Hawaiian island to another before we had learned how to handle her with any degree of skill, and well before we had made the voyage to Tahiti. Others questioned the need for authenticity and pushed to have modern keel fins installed on the hulls in order to ensure that we could sail close enough into the wind to reach Tahiti. Some even wanted to cancel the voyage altogether and use the canoe to "invade" Kahoolawe, a small island off Maui which the Navy uses as a bombing range and which had then become a target of protests by Hawaiian activists. To make matters worse, a number of *kahuna,* Hawaiian religious practitioners, prophesied that the canoe would meet with disaster, and one influential *kahuna* even attempted a crude form of blackmail by demanding a considerable sum of money to perform the rituals he claimed were necessary to enable to canoe and crew to make the voyage safely.

A strong element of "*Hōkūle'a* for Hawaiians only" entered into all this. Even among Hawaiian crewmen favorably disposed to the overall plan for the voyage, there was a growing sentiment that no *haole* (Caucasian) should sail on the canoe, and that research activities, as quintessentially *haole* behavior, had no place on a Hawaiian canoe. Thus, I found myself in the unenviable position of having to defend my participation in the project, as well as that of my co-organizer, Tommy Holmes, and of David Lerwis, the New Zealander who had just published a classic study of traditional Pacific navigation, *We the Navigators* (Lewis 1972), and who was scheduled to document how well the canoe could be navigated all the way to Tahiti and back without instruments. This resentment toward outsiders even came to be directed against Mau Piailug, the master Micronesian navigator I recruited to guide the canoe by traditional means, and to a Tahitian sailor I had invited to join the crew to pilot us through Tahitian waters, and particularly through the dangerous maze of Tuamotu atolls should we make our first landfall in that hazardous archipelago.

Had I owned the canoe outright, or at least had total control of the project, these pressures could have been shrugged off. However, the three of us who started the project were not always of like mind, and besides, *Hōkūle'a* was owned by the Polynesian Voyaging Society, a nonprofit corporation we had formed to raise funds and administer the project. Furthermore, we had deliberately encouraged wide public participation, particularly among Hawaiians. In fact, by proclaiming that one of our goals was to help revive Hawaiian cultural awareness we had opened the door wide for the move to kick all non-Hawaiians off the canoe.

This recipe for maritime disaster came to a head when *Hōkūle'a* swamped and was damaged on an interisland sail six months before our scheduled departure for Tahiti. Herb Kane, who had been campaigning the canoe around the islands, then withdrew from the project, leaving me to repair the canoe, get the project back on track, and carry out the voyage. The incongruity of having *haole* preside over the Polynesian Voyaging Society and direct an increasingly Hawaiian project was not lost on me, and certainly not on the Hawaiians who predominated on the crew as well as on the board of directors of the society. But the job had to be done and I saw no alternative to seeing it through myself—even though I realized I would be extremely vulnerable to any protests made in the name of Hawaiianness, particularly should I attempt to remove any of the crew-members who were then becoming increasingly rebellious.

As I feared, the troubles continued right down to the time of our sailing in May 1976 and throughout the voyage to Tahiti. On the eve of our departure a leading crewmember attempted to stage a mutiny and stop the canoe from sailing—all dramatically acted out before the television cameramen he had invited as witnesses. When we were finally able to sail some days later we still had on board crewmen who because of their disagreement with the goals of the project should not have been allowed to go, but who could not be dismissed in this highly polarized situation. Midway through the voyage these crewmen became so disaffected that they refused to stand watch and tried to bully everyone else—including the Hawaiian captain, whom they accused of being a "coconut" (brown on the outside, white on the inside), even though he was the only man on board who spoke fluent Hawaiian. To make a long story short, we did eventually make it to Tahiti, and though fights had broken out on board, without loss of life or limb.

But the project had been shattered. Our navigator, Mau Piailug, left us upon landing on Tahiti and flew back to Micronesia in disgust. Once ashore on Tahiti, rebellious crewmembers started agitating to depose the captain and take over the canoe. Although there was nothing I could do about getting Mau back, the offending crewmembers were put onto the first plane back to Honolulu and replaced with young Hawaiians who believed in the goals of the project. Then, to avoid further controversy over my role, I elected not to sail back on the canoe and devoted my energies to getting *Hōkūle'a* ready for departure. These and other measures worked, and the return was an uneventful voyage enjoyed by all.

Despite the safe return of the canoe, bitter divisions remained within the Polynesian Voyaging Society. Many were highly critical of me, either for being too high-handed or too lax, and I was totally exhausted from trying to keep the project together. It was time to step down, which I did as soon as I could get the society's finances in reasonable order.

While I set to work on writing articles on the findings of our voyage and working on a book for which the society had earlier received an advance, the Polynesian Voyaging Society was reorganized. The new leaders, virtually all Hawaiians, worked toward carrying out the promise to use *Hōkūle'a* as a floating classroom by sailing her from island to island within the Hawaiian group, and at each port of call by having the Hawaiian crew give lectures and demonstrations to students.

TO TAHITI AGAIN

Talk soon turned, however, to making another voyage to Tahiti—this time one that would be solely done by Hawaiians. So in 1978, two years after the first voyage, a heavily laden *Hōkūle'a* sailed from Honolulu bound for Tahiti. Unfortunately, this expedition was mounted with more enthusiasm than preparation and prudence. The canoe left one stormy evening and encountered gale winds in the treacherous channel between Oahu and Molokai. While the canoe was being driven hard to windward, the lee hull filled with water, and before the crew could react the force of the wind on the sails and the lifting motion of the huge seas turned the listing craft completely over. Although all crewmembers survived the capsize and were able to cling to the upturned hulls, without an escort vessel or an emergency radio beacon (which had been lost in the capsize) the situation was desperate. Because he feared that they had drifted south of shipping and air lanes, the next day Eddie Aikau, a world champion surfer, grabbed a surfboard and started paddling for the distant shore to raise the alarm. At dusk a passing aircraft spotted the canoe and the rescue of the remaining crewmembers and the canoe followed that night, but Eddie Aikau was never seen again.

This was certainly the low point in the project, particularly for those who had been trying so hard to make their voyage a success. To their credit, however, they did not give up. Under the firm tutelage of the Coast Guard, they worked to rebuild the battered canoe and to properly prepare for another attempt to sail to Tahiti. Once the canoe was relaunched, the crew sharpened their skills by countless sails offshore Oahu. In addition, with the help of Mau Piailug, who was brought back to Hawaii for this purpose, one of the crewmen, Nainoa Thompson, was able to develop his navigational skills to the point where he was ready to try to guide the canoe to Tahiti and return without instruments.

This time, in 1980, they succeeded admirably. Not only did they replicate the first voyage by making it to Tahiti and back, following approximately the same route as we had, but they completed the navigation experiment we had begun in 1976 by navigating both ways without instruments. What is more, the fact that a Hawaiian had actually learned how to navigate without instruments and was able to guide the canoe all the way to Tahiti and back made people forget the troubles and tragedy of the previous voyages and served to make the Hawaiians proud of their own maritime abilities.

VOYAGE OF REDISCOVERY

While the *Hōkūle'a* crew and other members of the society might legitimately have rested after this feat, within a few years they began talking about a much longer and more ambitious voyage. They wanted to sail throughout Polynesia, stopping at as many of the island centers as possible. They called the proposed venture the Voyage of Rediscovery, in that they wanted to investigate the various migration routes followed by the early voyagers by actually sailing over them, to feel the thrill of making landfalls on such historic islands as Rarotonga, Aotearoa, and Tongatapu, and to share those experiences with other Polynesians who would join the crew en route or would welcome the canoe upon its arrival at each successive island.

At this point, in 1984, I began to take an active role once more in the project. Although I had been called upon for help after the 1978 tragedy, I had confined my efforts primarily to giving advice and counsel, on the premise that the Hawaiians had to work things out for themselves. In addition, during this period I had become wholly engrossed in a new research project that grew out of my interests in Polynesian voyaging and expansion—developing anthropological insights on the impact on humanity of present and future ventures in space exploration and settlement—and had been spending a lot of time away from Hawaii. But in 1984 I returned to Hawaii to stay and felt like getting involved once more with the canoe.

I found the situation there to be vastly different from before. With the 1980 voyage under their belts, the Hawaiians were confident of their own abilities and the project was firmly in the charge of Myron Thompson, a vigorous Hawaiian patriot with extensive government and business experience, and his son, Nainoa, who after navigating the canoe to Tahiti and back had emerged as the leading seaman among the crew. Particularly as the Thompsons believed that the voyage should be fully documented and that the data gained should used to shed light on issues of Polynesian voyaging and migration, I was delighted to join the project again. This time, however, my role was that of research anthropologist instead of entrepreneur-administrator as before.

My job was to see that the voyage was properly documented and that the results were used to help us understand better how the original migration voyages took place and how the early Polynesians were able to sail and navigate over such a wide extent of sea. My first task was to go back to the partially analyzed data from the 1980 voyage, complete the analysis, and then prepare the results for publication as a model of what we were to do with the data on the Voyage of Rediscovery (Finney et al., 1986). Then I helped Nainoa Thompson plan the new voyage so we could learn as much as possible from it about Polynesian migrations and voyaging. I was also called upon to testify in the state legislature in favor of a bill to grant state funding for the project. There I discovered that, in the context of growing Hawaiian political power, *Hōkūle'a* had become a kind of "cultural motherhood" that legislators found it difficult to vote against.

By mid-1985, thanks to a large state appropriation plus donations from foundations, companies, and individuals, we had enough money to sail. The canoe sailed first to Tahiti, and from there to Rarotonga in the Cook Islands. In late November of that year I interrupted a sabbatical leave being spent at a NASA research center to fly to Rarotonga and join the crew for the next leg to New Zealand.

The sail to Aotearoa (the Maori name for the North Island of New Zealand) was a revelation. The crewmembers were confident, competent and a lot of fun to boot. Except for a Maori guest, all were from Hawaii. Most were veterans of the 1978 or 1980 ventures, and some had sailed in 1976 as well. In their years of sailing *Hōkūle'a* they had so developed their sailing skills and teamwork that even emergencies were handled with cool dispatch. Furthermore, the old resentment against outsiders was gone. There was no need for resentment; after all, they were clearly in charge and I was there as a guest investigator. They had accepted that research was a necessary activity, for they realized from previous voyages that unless their experiences are recorded they drop from view as memories fade. In fact, a number of crewmen vied for the job of debriefing the navigator, Nainoa Thompson, each dawn and dusk as to what course he had steered, as to what navigation decisions he had made, and as to where he thought we were—all data needed to analyze the performance of noninstrument navigation once the voyage was over.

After waiting out the cold New Zealand winter. *Hōkūle'a* was sailed to Tonga and then on to Samoa. Once the summer hurricane season had passed, *Hōkūle'a* was then headed toward the east to try to reach Tahiti—a formidable task in that the trades ordinarily blow from east to west. Taking advantage of spells of westerly winds, the crew was able to work the canoe first to the Cook Islands and then on to Tahiti to complete this most difficult leg of the entire voyage. Once in Tahiti, the canoe was again laid up to wait out the stormy summer season. The following April *Hōkūle'a* was sailed north from Tahiti to Rangiroa atoll in the Tuamotu Islands to await fair winds in order to sail north-northeast to the Marquesas, the islands from whence, hypothesize linguists and archaeologists, the first Hawaiian colonists sailed. But after waiting for weeks for favorable winds that never came, the plan to call on the Marquesas was abandoned and the canoe was sailed directly back to Hawaii, arriving at Kualoa Beach on May 23, 1987, twelve years after she had first been launched there and not quite two years since she had left Oahu to embark on the Voyage of Rediscovery.

Although my duties—assumed upon my return from the Aotearoa voyage—as chairman of the anthropology department at the University of Hawaii prevented me from sailing on any other legs of the voyage, I did manage to fly to Tahiti to greet the canoe upon her arrival from Samoa and then later see her off for Hawaii, and I continued to collect data recorded on the voyage.

These on-board data are now being compared with data on weather patterns en route derived from remote-sensing satellites, data from island weather stations, data on the actual track of the canoe as determined by position fixes made on board an escort vessel by analyzing transmissions from navigation satellites, and data gathered separately in France from automatic transmissions to special orbiting satellites from a sealed transmitter on board the canoe. We are therefore able to make detailed comparisons between, on one hand, the wind and weather conditions as perceived from the canoe, as well as Nainoa Thompson's dead-reckoning estimates based on his noninstrument navigation, and on the other hand, an oceanwide perspective of weather patterns as seen from weather satellites and ground meteorological stations, as well as precise position fixes determined by satellite transmissions. This unprecedented combination of the view from space with that from the deck of the canoe is allowing us to focus precisely on issues such as the accuracy of noninstrument navigation and the degree to which weather patterns determine sailing routes. Two articles based on this method of analysis have appeared so far (Finney 1988; Babayan et al. 1986), and more are in preparation for later inclusion in a book on the entire voyage.

DISCUSSION

Hōkūle'a has sailed over twenty-five thousand miles on three major experimental voyages, or more than enough to complete a circumnavigation of our globe at the equator. While these voyages cannot definitively prove or disprove any grand theory, by sailing over the migration routes indicated by linguistic, archaeological, and legendary evidence, and by navigating from island to island without instruments, we have been able to gain a wealth of practical experience which allows us to raise the discussion about Polynesian migrations and voyages to a much more informed level than has heretofore been possible.

There can be no doubt about the worth of double-hulled Polynesian canoes for long-range voyaging. Although they might not be able to point as high into the wind as a modern yacht, and although they are prone to swamping and capsize if not carefully handled, these canoes are nonetheless excellent sailing vehicles, ideally suited for blue-water voyaging in the tropics.

Similarly, setting a course by the stars, wind, and swells, keeping track of one's progress en route through purely mental dead reckoning, and detecting land by watching for the appearance of short-range land birds and other cues which serve to "expand the target" have been shown to be eminently practical—when carried out by such master navigators as Mau Piailug and his Hawaiian protege, Nainoa Thompson. Furthermore, despite the great potential for errors of observation and judgment inherent in this system, it appears more often than not that errors tend to cancel out one another so that long voyages can be navigated with a surprizing degree of accuracy.

The need to wait for the right wind conditions to sail over each particular route was brought home to us on virtually each leg of the voyage. For example, the sail from Samoa to Tahiti has been considered most difficult because the trade winds ordinarily blow from the east, the direction toward which a canoe must sail. Heyerdahl (1953), in fact, had declared that the steady trade winds and accompanying ocean currents would have prevented canoe sailors from sailing from west to east across the Pacific, and that therefore Polynesia had been settled from the Americas by voyages made drifting before the easterly trades and currents. However, we were able to sail from Samoa by waiting for and then exploiting the westerly wind shifts brought on by the passage of low pressure systems, a strategy which, according to Captain Cook and other early visitors, Polynesian sailors commonly used when they wanted to sail from west to east. And, to cite a negative example, we failed to reach the Marquesas from the Tuamotus because our schedule for returning to Hawaii did not allow enough time to wait for the advent of favorable winds needed to sail in that direction.

Finally, in voyaging over routes celebrated in legend, we have been able to gain some insight into the legends themselves. After being told for the last several decades that oral tales are merely mythical charters for current socio-political claims, or just structural designs devoid of practical meaning, it is refreshing to find that at least some of the voyaging legends make good sailing sense. For example, the much-disputed Maori tales of migration canoes indicate, by reference to lunar months and to the type of trees in bloom at the time of arrival, that the best time to sail to Aotearoa is just at the beginning of the southern hemisphere summer. We left Rarotonga at the recommended time, sailing southwest with the trades at our back. Then, once we left the tropics and entered temperate seas, instead of encountering the westerly headwinds which ordinarily prevail there, we found light easterly winds which sped us to Aoatearoa without delay. The legends, it turns out, are in tune with the meteorology of the southwest Pacific, for it is precisely in the early summer when passing high pressure systems block the westerlies and bring about an easterly air flow all the way to New Zealand.

Such insights are enabling us to develop a realistic picture of the voyaging technology so basic to Polynesian culture and its expansion over the Pacific and to begin to judge the feasibility of sailing, whether in terms of one-way settlement ventures or two-way communication, along specific interisland routes. Experimental voyaging research is thus taking its place alongside linguistics, archaeology, and other long-established fields of research in the common quest to understand the genesis and development of this unique phase in humanity's expansion over our globe.

But, the impact of our work goes far beyond the halls of academia and the pages of scientific journals. *Hōkūle'a* has become a powerful cultural symbol that is helping Hawaiians and other Polynesians anchor their battered cultural identity in a glorious history of oceanic discovery and settlement. Particularly for the Polynesians of Hawaii, Tahiti, and New Zealand, islands where the political and cultural losses have been the greatest, the image of *Hōkūle'a* evokes an earlier era when their ancestors were masters of their own destiny, and may even be helping some people to face their more complicated modern future. For example, the 1976 voyage helped spark a movement that has been hailed as the Hawaiian Renaissance, and the triumphant return of *Hōkūle'a* in 1987 was the highlight of the officially proclaimed "Year of the Hawaiian." The appearance of the curving sails of *Hōkūle'a* off Tahiti in 1976 stiffened Tahitian resolve during difficult political negotiations then taking place with the French and inspired them to make the double-hulled canoe the centerpiece of their new flag, standing for the voyaging heritage of Tahiti and surrounding islands. To the Maoris who greeted *Hōkūle'a* when she sailed into the Bay of Islands in 1985, the canoe was living proof of the seafaring abilities of their ancestors, proof that their migration traditions were not in error.

Crucial to the emergence of *Hōkūle'a* as a cultural symbol has been the Hawaiianization of the project. Starting virtually from scratch, a nucleus of expert Hawaiian canoe sailors has been developed, men and women who have been able to relearn the maritime arts of their ancestors so well that they have been able to sail the canoe to the far reaches of Polynesia and to navigate over thousands of miles of open ocean without compass, sextant, and other modern aids. After the troubles of 1976 and the tragedy of 1978, the Hawaiians have done much more than redeem their maritime heritage. They have given themselves a new pride in their own abilities as well as those of their ancestors.

Though this has been a primarily Hawaiian accomplishment, the Hawaiians have been most anxious to share their experience with other Polynesians. On each leg of the 1985–87 voyage, at least one person from the island to which the canoe was headed was included in the crew. Then, before going to a new island, cultural delegations were dispatched there to inform the people of the nature and goals of the voyage and to invite them to join in the project. Through these measures this last voyage has become much more than a Hawaiian adventure. It has truly become a voyage of cultural rediscovery for islanders throughout Polynesia.

The most intellectual accomplishment of this whole venture—that of guiding a canoe over thousands of miles of open ocean with only one's eyes and brain as instruments—has particularly caught people's attention. Nainoa Thompson, when originally recruited for the project in the early 1970s, knew nothing about navigation, modern or traditional. He has since become a cultural hero in Hawaii and other parts of Polynesia, particularly to schoolchildren. Mau Piailug, who rejoined the project in 1979 to teach Nainoa traditional wayfinding arts, is regarded with special esteem. In fact, in 1986 he was awarded an honorary doctorate from the University of Hawaii for his contributions to the preservation and revival of the art of traditional navigation. In what other anthropological project has an informant received a doctorate and other nonscientist participants gone on to take over the project and make it more productive?

Our project began with the twin goals of research and cultural revival. Both have been fulfilled, though not without difficulty. At times, when struggling to get the canoe ready for the initial departure to Tahiti and then when weathering the abuse of rebellious crewmembers while sailing to Tahiti, I regretted the decision to join cultural objectives with research ones. After the ill-fated attempt to sail to Tahiti in 1978, I imagine that at least some of the Hawaiian leaders thought long and hard about tying Hawaiian cultural identity to so risky a project. Fortunately, none of us gave up. Starting with the 1980 voyage, and particularly during the recently concluded Voyage of Rediscovery, research and cultural revival have fit together nicely, the one reinforcing the other. In fact, the synergy has been such that now the scope and significance of our research findings, and the degree to which Hawaiians and other Polynesians have developed a new understanding and pride in their maritime heritage, far surpasses our original expectations, even our most optimistic hopes. It has indeed been a long voyage, but one that has been worth it.

REFERENCES CITED

BABAYAN, CHAD, BEN FINNEY, BERNARD KILONSKI AND NAINOA THOMPSON
1986   Voyage to Aotearoa. Journal of the Polynesian Society 96(2):161–200.

FINNEY, BEN
1967   New Perspectives in Polynesian Voyaging. In Polynesian Cultural History. G. Highland, R. W. Force, A. Howard, M. Kelly, and Y. H. Sinoto, eds. Honolulu: Bishop Museum Press.
1977   Voyaging Canoes and the Settlement of Polynesia. Science 196(4296):1277–1285.
1979   Hokule'a: The Way to Tahiti. New York: Dodd, Mead.
1988   Voyaging Against the Direction of the TradeWinds: An Experimental Canoe Voyage from Samoa to Tahiti. American Anthropologist. (In Press.)

FINNEY, BEN R., BERNARD KILONSKY, STEVEN SOMSEN, AND E. DIXON STROUP
1986   Reviving a Vanishing Art. Journal of the Polynesian Society 95(1):41–90.

HEYERDAHL, THOR
1953   American Indians in the Pacific. Chicago: Rand McNally.

LEWIS, DAVID
1972   We, The Navigators. Honolulu: The University Press of Hawaii.

SHARP, ANDREW
1956   Ancient Voyagers in the Pacific. Wellington: The Polynesian Society.